THE HEALTHFUL GOURMET
Chinese Cookbook

Rose Lee

HPBooks

To my beloved mother, who lived until age ninety-three,
who raised us with simple, delicious and healthy foods.

HPBooks
are published by
The Berkley Publishing Group
A member of Penguin Putnam Inc.
375 Hudson Street
New York, New York 10014

Cover design by Jack Ribik
Cover photo by StockFood/Thom DeSanto
Chinese calligraphy by Rose Lee
Author photo by Photo Boutique
Interior Design by Lisa Stokes

First edition: January 1999

Published simultaneously in Canada.

The Penguin Putnam Inc. World Wide Web site address is
http://www.penguinputnam.com

Library of Congress Cataloging-in-Publication Data

Lee, Rose (Rose Li-Zhu)
    The healthful gourmet Chinese cookbook / Rose Lee. — 1st ed.
        p.   cm.
    Includes index.
    ISBN 1-55788-299-1
    1. Cookery, Chinese.   2. Low-fat diet—Recipes.   I. Title.
TX724.5.C5L463   1999
641.5'638—dc21   98-31191
                                                        CIP
Printed in the United States of America

10 9 8 7 6 5 4 3 2 1

Contents

Preface

THE FIRST QUESTION PEOPLE ALWAYS ASKED ME after I closed my restaurant was: "So what are you doing now?" When I said, "I am writing a cookbook," they replied, "Ten years ago you said you were going to write a cookbook." True. I wanted to write a cookbook ten years ago, but with demands that included teaching in my cooking school, running a restaurant, and raising a family, I did not have time to do so. After my children had grown, and I was no longer burdened by restaurant responsibilities, I was able to concentrate full time on writing this cookbook—and I enjoyed every minute of it.

During the years I spent teaching cooking and operating my restaurant, I saw a large number of international foods become standard American fare. I saw the American lifestyle change from a simple, more relaxed way of life to a more competitive, fast-paced one. I saw changes in the American diet and a growing desire to make smarter choices that have resulted in healthier eating habits. I saw a shift away from rich, fat-laden foods to more natural, fresher, and lighter cuisine. And I have noticed a growing Asian influence on the

American diet: More and more Asian foods are making their way into our kitchens. Ingredients that used to be hard to find are now readily available in supermarkets. Along with those changes, my own teaching repertoire has expanded; my range of cooking techniques has grown; I have refined my recipes to be more delicious yet lower in fats; and I have created new recipes that better meet today's healthier living standards.

Today more and more people everywhere are aware of the importance of maintaining a balance of proper nutrition and exercise for a healthful lifestyle. We often are told to eat foods that contain lower amounts of fat, sodium, and cholesterol to reduce the chances of developing chronic diet-related diseases.

With this goal in mind, I have written this cookbook to provide healthful recipes that are lower in fats, that have outstanding taste, and that are simple to prepare. I have included classic Chinese recipes as well as restaurant-popularized offerings and some contemporary twists to old standards. To make it easier to achieve dietary goals in keeping with today's lifestyle, each recipe is accompanied by a nutrition analysis. In addition, I have reduced the amount of cholesterol, saturated fats, and oils in these recipes to a minimum. Also, I have included chapters on the techniques that facilitate these reductions.

The great advantage of eating the Chinese way is that it is almost impossible not to eat a balanced diet. In the true Chinese diet, virtually every meal contains a healthy balance of grains, legumes, vegetables, and fruits. The recipes in this book are unlike the Chinese food served in restaurants, where the menu offerings have evolved toward richer foods and more meats. This book returns us, without sacrificing great taste, to a healthier, nutritional balance like that of the true Chinese diet.

Acknowledgments

I WANT TO THANK MY AGENT, BOB SILVERSTEIN, FOR his confidence in me; my editor, Jeanette Egan, for sharing with me the vision of publishing a healthful low-fat Chinese cookbook for today's lifestyle: her skillful editing and knowledgeable input were always right on target; my cooking class student, Randy Chaney, for his enthusiasm and for analyzing some of the nutritional data; my friend, Nancy Wang, for her critique and suggestions; and all of my cooking class students for their encouragement and for sharing so many cooking experiences with me. I also want to thank my children, Freddie, Lillian, and Matt, for their encouragement and support, for their tireless tasting and criticism, and for enduring chores and helping at the restaurant for more than ten years while still bringing home top grades and awards throughout their school years. I love them dearly; my legacy to them is this cookbook.

Above all, I am most grateful to my husband, Fred, who supported me in so many ways. He is always there when I need help or advice. He helped me unravel the intricacies of my multimedia computer and printer, without which the writing of this book would have been a daunting task. After using them to record hundreds of recipes, my computer and typing skills have improved enormously and I am ready for my next book.

Introduction

THE TRUE CHINESE DIET

*F*OR CENTURIES PEOPLE IN CHINA HAVE BEEN eating what doctors and researchers now recognize to be a healthy diet—small amounts of meat, and several servings of carbohydrates, fruits, and vegetables. The Chinese eat several rice servings at every meal. The main dishes are there to please the palate. Fresh fruits, such as melons, oranges, papayas, peaches, plums, and many others, are always served after each meal and are used for snacks.

Due to the lack of grazing land, meats have been relatively scarce. Meat is cut into small pieces and cooked with several fresh vegetables and a delicious sauce. The food platters are placed in the middle of the dining table and shared by the whole family. The Chinese diet includes more vegetables than meat. China's extensive coastline makes an enormous variety of fish and shellfish affordably available year-round, so seafood often appears on the dinner table.

Beans are used extensively in Chinese cooking. Red adzuki beans are used widely both for cooking and for making many kinds of sweet snacks. Black beans are used in cooking, and in brewing soy sauce, or they are fermented to be used as a seasoning. Soybean products are on the dinner table at almost every meal. Soybean is the single most important protein resource in the Chinese diet—soybean milk, soybean curd (tofu), soybean cake, soy sauce, soybean paste, and soy flour.

The Chinese use peanut oil or soybean oil for cooking, and toasted sesame oil for flavoring. They are heart-healthy oils. Butter and cheeses are not available and are not used in Chinese cooking.

The true Chinese diet is in perfect keeping with the balanced-diet recommendations of the American government's Food Guide Pyramid. This book is a quest to return us, without sacrificing great taste, to healthier and more nutritionally balanced dishes, like those in the true Chinese diet.

LOW-FAT COOKING TECHNIQUES

Chinese cooking need not be a trying experience for cooks new to it. A wok is not required. I do most of my stir-frying in heavy-bottomed, 10-inch skillets. Chinese cuisine has become very popular throughout the country, and as a result many of the better supermarket produce sections have blossomed with arrays of ethnic offerings. Asian vegetables and fruits have become mainstream. You need not worry about whether you are using the correct technique. This cookbook provides you with insights into the techniques of successful Chinese cooking.

· Blanching ·
A precooking process. The meat or vegetable is dropped into a pot of boiling water and left only until the color changes. Then it is immediately removed or drained and rinsed with cold water to stop further cooking. Sometimes seafood can be blanched in boiling water to partially cook it before the final cooking. Blanching is also used to preserve the bright color and nutrients of vegetables, especially tougher vegetables like broccoli and peeled carrots.

· Braising ·

An easy, aromatic, flavorful, delicious, and economical technique. A piece of meat is generally browned on all sides first, then slowly cooked whole in a pot, and cut into slices or cubes to serve. Occasionally the meat is cut up first to speed the cooking time. Soy sauce, dry sherry, sugar, spices such as star anise, fennel seeds, cinnamon sticks, and ginger and scallion, are added along with a small amount of water. The meat is turned and basted in the sauce several times during cooking.

· Oven Baking and Broiling ·

Cooking methods not common in China. Ovens are not available in standard Chinese kitchens. They have never been incorporated into home cooking. Traditionally deep-frying was used for browning and crisping. In the West we have ovens in our kitchens, and I have changed all of the deep-frying recipes in this cookbook to use baking and broiling, which are more consistent with a low-fat healthful diet. In these recipes I have preserved the character, great taste, and texture of these dishes.

· Smoke Cooking ·

A technique that is more a flavoring than a cooking process. Detailed smoking techniques are provided in the Smoked Duck recipe (page 188). The food to be smoked is generally seasoned and precooked or steamed first. The smoking agents—tea leaves, rice, and brown sugar—are readily available.

· Steaming ·

A cooking method used frequently in China that retains the pure, natural flavor and color of the food. It does not require the use of oil and is an ideal method of cooking for a healthy diet. A good-quality steamer is a wise investment.

When steaming, the water in the steamer should be boiling before the food is placed in the steamer. The food should be well above the surface of the boiling water so that the water does not bubble over it. The steaming pot should be large enough to hold enough water and provide sufficient space for the intense steam to circulate around the food. A steady volume of steam should be maintained throughout the cooking time. Put a small heatproof dish in the water; it will make some noise when the water is bubbling. If the noise ceases, it is a signal that the water has evaporated and will need to be replenished, with boiling water, if the cooking is still in progress.

· Stir-frying ·

A technique used to cook food quickly over high heat in a nonstick hot metal skillet. Chinese cooks use natural vegetable oils such as peanut, corn, safflower, canola, and soybean in stir-frying. Peanut oil and corn oil can withstand high heat without smoking and have a very good flavor. Soybean oil is good for you but tends to leave an odor that can linger in your house for a long period of time. Olive oil can also be used for stir-frying, but not with high heat; it burns easily. For nearly fat-free cooking, use nonstick cooking spray.

In stir-frying, the meats and vegetables are cut into small pieces before cooking; thus the cooking time is short, about 3 to 5 minutes. Don't cook too big a batch or you will be steaming instead of stir-frying. Divide large amounts and cook in several batches. Meat and poultry should be cut across the grain and marinated before stir-frying. Marinating gives meats or poultry a flavor they could not otherwise acquire in the short cooking time.

In low-fat stir-frying, little or none of the nutrients are lost in the cooking process. Begin by heating the nonstick wok or heavy nonstick frying pan over medium-high heat until it is hot, and only then add the oil. After adding the oil, let it heat for another 5 to 15 seconds, then add your flavoring agents (ginger, scallions, garlic, dried chilies) and cook until they become aromatic, about ten seconds. Then add your stir-fry ingredients and proceed to stir-fry with stirring, tossing, flipping, and turning motions. When stir-frying, at the beginning have the frying-pan lid within easy reach to use as a shield against spattering and smoking if necessary. Hold the lid a few inches over the frying pan, or rest the cover on the frying pan, leaving it partially open.

Basic Cooking Utensils

A well-equipped American kitchen is more than adequate for Chinese cooking. With today's improved technology, and our new knowledge and awareness of health and diet, your best investment would be in good-quality, heavy-bottomed nonstick cookware to reduce the need for added oil. There are a few special Chinese utensils that you can do without but would find versatile, convenient, and great fun to use.

· Wok or Nonstick Frying Pan ·

I have heard many people say: "I can't cook Chinese food because I don't have a wok," or "I bought a wok so I can do Chinese cooking." The fact is that you do not really need to have a wok to prepare great-tasting Chinese meals. A large nonstick deep frying pan can serve you well for stir-frying. In fact the wok, round bottom or flat bottom, is not built to work on the Western-style stove, which is better suited to heating flat-bottomed pans. Western stoves are not powerful enough to provide the high heat required to keep the whole curved surface of a wok at stir-frying temperature. If you do want to buy a wok, select a 14-inch heavy nonstick or thin, tempered iron wok, which can conduct and distribute heat evenly. I have thin, tempered iron woks, but for low-fat cooking, where I use very little oil, I use a heavy-bottomed, nonstick frying pan for stir-frying and pan-frying.

· Cleaver ·

A Chinese cleaver is a very convenient tool to have in the kitchen. Its sharp edge cuts, chops, and slices, and its blunt edge tenderizes meat. The flat side of the cleaver is used for crushing garlic, ginger, or water chestnuts, and for scooping prepared ingredients from the cutting board into the frying pan. And the end of the wooden handle can be used as a pestle to grind, crush, and pulverize. Chinese cleavers are available in a variety of sizes. The blade, made with a very slightly curved edge, is generally 7 to 8 inches in length and 3 to 5 inches in width. The 4-inch handle generally provides a comfortable grip. Chinese cleavers come in three weights: light, medium, and heavy. A *light* cleaver has a thin blade that is about $\frac{1}{16}$ inch thick and weighs $\frac{1}{2}$ to $\frac{3}{4}$ pound. It is for extremely fine and fancy cutting. A *medium* cleaver is about $\frac{1}{8}$ inch thick and weighs $\frac{3}{4}$ to $1\frac{1}{4}$ pounds. It is used for standard cutting and for light mincing and chopping. The *heavy* cleaver is about $\frac{1}{4}$ inch thick and weighs $1\frac{1}{4}$ to 2 pounds. It is used for power mincing and for chopping through meat bones.

· Steamer ·

Steaming, a very popular cooking method, is recommended for people on special diets. The Chinese manufacture two kinds of steamers—bamboo and metal. Bamboo steamers come in sizes ranging from miniature to very large. They are round trays with woven bamboo bottoms that stack tightly, one over another, in sets of two or three tiers; a solid woven cover fits on top. The steamer should be placed snugly inside a base pan, either a wok or a soup kettle, that is about 2 inches wider. The most practical bamboo steamer for your kitchen is a 12-inch steamer with two tiers and a cover, for which you would use a 14-inch-diameter wok as a base. Or you can use an aluminum 15-inch steamer set composed of two tiers, a base pot, and a cover. These are very handy for steaming large amounts of ingredients. Also available is a single-layer, 11-inch, stainless-steel steaming basket, which will fit inside a 12-inch skillet with a lid. This works perfectly for steaming small amounts of ingredients.

NUTRITIONAL ANALYSIS

The nutrition analyses can be used as a guide for putting together menus that keep nutrition within the daily guidelines for a 2,000- or 2,500-calorie diet. The current daily 2,000-calorie guidelines are: Total Fat less than 65 grams, Saturated Fat (which is part of the total fat) less than 20 grams, Cholesterol less than 300 milligrams, Sodium less than 2,400 milligrams, Total Carbohydrates target 300 grams, and Dietary Fiber target 25 grams. The guidelines, for a 2,000- and a 2,500-calorie diet, are printed on the labels of many food products.

The nutrition analyses in this book were determined by using the microcomputer dietary analysis software, SANTÉ, from Hopkins Technology. Dietary software makes use of published USDA and manufacturers' nutritional data to estimate the nutrients per serving from the ingredients and quantities that an inquirer specifies.

About the nutrition analyses in this book:

- If a range of servings is given in the recipe, e.g., four to six servings, the nutrition data apply to the lower number of servings.

- The nutrition analyses do not include ingredients listed as "optional," "for garnish," or "if desired."

- If an ingredient is listed with one or more alternatives or substitutes, the nutrition analysis includes only the first of the alternatives mentioned.

- Suggested accompaniments are not included in the nutrition analysis unless they are also in the ingredients list, but not optional ones.

- If a recipe has salt in the ingredients list and also says "salt to taste," then only the amount of salt listed is included and any additional (optional) salt to taste is not included in the nutrition analysis.

- For recipes that use marinades that are not consumed, only a fraction of the sodium contained in the marinade is actually absorbed into the food that is marinated. No nutrition analysis software reliably predicts the amount of sodium per serving in these circumstances. Thus the sodium levels listed for recipes that use marinades are only estimates.

- Some of the recipes that have no salt in the ingredients list, do show sodium in their nutrition analysis. This is because some ingredients already contain their own sodium. A few contain a lot of sodium. You will thus know how much sodium these recipes contain before adding the optional salt to taste, and you can decide whether or not it would be wise to add salt. (Tip: One level teaspoon measure contains 2,131 milligrams of sodium. The daily per person guideline is 2,400 milligrams.)

Note: Many factors in the manufacture of ingredients can result in variations in their nutrition levels, and the nutrition analyses may only approximate the nutrients in prepared dishes.

These recipes will help maintain a healthy lifestyle that observes dietary guidelines and includes proper exercise. They are not a substitute for medical advice or medically based diet plans. Individuals who need sodium-, fat-, or cholesterol-restricted diets should get medical supervision.

Appetizers and Dim Sum

Throughout China there are teahouses where people can meet and enjoy dumplings, varieties of vegetables in small servings, and morsels of meats and pastries.

These are meant to be snacks or light meals and are called *dim sum*. For a midday snack, some Crystal Shrimp Dumplings or Crispy Spring Rolls can satisfy your appetite.

For a perfect way to start a meal, or for a dim sum snack, this chapter contains low-fat, great-tasting recipes such as Golden Cups, Dumpling Blossoms, Teriyaki Mini Kabobs, and Shrimp Toast. Most of these recipes satisfy today's desire for fewer calories and reduced fat. No deep-frying is used.

Dim sum are great fun to eat. They can be served as appetizers or in larger amounts as an entree with salad and rice. Chinese dim sum blend beautifully with Western meals, so do not hesitate to incorporate a dish here and there into your luncheon, dinner, or party fare. They will truly delight family and guests.

Galloping Horses

These refreshing hors d'oeuvres have always been a hit at parties that I have catered. They are made from a combination of pork and tropical fruits and have a delightful flavor and texture.

MAKES 40 PIECES

1 small ripe pineapple, rinsed
3 small carambolas (star fruit), rinsed
1 tablespoon olive oil
3 cloves garlic, minced
3 cilantro roots, finely minced (see Note below)
1 shallot, minced
1 pound ground pork tenderloin

3 tablespoons fish sauce
4 tablespoons light brown sugar
Freshly ground black pepper to taste
½ cup crushed dry-roasted peanuts
2 fresh red chilies, seeded and thinly sliced
1 tablespoon chopped fresh spearmint or cilantro

Cut off and discard skin and both ends of pineapple. Quarter pineapple lengthwise and trim off core. Cut each quarter crosswise into ⅜-inch-thick slices and set aside. Cut carambolas crosswise into ¼-inch-thick star-shaped slices and set aside.

Heat a heavy 10-inch nonstick frying pan over medium-high heat until hot. Add oil, swirl to coat pan, and heat 15 seconds. Add garlic, cilantro roots, and shallot and cook, stirring, 30 seconds, or until aromatic. Add pork and cook, stirring to break up pork, about 2 minutes, or until pork is cooked through. Add fish sauce, sugar, pepper, and peanuts; stir and toss until thoroughly mixed.

Place a heaping teaspoonful of the pork mixture on each pineapple and carambola slice. Garnish each with a sliver of red chili and mint or cilantro.

Per piece: 47 Calories, 3.3 g Protein, 1.7 g Total Fat (32% of Calories), 0 g Saturated Fat, 5 g Carbohydrates, 0.6 g Dietary Fiber, 7 mg Cholesterol, 128 mg Sodium

Note: If cilantro roots are not available, use 2 tablespoons chopped cilantro stems.

Cinnamon-Honey Walnuts

Originally these walnuts were deep fried, but I find this baked version to be very satisfactory. A hint of cinnamon makes these candied nuts truly special. Walnuts, like all nuts, are high in fat content, but it is mainly polyunsaturated. Enjoy the great taste of walnuts, but eat them in small amounts.

MAKES 4 CUPS

4 cups walnuts
1 teaspoon vegetable oil
1/2 cup sugar

1/4 cup honey
1 piece (2-inch long) cinnamon stick
1/4 cup water

Place walnuts in a colander over the sink; shake a few times to rid them of any powder residue.

In a 3-quart pot, bring 4 cups water to a boil; add the walnuts, turn off heat, and let walnuts soak 5 minutes to remove bitterness. Drain walnuts in a colander and shake well to remove any excess water. Spread the walnuts on a large baking sheet and air-dry 30 minutes.

Preheat oven to 325F (165C). Heat a wok over medium heat; add oil and swirl to cover the lower third of the wok. Add the sugar, honey, cinnamon stick, and 1/4 cup water; bring to a boil over medium heat, stirring to dissolve sugar. Boil, without stirring, 2 minutes, or until some moisture has evaporated and the sugar syrup can coat a spoon.

Add the walnuts and increase the heat to medium-high; cook, tossing mixture constantly, about 5 minutes, or until walnuts are evenly coated and excess liquid has evaporated. Immediately transfer walnuts to a nonstick baking sheet. Spread walnuts in a thin, even layer without clumping to within an inch of the edge, separating them into individual pieces.

Bake the walnuts 10 minutes. Stir walnuts and rotate the baking sheet from front to back and bake 4 to 5 minutes longer, until walnuts are light brown and sugar coating is glistening and almost caramelized. (The walnuts will continue to darken from their own heat after they are removed from the oven. If too dark, they will be bitter.) Immediately transfer walnuts to another baking sheet to cool and harden.

Refrigerate walnuts in an airtight container. They will stay crisp and delicious for weeks.

Tofu- and Cheese-Filled Vegetables

Here is a low-calorie dip that I created for a party. The guests loved it. Tofu gives the dip its spreadable consistency, and the blue cheese gives it flavor. Together they make a great dip for vegetables or a spread for party breads, wonton chips, or crackers. Here I use it as a filling for stuffed celery and stuffed cherry tomatoes.

MAKES 4 SERVINGS

¼ pound fresh firm tofu
⅛ teaspoon salt
⅛ teaspoon sugar
⅛ teaspoon ground cumin
⅛ teaspoon hot chili sauce
¼ teaspoon white wine vinegar
1 small scallion, including top, chopped

1 tablespoon chopped fresh cilantro
1 tablespoon crumbled blue cheese
2 stalks tender celery, trimmed and cut into 1½-inch lengths
10 cherry tomatoes, tops and seeds removed

Place tofu in a microwave-safe dish. Cook in a microwave oven on HIGH 1 minute. Press gently to extract excess water and pat dry with paper towels. Mash the tofu in a small bowl; transfer to a strainer to drain 15 minutes or longer.

Return tofu to bowl. Add salt, sugar, cumin, chili sauce, vinegar, scallion, and cilantro; stir to blend well. Fold in blue cheese. Spoon mixture into the celery and tomatoes.

Crab Rangoons

These rangoons are crisp on the outside and soft and flavorful on the inside. They make ideal appetizers or snacks, and are wonderful hors d'oeuvres for a party.

MAKES 24 CRAB RANGOONS

4 ounces reduced-fat cream cheese, softened
6 ounces cooked crabmeat
1 teaspoon minced garlic
1 teaspoon Worcestershire sauce
1/2 teaspoon sugar
1/2 teaspoon salt

1/8 to 1/4 teaspoon cayenne pepper
2 tablespoons thinly sliced chives
24 fresh wonton wrappers, chilled
1 egg white, lightly beaten
Cooking spray
Spicy Orange Sauce (page 298) (optional)

In a medium bowl, stir together cheese, crabmeat, garlic, Worcestershire sauce, sugar, salt, and cayenne until combined. Stir in chives. Cover and refrigerate 4 hours or overnight to firm up.

Place 1 rounded teaspoonful of the cheese mixture on each wonton wrapper. Brush edges with egg white. Pick up 2 diagonally opposite corners and press edges together to seal and form a triangle shape. Holding the triangle vertically at the top, tap bottom gently on your work surface to flatten it somewhat and bend the 2 ends toward you so that the rangoon sits up straight (like the arms and back of an armchair). Repeat until all rangoons are shaped.

Arrange the rangoons without touching on an ungreased baking sheet and spray them with cooking spray. Place in the freezer 1 hour to firm and set their shapes.

Preheat oven to 350F (175C). Bake rangoons 11 minutes, or until light brown and crisp. Serve hot with Spicy Orange Sauce, if desired.

Per rangoon: 35 Calories, 2.4 g Protein, 1 g Total Fat (25% of Calories), 0.6 g Saturated Fat, 3.8 g Carbohydrates, 0 g Dietary Fiber, 10 mg Cholesterol, 103 mg Sodium

When filling the rangoons, have both the wonton wrappers and chilled cheese mixture very cold, and bake them immediately after freezing. These will help to keep their shapes and prevent the cheese from oozing out during baking.

Wonton Chips

These wonton chips make great low-calorie munchies. They are easy and quick to make and contain no fat. Serve them as snacks or with dips or salsa.

MAKES 100 CHIPS

8 ounces fresh wonton wrappers
Cooking spray
1/4 teaspoon sugar or to taste

1 teaspoon ground cinnamon
1/8 teaspoon salt

Preheat oven to 350F (175C). Lightly coat baking sheets with cooking spray.

Cut each wonton wrapper diagonally into 4 small triangles. Place the triangles in a single layer on prepared baking sheets. Spray the wrappers lightly with cooking spray. Sprinkle sugar, cinnamon, and a dash of salt lightly all over the triangles.

Bake 5 to 7 minutes or until light brown. Remove from oven. Repeat until all the wonton triangles are baked.

Per 10 chips: 67 Calories, 2 g Protein, 0 g Total Fat (0% of Calories), 0 g Saturated Fat, 13 g Carbohydrates, 0.6 g Dietary Fiber, 3 mg Cholesterol, 127 mg Sodium

Golden Cups

These little bite-size cups are filled with a savory mixture of minced chicken and diced vegetables. They are ideal finger foods. For a variation, shrimp may be used instead of chicken.

MAKES 24 FILLED CUPS

24 fresh wonton wrappers, cut into
   3-inch circles
Cooking spray
2 teaspoons canola oil
1 small potato, cut into ¼-inch cubes
¼ cup diced carrots
¼ cup frozen green peas
¼ cup corn kernels
2 tablespoons water
1 teaspoon minced lemongrass

¾ cup minced chicken
½ teaspoon curry powder
1 teaspoon fish sauce
¼ teaspoon sugar
1 teaspoon lime juice
2 heaping tablespoons coarsely chopped
   fresh cilantro
Salt and freshly ground black pepper to
   taste

Preheat oven to 375F (190C).

Spread out wonton wrappers individually on a baking sheet and spray each lightly with cooking spray. Turn them over and spray the other side. Gently press 1 wonton wrapper into each cup of a mini muffin pan, making sure the bottom is evenly flat. Bake 7 to 8 minutes, or until slightly golden.

Heat an 8-inch nonstick frying pan over medium heat until hot. Add 1 teaspoon oil, swirl to coat pan, and heat 10 seconds. Add diced potato; shake, flip, and cook 1 minute. Add carrots, peas, corn, and water. Cover and cook 1 minute, or until potato is tender. Transfer to a plate and set aside.

Wipe pan clean. Add remaining 1 teaspoon oil and heat over medium heat until hot. Add lemongrass; stir a few seconds. Add chicken; cook, stirring to separate the chicken pieces, until chicken turns white, about 1 minute. Add curry powder, fish sauce, sugar, and lime juice; stir and flip a few times. Return the vegetable mixture to the pan and stir in cilantro. Taste and adjust seasonings with salt and pepper, if necessary.

Fill each cup with 1 tablespoon of the chicken mixture and serve.

Per cup: 36 Calories, 2.5 g Protein, 0.5 g Total Fat (13% of Calories), 0 g Saturated Fat, 5 g Carbohydrates, 0 g Dietary Fiber, 5 mg Cholesterol, 51 mg Sodium

VARIATION

Golden Cup shells also make wonderful dessert shells. Fill them with custard, pudding, or cherry pie or other fruit pie filling; add some garnishes; and you will have another artistic palate pleaser.

Tricolored Meat Dumplings (Guo Tie)

During my college years in Taiwan, on long weekends the students often made dumplings for fun and to satisfy our appetites. We shared the job of making the dough, preparing the filling, rolling the dough, and shaping the dumplings. We talked and laughed while working and had a lot of fun. After we ate we would count how many each person had eaten. On an average each person would eat ten to fifteen pieces. These dumplings, which we call "guo tie" in Mandarin, are served as a meal by themselves in China. In America they are known as Peking raviolis or pot stickers, and are served in Chinese restaurants as appetizers.

MAKES 50 DUMPLINGS

FILLING

½ pound (2 cups) chopped green
    cabbage
½ teaspoon salt
1 pound ground turkey
2 tablespoons reduced-sodium soy sauce
1 tablespoon dry sherry
½ teaspoon sugar
¼ teaspoon freshly ground black pepper
1 tablespoon finely minced fresh ginger
3 scallions, including tops, thinly sliced
1 tablespoon cornstarch dissolved in 4
    tablespoons fat-free chicken broth
1 tablespoon oriental sesame oil

BASIC DUMPLING DOUGH

1 cup unbleached flour
⅓ cup boiling water
½ teaspoon olive oil

CARROT DUMPLING DOUGH

1 cup unbleached flour
½ cup pureed blanched carrot
3 cloves garlic, minced
1 teaspoon cracked black pepper
¼ teaspoon salt
½ teaspoon olive oil

GREEN PEA DUMPLING DOUGH

1 cup unbleached flour
½ cup pureed thawed frozen green peas
⅓ cup sweet basil, shredded
¼ teaspoon salt
½ teaspoon olive oil

ACCOMPANIMENT

Ginger Sauce I (page 288)

Filling: Sprinkle cabbage with salt in a medium bowl, toss, and let stand 15 minutes. Squeeze cabbage firmly between your palms to remove excess water; toss cabbage into a large bowl.

Add ground turkey and remaining filling ingredients; stir in one direction until mixture is thoroughly blended. Cover and refrigerate 3 to 4 hours or overnight.

Basic dough: Measure flour into a small bowl and make a well in the center. Add boiling water and oil. Stir with chopsticks until the flour is evenly moistened by the liquid. Turn dough onto a floured work surface and knead with your hands until elastic, smooth, and earlobe soft, about 5 minutes. (Or transfer the flour mixture to a food processor fitted with metal blade and process, adding 1 to 2 tablespoons of water, as needed, until dough forms a ball, about 30 seconds.) Cover dough with a damp cloth and let it rest 30 minutes.

Carrot dough: Measure flour into a small bowl and make a well in the center. Add carrot puree, garlic, pepper, salt, and oil. Continue as above for basic dough.

Green pea dough: Measure flour into a small bowl and make a well in the center. Add green pea puree, basil, salt, and oil. Continue as above for basic dough.

On a lightly floured board, work with 1 dough at a time, keeping the others covered. Press dough into a flat disk and roll out to an even 1/16-inch thickness, dusting the dough and the board lightly with flour as needed to prevent sticking and to allow the dough to stretch smoothly. Using a 3-inch round cutter, cut out as many rounds as possible, cutting them as closely as possible to minimize scraps. Form scraps into a ball; reroll, and cut into rounds.

Place rounds on a lightly floured surface and cover them with a dry cloth. Repeat with remaining 2 doughs.

Place 1 rounded teaspoonful of filling in center of 1 round, fold in half to enclose filling, and pinch open edges together at their midpoint. Pinch-pleat 1/2 of the circle, with 2 small pleats on either side of the pinched middle pointing toward the middle, and leave the other half-circle edge unpleated. Seal pleated and unpleated sides together by pinching along top. The pleated dumpling should curl naturally into an arc. Slightly tap bottom flat on work surface and rest it flat on its bottom. Repeat with remaining filling and rounds.

Heat a heavy 10-inch nonstick skillet over high heat until hot. Add 2 teaspoons oil, swirl to coat pan, and remove skillet from heat. Arrange dumplings close together, flat side down, in a single layer in the skillet, making concentric rings starting from the center and working out toward rim. (Use 2 skillets or cook in 2 batches.)

Return skillet to high heat. Shake skillet back and forth several times to prevent dumplings from sticking. Pour 1/2 cup water over the dumplings, cover immediately, and bring to a rolling boil. Reduce heat to medium and steam-cook 10 minutes. Uncover, increase heat to medium-high to evaporate any remaining water, and let dumplings fry, shaking pan often, about 1 minute, until bottoms are golden brown, watching carefully to make sure bottoms do not burn. If dumplings stick, use chopsticks to push at their ends to loosen them.

To serve, invert a large platter big enough to completely cover pan over the skillet and then, holding platter and pan securely, turn both upside down together. If you have done the job well, the dumplings on the plate will cling together in a spiral for a nice presentation. Serve immediately with Ginger Sauce on the side.

Per dumpling: 45 Calories, 3 g Protein, 0.8 g Total Fat (25.64% of Calories), 0.2 g Saturated Fat, 6.5 g Carbohydrates, 0 g Dietary Fiber, 6 mg Cholesterol, 78 mg Sodium

VARIATIONS
STEAMED DUMPLINGS

To steam the dumplings: Spray steaming basket lightly with cooking spray. Arrange dumplings, close together but not touching, in the basket over boiling water; steam, covered, over high heat 10 minutes. Turn off heat and let stand 1 minute to allow steam to subside before lifting the cover. Transfer dumplings to a serving plate.

Substitute coarsely chopped chicken for the turkey and 10 ounces thawed, frozen spinach, well drained, for the cabbage.

PLAIN DOUGH

Measure 2½ cups unbleached flour into a medium bowl. Pour in ⅔ cup boiling water. Mix and let stand 2 minutes. Stir in ⅓ cup cold water. Knead dough on a floured surface until smooth; cover and let rest at least 15 minutes. Knead again until dough is elastic, smooth, and earlobe soft. Make wrappers and fill as above. Ready-made Shanghai dumpling wrappers from Asian markets, made with flour and water only, can be used instead. Do not use wonton wrappers, which are made with eggs.

TIP
The uncooked dumplings freeze very well. Place dumplings, close together but not touching, on a plastic wrap–covered baking sheet and freeze. After freezing, put them into a plastic bag and seal. They can be cooked right from the freezer without thawing first.

Dumpling Blossoms (Shao Mai)

Dumpling Blossoms can be made in advance, frozen, and steamed right from the freezer. Garnish them with chopped parsley, carrots, ripe olives, green peas, or edible flowers for a beautiful presentation.

MAKES 20 DUMPLINGS

1 cup lean ground chicken or turkey breast

1/3 cup fresh shrimp, peeled, deveined, and chopped

1/4 cup minced bamboo shoots

2 Chinese dried mushrooms, soaked in hot water 30 minutes, drained, and chopped

1 tablespoon reduced-sodium soy sauce

1/4 teaspoon sugar

Pinch of white pepper

1 egg white, lightly beaten

1 teaspoon oriental sesame oil

20 wonton wrappers

Garnishes: chopped fresh parsley, chopped carrots, chopped ripe olives, green peas

Ginger Sauce II (page 288) (optional)

In a small bowl, combine all of the ingredients except wonton wrappers, garnishes, and sauce. Mix with a circular motion in one direction until well combined. Cover and refrigerate 4 hours to firm up mixture.

Trim wonton wrappers into 3-inch circles. Working with 1 piece at a time, moisten the top surface of the wonton wrapper lightly with water (this enables the wrapper to stick to the meat mixture securely). Using a butter knife, spread a spoonful of the meat mixture on each round to within 1/2 inch of the edge. With your hands, gather up wrapper to form a cup with the open end up and with your fingers wrapped around it, squeeze gently, leaving wrapper slightly open at the top and the edges flared. Tap each dumpling on the work surface a few times to flatten the bottom so that it will stand upright in the steamer.

Lightly coat a steamer basket with cooking spray. Place dumplings in the basket over boiling water; cover and steam over medium-high heat 15 minutes. Transfer dumplings to a serving plate and garnish tops creatively. Serve hot with Ginger Sauce, if desired.

Per dumpling: 42 Calories, 5 g Protein, 0.5 g Total Fat (10% of Calories), 0 g Saturated Fat, 4 g Carbohydrates, 0 g Dietary Fiber, 20 mg Cholesterol, 80 mg Sodium

Crystal Shrimp Dumplings

Wheat starch and tapioca starch turn translucent after they are cooked, allowing the pink shrimp and colorful vegetables to show through. These little mouthfuls look almost too pretty to be eaten. A touch of oil in the dough gives the dumplings a sheen.

It is simple but a little tricky to make them: You must work fast while the dough is still warm; once the dough is cold it becomes flaky.

MAKES 24 DUMPLINGS

FILLING

½ pound small fresh shrimp, peeled, deveined, and diced
½ teaspoon salt
1 teaspoon sugar
1 teaspoon premium oyster sauce
1 small egg white, lightly beaten
½ tablespoon tapioca flour
White pepper to taste
⅓ cup finely diced bamboo shoots
1 small scallion, including top, thinly sliced
1 teaspoon oriental sesame oil

DOUGH

1 cup wheat starch
½ cup tapioca starch
¼ teaspoon salt
¾ cup boiling water
1 teaspoon safflower oil

ACCOMPANIMENT

Ginger Sauce I (page 288) (optional)

In a medium bowl, combine all the filling ingredients; stir evenly and thoroughly. Cover and refrigerate 2 hours.

In a small bowl, combine wheat starch, tapioca starch, and salt and make a well in the center. Slowly add boiling water while mixing with chopsticks. Add oil and mix together thoroughly. If dough is too dry, stir in 1 teaspoon water at a time until dough is moist enough to come together. Turn dough onto a lightly floured surface and knead a few times until smooth. Divide dough into 2 pieces and place them in plastic bags to prevent them from drying out and to keep them pliable.

Lightly spray a work surface and the broad side of a cleaver with cooking spray to prevent sticking; repeat as necessary. Roll dough into sausage-shaped lengths about 6 inches long and 1 inch in diameter. Cut crosswise into ½-inch-thick rounds. Lay each round on its side and press flat with the broad side of the cleaver to create a thin, round disk, about 2¼ inches in diameter.

Place 1 teaspoon of shrimp mixture in center of each disk, then fold the disk in half, forming a crescent shape. Hold the open dumpling securely in the fingers of your left hand, then begin to form 2 or 3 pleats at the edge of one half of the skin, using the fingers of your right hand. Then bring the 2 halves to meet, enclosing the filling, and pinch edges together to seal completely.

Lightly coat a steamer basket with cooking spray. Place dumplings, close together but not touching, in the basket over boiling water; cover and steam over high heat 5 minutes. Turn off heat and let stand 1 minute to allow steam to subside before lifting the cover. Serve hot with Ginger Sauce, if desired.

Per dumpling: 37 Calories, 2.2 g Protein, 0.5 g Total Fat (12% of Calories), 0 g Saturated Fat, 5.8 g Carbohydrates, 0 g Dietary Fiber, 14 mg Cholesterol, 78 mg Sodium

Fantail Shrimp

Quick and easy, this eye-catching shrimp is an absolutely delicious appetizer. Serve with Plum Sauce (page 291) or Spicy Orange Sauce (page 298). Try a variation using your own favorite herbs.

MAKES 30 SHRIMP

1 pound (26 to 30 per pound) unpeeled
   large shrimp
1 tablespoon dry sherry
1/4 teaspoon garlic powder
1/2 teaspoon sugar
1 egg white, lightly beaten
1 tablespoon cornstarch
3/4 cup Japanese fine dry bread crumbs

1/4 cup sesame seeds
1/4 teaspoon salt
1/2 teaspoon ground black pepper
1/4 teaspoon paprika
1 tablespoon finely chopped fresh
   cilantro
1 tablespoon olive oil

Rinse shrimp and pat dry with paper towels; peel and devein shrimp, leaving last segment of shell and tail attached. Using a small sharp knife, make a small incision along inner curve of shrimp, but do not cut all the way through. Spread each shrimp out flat and tap lightly with the broad side of a heavy knife.

In a medium bowl, mix together sherry, garlic powder, sugar, egg white, and cornstarch. Add shrimp and stir gently to coat well.

In a small bowl, mix the bread crumbs, sesame seeds, salt, black pepper, paprika, and cilantro. Stir in oil and mix to distribute evenly.

Preheat oven to 425F (220C). Spray a baking sheet lightly with cooking spray.

Holding each shrimp by the tail, dredge both sides in the crumb mixture to coat well. Place shrimp in a single layer on prepared baking sheet, leaving a little space between them. Bake 7 minutes. Turn shrimp over and bake 2 minutes more, or until light brown and crisp (do not overcook the shrimp). Serve hot with a dipping sauce, if desired.

Per shrimp: 31 Calories, 3 g Protein, 0.6 g Total Fat (17% of Calories), 0 g Saturated Fat, 2 g Carbohydrates, 0 g Dietary Fiber, 23 mg Cholesterol, 52 mg Sodium

TIP

Cutting along the inner curve of a shrimp keeps the shrimp from curling when cooked.

Five-Spiced Pepper Salt

Sichuan peppercorn and five-spice add an exquisite flavor to the table salt, turning an ordinary food into a delicacy. Use it on roasted meats or broiled seafood, such as shrimp, scallops, or calamari.

MAKES ABOUT 4 TEASPOONS PEPPER-SALT

1 tablespoon kosher salt   ¼ teaspoon five-spice powder
½ teaspoon ground Sichuan pepper

Heat salt in a small dry skillet over low heat, stirring constantly, until salt turns off-white. Transfer to a small dish. Add Sichuan pepper and five-spice powder and mix thoroughly. Store in an airtight jar.

Per ¼ teaspoon: 0.2 Calories, 0 g Protein, 0 g Total Fat (0% of Calories), 0 g Saturated Fat, 0.1 g Carbohydrates, 0g Dietary Fiber, 0 mg Cholesterol, 376 mg Sodium

Shrimp Toast

This combination of chopped shrimp and crunchy water chestnuts produces a sensational flavor and texture. Shrimp toast is delicious as an appetizer and these are baked instead of deep-fried, so you can eat more. The basic shrimp paste can be used in many different ways, e.g., for stuffed peppers, stuffed mushrooms, and stuffed tofu; shrimp balls; and shrimp rolls.

MAKES 48 PIECES

12 slices densely textured thin sandwich
   bread, crusts trimmed
Basic Shrimp Paste (see below)
Garnishes: chopped ham, sesame seeds,
   or cilantro leaves
Cooking spray
Spicy Orange Sauce (page 298) (optional)

BASIC SHRIMP PASTE

1 pound medium fresh shrimp, peeled
   and deveined

1 tablespoon safflower oil
1 tablespoon finely minced fresh ginger
2 large scallions, including tops, thinly
   sliced
¾ teaspoon salt
½ teaspoon sugar
⅛ teaspoon white pepper
1 tablespoon cornstarch
1 large egg white
6 water chestnuts, chopped

Cut each bread slice diagonally into 4 small triangles, making a total of 48 triangles. Spread them on a baking sheet in a single layer and set aside to dry for 1 day.

Prepare Basic Shrimp Paste: In the bowl of a food processor fitted with the steel blade, combine shrimp, oil, ginger, scallions, salt, sugar, white pepper, cornstarch, and egg white. Process 30 seconds, or until shrimp are coarsely chopped, scraping down the sides of bowl as necessary. Transfer mixture to a bowl and fold in the water chestnuts. Cover and refrigerate 2 hours.

Preheat oven to 350F (175C). Using a butter knife, mound a portion of shrimp paste on each bread triangle, making it high in the center and tapering to the edges. Garnish each piece with either chopped ham or sesame seeds (or leave some plain and garnish with cilantro leaves after cooking).

Place triangles on an ungreased baking sheet, shrimp side up, and spray lightly with cooking spray. Bake 15 to 20 minutes, or until shrimp paste has puffed up and is firm to the touch at the centers. Serve hot with Spicy Orange Sauce, if desired.

Per piece: 22 Calories, 2 g Protein, 0.4 g Total Fat (16% of Calories), 0 g Saturated Fat, 2 g Carbohydrates, 0 g Dietary Fiber, 14 mg Cholesterol, 68 mg Sodium

VARIATIONS
SHRIMP BALLS

Shape 1 recipe Basic Shrimp Paste into 26 walnut-size balls. Roll some of them in 1 cup Japanese dry bread crumbs and some of them in a mixture of 2 tablespoons *each* white and black sesame seeds. Place balls on an ungreased baking sheet and spray with cooking spray. Bake in a preheated 350F (175C) oven 17 minutes, or until browned. Serve hot.

STUFFED PEPPERS

Shape 1 recipe Basic Shrimp Paste into 36 walnut-size balls. Remove cores and seeds from 1 small green bell pepper, 1 small red bell pepper, and 1 small yellow bell pepper. Cut each bell pepper into 8 equal squares. Dust bell pepper squares lightly with cornstarch. Top each bell pepper square with 1 portion of shrimp paste. Place filled pepper squares on a heat-resistant plate. Place plate over boiling water, cover, and steam over medium heat about 7 minutes, or until cooked through. Serve hot.

STUFFED MUSHROOMS

Soak 48 small, equal-size Chinese dried mushrooms in hot water 30 minutes; drain and squeeze gently to remove excess water. Remove stems. Shape 1 recipe Basic Shrimp Paste into 48 walnut-size balls. Place 1 portion of shrimp paste on bottom of each mushroom. Place on a heat-resistant plate. Place plate over boiling water, cover, and steam over medium heat about 7 minutes, or until cooked through. Serve hot.

Chicken Fingers

These small chicken strips are marinated, coated with light bread crumbs mixed with just a little oil, and then baked in a hot oven. Serve these delicious morsels with Plum Sauce and watch them disappear.

MAKES 6 SERVINGS

1 tablespoon dry sherry
1 tablespoon reduced-sodium soy sauce
½ teaspoon sugar
¼ teaspoon white pepper
2 teaspoons cornstarch
1 tablespoon egg white, lightly beaten
¾ pound boneless, skinless chicken breast, cut into 2½-inch long strips

½ cup plain dry bread crumbs
¼ cup sesame seeds
⅛ teaspoon salt
1 tablespoon finely chopped fresh cilantro (optional)
1 tablespoon peanut oil
Plum Sauce (page 291) (optional)

In a plastic bag, mix together sherry, soy sauce, sugar, white pepper, cornstarch, and egg white. Add chicken, seal bag, and turn to coat well. Set aside 30 minutes.

In a small bowl, mix bread crumbs, sesame seeds, salt, and cilantro, if using. Stir in oil and mix to distribute it evenly.

Preheat oven to 425F (220C). Coat a baking sheet with cooking spray.

Dredge chicken strips, one at a time, in bread crumb mixture, then arrange on prepared baking sheet in a single layer, leaving a little space between them. Bake 10 minutes. Turn chicken over and bake 5 minutes longer, or until lightly browned and crisp. Serve hot with Plum Sauce, if desired.

Per serving: 170 Calories, 21.8 g Protein, 6 g Total Fat (31% of Calories), 1 g Saturated Fat, 5.4 g Carbohydrates, 0 g Dietary Fiber, 49 mg Cholesterol, 322 mg Sodium

Walnut Chicken

Flavorful and crunchy, these chicken strips are seasoned with five-spice seasoning and coated with chopped walnuts. They make wonderful nibblers for a party. Although over half of the calories are from fat, nearly all of this is polyunsaturated fat from the walnuts. Still, eat these delicious walnut chicken strips in moderation!

MAKES 30 CHICKEN PIECES

¾ pound boneless, skinless chicken breast
1 tablespoon dry sherry
1 egg white, lightly beaten
2 tablespoons cornstarch

¼ pound (1 cup) shelled walnuts
Five-Spiced Pepper Salt (page 23) to taste
Plum Sauce (page 291) (optional)

Using the broad side of a cleaver or knife, gently flatten chicken breast to a scant ¼-inch-thick large piece, then cut into ½-inch-wide, 2-inch-long strips. Place in a medium bowl. Add sherry, egg white, and cornstarch; stir to coat the slices evenly. Cover and refrigerate 1 hour or longer.

Preheat oven to 375F (190C). Spray a baking sheet with cooking spray. Using a cleaver or knife, chop walnuts into small even pieces and place in a small bowl.

Stir chicken again to distribute the coating. Dredge chicken strips, one at a time, in chopped walnuts, then arrange on prepared baking sheet in a single layer, leaving a little space between them. Bake 7 to 8 minutes, or until walnuts are lightly toasted and chicken is cooked through. Remove from oven and sprinkle chicken with Five-Spiced Pepper Salt to taste. Serve with Plum Sauce, if desired.

Per piece: 39 Calories, 3.3 g Protein, 2.5 g Total Fat (58% of Calories), 0.3 g Saturated Fat, 1.1 g Carbohydrates, 0 g Dietary Fiber, 7 mg Cholesterol, 9 mg Sodium

Fresh Spring Rolls

The pink shrimp and striking green vegetables show through their translucent rice paper wrapper. These spring rolls are not deep-fried or baked, they are served fresh at room temperature. They are visually tempting and quite delicious.

MAKES 8 SPRING ROLLS

½ pound cooked pork tenderloin, trimmed of all visible fat

8 large cooked shrimp, peeled

2 ounces dried rice noodles, blanched in boiling water 2 minutes and cut into 3-inch lengths

1 large carrot, finely shredded

1 cup (about 2½ ounces) fresh bean sprouts

16 fresh mint leaves

15 to 20 sprigs fresh cilantro

8 (9-inch-round) perfect rice papers

8 green-leaf lettuce leaves, trimmed and cut in half

Garlic-Chili Dipping Sauce (opposite page) (optional)

Cut pork across the grain into ⅛-inch-thick slices; set aside. Cut each shrimp lengthwise in half; set aside.

Divide noodles, carrots, pork, bean sprouts, and mint leaves into 8 equal portions and combine them in 8 separate piles on a baking sheet.

Pour 1 inch of hot water into a 10-inch skillet. Immerse 1 rice paper in the hot water for 5 seconds. Remove paper from water and place on a damp kitchen towel. Let stand 15 seconds (rice paper should be soft and pliable; if still stiff, sprinkle with more hot water).

Fold up bottom third of 1 rice paper. Lay 1 lettuce leaf half over the folded portion; top with 1 pile of the noodle mixture. Shape filling into 4-inch-long log centered on the lettuce leaf and parallel to the folded edge of wrapper. Fold left and right sides of rice paper over filling. Starting at the filled end, roll up rice paper halfway into a cylinder enclosing filling completely. Lay 2 shrimp halves, cut side down, lengthwise on roll. Place several cilantro leaves next to the shrimp row. Finish rolling wrapper into a cylinder to incorporate the shrimp and cilantro and press final edge lightly to seal. Repeat with remaining rice papers and filling until all 8 rolls are made.

Line a serving platter with the extra lettuce leaves, and place rolls, shrimp side up, on the lettuce. Serve with Garlic-Chili Dipping Sauce, if desired.

Per ½ roll: 63 Calories, 5.6 g Protein, 0.5 g Total Fat (7% of Calories), 0 g Saturated Fat, 8.8 g Carbohydrates, 0.4 g Dietary Fiber, 24 mg Cholesterol, 66 mg Sodium

Garlic-Chili Dipping Sauce

This sauce is served to accompany fresh spring rolls, lobster rolls, or any steamed, poached, or barbecued seafood.

MAKES 1 CUP

2 small garlic cloves, crushed
1 small fresh hot chili, seeded and
   minced
2 tablespoons sugar
2 tablespoons lime juice
¼ cup rice vinegar

¼ cup fish sauce
¼ cup water
¼ cup finely shredded carrot (optional)
¼ cup finely shredded daikon radish
   (optional)

Combine garlic, chili, and sugar in a mortar. Pound with pestle to a fine paste. Add lime juice, vinegar, fish sauce and water; stir to combine. Transfer mixture to a small dish. Add shredded carrot and daikon, if using.

Alternatively, puree first 7 ingredients in a blender or processor; pour into a small bowl. Add shredded carrot and daikon, if using.

Per 2 tablespoons: 26 Calories, 1.2 g Protein, 0 g Total Fat (1% of Calories), 0 g Saturated Fat, 6 g Carbohydrates, 0.2 g Dietary Fiber, 0 mg Cholesterol, 710 mg Sodium

Crispy Spring Rolls

No more deep-frying! These baked spring rolls are delicious and crisp. You can cut them in half to serve as appetizers, or serve them whole for snacks. They can be made days in advance, frozen, and baked just before serving.

MAKES 20 SPRING ROLLS

6 ounces boneless, skinless chicken breast, shredded
1¾ teaspoons cornstarch
¼ pound fresh shrimp, peeled, deveined, and coarsely chopped
1 teaspoon vegetable oil
1 teaspoon grated fresh ginger
1 tablespoon dry sherry
4 Chinese dried mushrooms, soaked in hot water 30 minutes, drained, and shredded

⅓ cup shredded carrot
½ pound cabbage, shredded
6 ounces fresh bean sprouts
1 tablespoon reduced-sodium soy sauce
1 tablespoon cornstarch dissolved in 1 tablespoon water
20 spring roll wrappers
Cooking spray

In a bowl, combine chicken with 1 teaspoon of the cornstarch; set aside. In another bowl, combine shrimp with remaining ¾ teaspoon cornstarch; set aside.

Heat a heavy 10-inch nonstick skillet over medium-high heat until hot. Add oil and swirl to coat. Add ginger and cook, stirring, 10 seconds. Sprinkle chicken over ginger and stir-fry 1 minute, or until chicken is white. Push chicken to one side of the skillet. Add shrimp and sherry; stir-fry until shrimp are opaque. Transfer chicken and shrimp to a bowl.

Add mushrooms to skillet, stir a few times. Stir in carrot and cabbage; cover and cook 1 minute. Return chicken and shrimp to the vegetable mixture. Sprinkle bean sprouts and soy sauce over mixture and stir well. Stir cornstarch mixture and add to skillet; cook, stirring, until liquid thickens. Transfer mixture to a large platter and spread out. Cover and refrigerate several hours. (You can do this a day in advance.)

Preheat oven to 400F (205C). Spray a baking sheet with cooking spray. On a work surface, lay out several individual spring roll skins with a corner pointing toward you, keeping the rest covered with a damp cloth to keep them from drying out. Place ⅓ cup filling in a line about 4 inches long in the center of each spring roll skin. Pick up the corner closest to you and fold it over the mixture. Fold right corner of wrapper over mixture, then left corner—like folding an envelope around a letter. Moisten edges of top corner flap with water. Roll up from bottom into a cylinder, pressing lightly to seal roll. Arrange spring rolls, sealed side down, on prepared baking sheet. Repeat until all spring rolls are formed.

Spray rolls lightly with cooking spray. Bake 15 minutes, or until wrappers are light brown and crisp. Serve hot.

Per roll: 67 Calories, 5 g Protein, 0.3 g Total Fat (4% of Calories), 0 g Saturated Fat, 10.9 g Carbohydrates, 0.7 g Dietary Fiber, 13 mg Cholesterol, 94 mg Sodium

VARIATIONS
TAIWANESE SPRING ROLLS

Place ½ cup filling in a line about 4 inches long in the center of each spring roll skin. Spread 1 teaspoon hoisin sauce on the wrapper along the filling and sprinkle 1 tablespoon finely chopped roasted peanuts and some cilantro leaves on top of the mixture. Roll up spring rolls as above and eat them with your fingers (no baking needed here). These spring rolls are good made with a hot filling or at room temperature. Traditionally they are served during Chinese New Year to guests and holiday well-wishers.

Note: Spring roll wrappers are made from flour and water, and are precooked and edible right out of the package. Egg roll skins are uncooked, contain raw egg, and should not be eaten unless cooked.

Crispy Fish Rolls

$\int$erve these delicious fish rolls, cut in half, as appetizers or snacks with a sweet and sour sauce.

1 pound fish fillet, such as haddock, cod, or any firm white fish
1 tablespoon dry sherry
1 teaspoon oriental sesame oil
Salt and freshly ground white pepper to taste
1 tablespoon egg white, lightly beaten
2 scallions, including tops, finely sliced

1 teaspoon grated fresh ginger
12 spring roll wrappers
1 tablespoon cornstarch dissolved in 2 tablespoons water, for sealing
Cooking spray
Sweet and Sour Sauce (page 294) (optional)

Preheat oven to 400F (205C). Spray a baking sheet with cooking spray.

Cut fish into twelve 4-inch-long strips; place in a medium bowl. Add sherry, sesame oil, salt and white pepper to taste, and egg white and stir gently to blend well. Fold in scallions and ginger.

On a work surface, lay out several individual spring roll skins with a corner pointing toward you, keeping the rest covered with a damp cloth to keep them from drying out. Place $\frac{1}{12}$ of the fish mixture in a line about 4 inches long in the center of each spring roll skin. Pick up the corner closest to you and fold it over the mixture. Fold right corner of wrapper over mixture, then left corner—like folding an envelope around a letter. Moisten edges of top corner flap with cornstarch mixture. Roll up from bottom into a cylinder, pressing lightly to seal roll. Arrange fish rolls, sealed side down, on prepared baking sheet. Repeat until all fish rolls are formed.

Spray fish rolls lightly with cooking spray. Bake 20 minutes, or until wrappers are slightly brown and crisp. Serve with Sweet and Sour Sauce, if desired.

Per roll: 80 Calories, 8.5 g Protein, 0.8 g Total Fat (9% of Calories), 0 g Saturated Fat, 9.3 g Carbohydrates, 0.4 g Dietary Fiber, 23 mg Cholesterol, 68 mg Sodium

Lobster Rolls

These lobster rolls can be cut on the bias into small halves and served, cut side up, for hors d'oeuvres, or they can be served whole for a light lunch.

MAKES 4 LOBSTER ROLLS

4 perfect 9-inch round rice papers
4 large perfect Boston lettuce leaves, cut in half
1 cup thinly shredded carrots
1 cup shredded peeled cucumbers
24 fresh mint or basil leaves
¾ pound cooked lobster meat

1 lemon
Freshly ground black pepper
4 scallions, including tops, cut into 4-inch lengths
½ cup fresh cilantro leaves
Garlic-Chili Dipping Sauce (page 29)

Divide lobster meat and each kind of vegetable into 4 equal portions on a baking sheet.

Pour 1 inch of hot water into a 10-inch skillet. Immerse 1 rice paper in the hot water for 5 seconds. Remove paper from water and place on a damp kitchen towel. Let stand 15 seconds (rice paper should be soft and pliable; if still stiff, sprinkle with more hot water).

Fold up bottom third of 1 rice paper. Lay 1 lettuce leaf half over the folded portion; top with ¼ of the shredded carrots, ¼ of the shredded cucumbers, and 6 mint or basil leaves. Spoon ¼ of the lobster meat in a row in the middle of the vegetables. Sprinkle lobster with some lemon juice and freshly ground black pepper, then cover the lobster with ¼ of the scallions and cilantro leaves. Shape filling into a 5-inch-long log centered on the lettuce leaf and parallel to the folded edge of wrapper. Fold left and right sides of rice paper over filling. Starting at filled end, roll up rice paper into a cylinder, enclosing filling completely. Repeat with remaining rice papers and filling until all rolls are made, keeping finished rolls covered with a damp towel so they will stay moist. Pour dipping sauce into small individual bowls and serve with the lobster rolls.

Per ½ lobster roll (without dipping sauce): 73 Calories, 8.7 g Protein, 0.8 g Total Fat (9% of Calories), 0 g Saturated Fat, 7.7 g Carbohydrates, 1 g Dietary Fiber, 36 mg Cholesterol, 138 mg Sodium

Vegetarian Rolls

These vegetarian rolls can be served as appetizers or snacks at any time. They also make good accompaniments for barbecued chicken or steaks. When soaking bean threads, keep the string on the bundle tied. Discard the string after you cut the noodles into short lengths. It's easier to cut the noodles while they are still tied.

MAKES 12 ROLLS

1 bundle (2 ounces) bean threads, tied with string, soaked in cold water 30 minutes

8 large Chinese dried mushrooms, soaked in hot water 30 minutes, liquid reserved, and shredded

1 cup shredded carrots

1 cup shredded snow peas

1 cup shredded winter bamboo shoots

12 perfect 9-inch-round rice papers

12 perfect fresh cilantro sprigs with leaves, each 5 inches long

1 head leaf lettuce, separated and washed

Ginger Sauce I (page 288) (optional)

Drain bean threads and cut into 2-inch lengths; discard string. In a large pot, bring 2 quarts water to a boil. Add bean threads and cook until al dente, about 1 minute. Drain and set aside.

Heat a 10-inch frying pan over medium heat. Add mushrooms, carrots, snow peas, bamboo shoots in separate groups without mixing, and 1 cup of the reserved mushroom soaking liquid. Cover and cook 1 minute, or until vegetables are brighter in color and heated through. Drain vegetables and let cool.

Divide bean threads and each vegetable into 12 equal portions and place them in separate piles on a baking sheet for easier handling.

Pour 1 inch of hot water into a 10-inch skillet. Immerse 1 piece of rice paper in the hot water for 5 seconds. Remove paper from water and place on a moist kitchen towel; let stand 15 seconds (rice paper should be soft and pliable; if still stiff, sprinkle with more hot water).

Fold up bottom third of 1 rice paper. Lay $1/12$ of the bean threads, mushrooms, carrots, snow peas, and bamboo shoots neatly in a row over the folded portion; shape filling into a 4-inch-long line parallel to the folded edge. Fold left and right sides of rice paper over filling. Starting at filled end, roll up rice paper 1 turn to form a tight cylinder, enclosing filling completely. Once you complete 1 turn, place a sprig of cilantro on the cylinder and continue rolling to complete roll; press end of wrapper lightly to seal. Repeat with remaining rice papers, and vegetables.

Line a serving platter with lettuce leaves. Place vegetarian rolls, cilantro side up, on the lettuce. Serve with Ginger Sauce, if desired.

Per roll: 162 Calories, 1.7 g Protein, 0.1 g Total Fat (1% of Calories), 0 g Saturated Fat, 40 g Carbohydrates, 2.4 g Dietary Fiber, 0 mg Cholesterol, 111 mg Sodium

Pearl Balls

Regular meatballs are just ordinary, but when coated with pearl-white grains of rice and garnished, they become extraordinary. When I catered for birthday parties, I found that children love these special meatballs, and they love to make them too, as a party activity.

MAKES 26 PEARL BALLS

¾ cup glutinous rice, soaked in water overnight

4 Chinese dried black mushrooms, soaked in hot water for 30 minutes, drained, and chopped

1 pound ground turkey

1 tablespoon reduced-sodium soy sauce

1 tablespoon dry sherry

½ teaspoon salt

½ teaspoon sugar

Freshly ground black pepper to taste

1 large egg white, lightly beaten

⅓ cup minced water chestnuts

2 teaspoons finely minced fresh ginger

1 scallion, including top, thinly sliced

1 tablespoon cornstarch dissolved in ¼ cup water

Finely chopped carrot and chopped fresh cilantro, for garnish

Garlic-Soy Dipping Sauce (page 287)

Drain rice and rinse several times until water runs clear. Drain and place in a small bowl; set aside.

In a medium bowl, combine mushrooms, turkey, soy sauce, sherry, salt, sugar, black pepper, egg white, water chestnuts, ginger, scallion, and cornstarch; stir in a circular direction until mixture is smooth and cohesive.

Form mixture into 26 walnut-size meatballs. Roll each meatball in rice until evenly coated. Place meatballs ¾ inch apart on a heatproof plate coated with cooking spray. Place plate in steamer over boiling water; cover and steam over medium heat until rice is tender, about 30 minutes.

Transfer pearl balls to a serving dish. Sprinkle chopped carrot and cilantro on top of the pearl balls to contrast with the ivory luster of the rice. Serve hot with Garlic-Soy Dipping Sauce, if desired.

Per ball: 49 Calories, 4.6 g Protein, 0.6 g Total Fat (19% of Calories), 0.2 g Saturated Fat, 5.7 g Carbohydrates, 0.3 g Dietary Fiber, 11 mg Cholesterol, 93 mg Sodium

VARIATION

Divide rice among 3 bowls. Add 1 drop of red food coloring to one bowl, 1 drop of green food coloring to second bowl, and keep the rice in the third bowl natural. Coat one-third of meatballs with each color of rice. Cook as above. The result is beautiful coral-, jade-, and ivory-colored meatballs.

Vegetarian Balls

Instead of meat, these mock meatballs contain tofu. They are very satisfying and can be served in many ways. Serve them with Sweet and Sour Sauce (page 294) for appetizers, or serve them with General Zuo's Chicken (page 172) accompanied by steamed broccoli and rice for a quick meal. Tofu has only 4 grams of fat, mostly polyunsaturated, per 3½ ounces.

MAKES 26 BALLS

16 ounces firm tofu, drained
1 tablespoon reduced-sodium soy sauce
¼ teaspoon salt
¼ teaspoon sugar
¼ teaspoon celery seeds
½ teaspoon hot chili sauce
1 scallion, including top, finely sliced
1 teaspoon finely minced fresh ginger

4 Chinese dried mushrooms, soaked in hot water 30 minutes, drained, and finely diced
⅓ cup finely chopped carrot
⅓ cup finely crushed corn flakes
2 large egg whites, lightly beaten
1 teaspoon oriental sesame oil
Cooking spray

Mash tofu in a medium microwave-safe bowl with a fork until there are no more big pieces. Heat tofu in a microwave oven on HIGH 2 minutes. Transfer to a strainer to drain excess water.

In a large bowl, combine tofu, soy sauce, salt, sugar, celery seeds, and chili sauce and mix well. Add scallion, ginger, mushrooms, carrot, corn flakes, egg whites, and sesame oil and mix well. Cover and set aside 30 minutes.

Preheat oven to 450F (230C). Spray a baking sheet with cooking spray.

Using a melon baller, form mixture into 26 walnut-size balls and place them on prepared baking sheet. Spray tofu balls with cooking spray and bake 20 minutes, or until light brown and crisp. Serve hot.

Per ball: 21 Calories, 1.7 g Protein, 0.7 g Total Fat (29% of Calories), 0 g Saturated Fat, 2.2 g Carbohydrates, 0 g Dietary Fiber, 0 mg Cholesterol, 72 mg Sodium

Teriyaki Mini Kabobs

These chicken kabobs are irresistibly delicious. The marinade, which is thickened slightly with flour to help it cling, provides the chicken with a moist and luscious coating. Serve these kabob cubes on wooden picks as appetizers, or serve them on skewers and accompany them with a tossed green salad and hot steamed rice for a light meal.

MAKES 6 SERVINGS

⅓ cup reduced-sodium soy sauce

¼ cup dry sherry

¼ cup sugar

1 tablespoon all-purpose flour

1½ pounds boneless, skinless chicken leg meat, trimmed of all visible fat and tendons and cut into about ¾-inch cubes

1½ tablespoons grated fresh ginger

¼ teaspoon freshly ground black pepper or to taste

1 green bell pepper, cut into ¾-inch squares

1 yellow bell pepper, cut into ¾-inch squares

1 large onion, cut into ¾-inch squares

In a small saucepan, whisk together soy sauce, sherry, sugar, and flour and cook over medium heat until mixture comes to a boil and is slightly thickened, about 1 minute. Remove from heat and let cool.

Add chicken cubes, grated ginger, and black pepper to the soy sauce mixture and stir to coat chicken well. Cover and refrigerate, stirring occasionally, 2 hours.

Prepare grill or preheat broiler. Thread bell peppers, onion, and marinated chicken cubes onto 6 long stainless-steel skewers. Finish each skewer with a piece of onion to secure the kabobs. Reserve remaining marinade.

Grill or broil kabobs 5 minutes. Brush with remaining marinade. Turn chicken over and cook another 4 minutes, or until the chicken is golden brown and cooked through.

Per serving: 254 Calories, 24 g Protein, 7 g Total Fat (24% of Calories), 2 g Saturated Fat, 22 g Carbohydrates, 1 g Dietary Fiber, 92 mg Cholesterol, 694 mg Sodium

Soups

In China, soup is served at every meal. In contrast to the Western meal, soup is not served at the beginning of a meal. During a Chinese family meal, a large bowl or tureen of soup is placed in the center of the table, presiding over the surrounding dishes. Diners spoon a little soup into their soup or rice bowls as their beverage from time to time throughout the meal. Water or tea is not served with a meal. Tea is always served after the meal, for the Chinese believe that tea aids in digestion and cleanses the palate.

Some of the soups are light and clear, and some are thick and hearty. Some, such as a noodle soup or a dumpling soup, can be a snack or light meal. Then there are soups containing a whole chicken or fish that are cooked and served in earthenware in a rich broth, sometimes with bean threads, tofu, and vegetables added. These are meals in themselves.

The soups I have selected here are diverse, easy to make, and delicious. All soups, including the simplest ones, should be based on a good strong stock that is homemade. If time does not allow this, use a commercially canned low-fat, low-sodium chicken broth.

Egg Drop Soup

Fast and economical, this delicate soup needs no more than a pot of good homemade chicken broth and careful technique.

MAKES 4 SERVINGS

2 large egg whites
½ teaspoon oriental sesame oil
4 cups fat-free, low-sodium chicken broth
⅛ teaspoon sugar

Salt and black pepper to taste
4 teaspoons cornstarch dissolved in 2 tablespoons water
1 scallion, including top, thinly sliced

Beat egg whites with sesame oil until blended but not frothy; set aside.

In a 2-quart soup pot, bring chicken broth to a boil, then lower heat to a simmer; add sugar, salt, and pepper to taste. Stir cornstarch mixture and stir into the soup; bring to a boil again, stirring constantly. Remove pot from heat. Pour egg-white mixture in a thin stream in a wide circle over the surface of the broth. Stir gently a few times and see the egg ribbons float to the surface. Sprinkle in scallion and serve.

Per serving: 47 Calories, 4 g Protein, 1.3 g Total Fat (26% of Calories), 0 g Saturated Fat, 4.4 g Carbohydrates, 0 g Dietary Fiber, 0 mg Cholesterol, 90 mg Sodium

VARIATION
SEAWEED EGG DROP SOUP

Add 1 large ripe tomato, cut into thin wedges; 1 cup torn seaweed; and 2 scallions, including tops, cut into 1-inch lengths, to the egg drop soup.

TIPS

The soup must be hot enough to cook the egg white to form ribbons. If too cool, the egg will just mix into the broth without making ribbons.

If you want to make the egg drop soup several hours ahead, stir 1 teaspoon white vinegar into the soup to prevent the egg drops from turning dark.

 Wonton Soup

Wonton soup traditionally was eaten as a snack food. Wontons are versatile: They can be boiled and tossed with soy sauce, sesame oil, and hot chili sauce and served as Sichuan dumplings, or they can be baked and served as appetizers in addition to being added to soups. Sometimes cooked noodles are added to wonton soup with a few green vegetables. This wonton noodle soup can be a light meal by itself.

1 Chinese dried mushroom, soaked in hot water 30 minutes, drained, and minced
¼ pound lean ground pork
¼ pound raw shrimp, peeled, deveined, and chopped
1 tablespoon minced water chestnut
1 small scallion, including top, finely sliced
½ teaspoon finely minced fresh ginger

1 teaspoon dry sherry
¼ teaspoon salt
Pinch *each* of sugar and white pepper
32 wonton wrappers
8 cups fat-free, low-sodium chicken broth
2 scallions, including tops, thinly sliced, for garnish
2 teaspoons oriental sesame oil, for garnish

In a small bowl, combine mushroom, pork, shrimp, water chestnut, scallion, ginger, sherry, salt, sugar, and white pepper; cover and set aside 30 minutes.

Place 1 wonton wrapper on work surface with 1 corner pointing toward you; place 1 teaspoon of filling a little off center and slightly away from you on wrapper. Brush edges of the wrapper lightly with water. Fold the far corner over the filling to meet the corner that points toward you, but let it fall ½ inch short of meeting, and pinch to seal at edges of the inner triangle. Brush a little water on left corner. Bring right corner up to overlap slightly on left corner and press overlap together to seal. Repeat until all wontons are formed.

In a large pot, bring 4 quarts water to a boil. Stir water gently in a circular motion while you drop in wontons a few at a time so they will not stick to bottom of pot. Simmer 7 to 10 minutes, until wontons float to the surface. Drain wontons and discard water.

Meanwhile, in another large pot, bring chicken broth to a boil. Place 4 cooked wontons in each of 8 individual soup bowls. Ladle the hot chicken broth over the wontons, garnish with chopped scallions, and drizzle a few drops of sesame oil on top. Serve immediately.

Per serving: 69 Calories, 6.8 g Protein, 3 g Total Fat (39.70% of Calories), 0.5 g Saturated Fat, 3 g Carbohydrates, 0 g Dietary Fiber, 20 mg Cholesterol, 163 mg Sodium

Hot and Sour Soup

This hearty Beijing hot and sour soup together with some fried rice or scallion pancakes and a tossed green salad make a wonderful luncheon or light meal.

4 cups fat-free, low-sodium chicken broth

6 Chinese dried mushrooms, soaked in hot water 30 minutes, drained, and shredded

1 tablespoon wood ear mushrooms, soaked in hot water, drained, and shredded

10 dried tiger lily buds, soaked, cut into 1-inch lengths, and hard stems removed

1/3 cup shredded bamboo shoots

1/2 cup thinly shredded chicken breast

1/2 pound regular tofu, cut into thin shreds

2 tablespoons reduced-sodium soy sauce

1/2 teaspoon sugar

1/2 to 1 teaspoon white pepper or cayenne pepper

3 tablespoons cornstarch dissolved in 1/4 cup water

2 large egg whites, lightly beaten

3 tablespoons white distilled vinegar or to taste

1 teaspoon oriental sesame oil

2 scallions, including tops, finely sliced, or 2 tablespoons chopped fresh cilantro

Salt and freshly ground black pepper to taste

In a large pot, bring chicken broth to a boil over high heat. Add mushrooms, lily buds, and bamboo shoots; stir a few times and cook 1 minute. Add chicken; stir gently to separate the pieces and cook 1 minute. Add tofu, soy sauce, sugar, and pepper. Reduce heat; stir gently a few times and simmer 2 minutes.

Stir cornstarch mixture and add to the soup. Increase heat to medium and cook, stirring, until soup is slightly thickened and comes to a boil again.

Turn off heat and immediately pour egg whites in a thin stream over the surface of the broth. As egg whites begin to congeal, stir gently a few times to break them into silken ribbons. Add vinegar, sesame oil, and chopped scallion or cilantro. Serve immediately.

TIP

The soup must be hot enough to cook the egg white to form ribbons. If not, the egg whites will simply mix with the soup.

Ginger Clam Soup

Ginger and clam flavors are very complementary and make a refreshing and delicious soup. The clams must be live and closed before cooking; they should open during cooking. Discard any clams that do not open.

MAKES 4 SERVINGS

12 live littleneck clams, scrubbed clean under running water
4 cups water
1 (¼-inch-thick) slice fresh ginger, lightly smashed

8 watercress sprigs, trimmed
4 very thin lime or lemon slices
Salt and freshly ground pepper to taste

In a heavy 10-inch skillet over high heat, combine clams, water, and ginger; cover and bring to a boil, but watch carefully, as the soup can boil over very quickly. Reduce heat slightly and, keeping lid askew, simmer until clams open, 1 to 2 minutes. Skim off any scum that rises to the surface. Remove pan from heat.

In each of 4 soup bowls, place 3 clams in their shells. Garnish with 2 watercress sprigs and a slice of lime or lemon. Fill each bowl with hot broth. Discard ginger and any sand at bottom of the pan. Serve at once. Pass salt and pepper so each person can season the soup as desired.

Swordfish Miso Soup

This soup is made with miso, which is fermented soy bean paste, a flavoring used widely in the Orient in cooking, marinades, and dressings. You can add just about anything from the sea into this soup. Try it with haddock, bluefish, or clams. Serve this soup with hot steamed rice; it is an excellent warming snack or light meal on a cold day. Or serve this soup as part of a multicourse meal.

MAKES 4 SERVINGS

¼ pound swordfish, cut into ¾-inch cubes
1 teaspoon reduced-sodium soy sauce
Pinch of sugar
1 teaspoon cornstarch
3 cups fish stock or water
½ pound tofu, cut into ¾-inch cubes and drained

2 tablespoons light (white) miso
¼ teaspoon sugar
Freshly ground black pepper to taste
1 whole large scallion, cut into 1-inch lengths

Stir together the swordfish, soy sauce, sugar, and cornstarch in a small bowl. Marinate 15 minutes.

Bring the stock or water to a boil in a 2-quart soup pot; add swordfish and tofu. Cook over medium heat 2 minutes, or until fish turns white. Reduce heat to low. Remove ½ cup of the broth to a bowl; add miso paste and press with the back of a spoon until dissolved. Add miso mixture to the soup. Sprinkle in sugar and pepper. Add scallion and stir briefly. Serve immediately.

Per serving: 84.9 Calories, 9 g Protein, 3.1 g Total Fat (33% of Calories), 0.5 g Saturated Fat, 4.7 g Carbohydrates, 0.6 g Dietary Fiber, 16 mg Cholesterol, 441 mg Sodium

Pressing miso through a metal strainer will make it easier to dissolve the paste.

To derive the greatest health benefits from miso soup, do not bring the miso to a boil; it will destroy the lactobacillus enzymes. Instead, make the soup, then remove a few cups of broth. Stir the miso into the broth until it dissolves, then return the mixture to the soup. Heat until hot without boiling.

Tilapia and Vegetable Soup

Tilapia is a light flavorful fish with a pleasing texture. It is ideal for making fish chowder or fish stew. Use medium heat and simmer it slowly to bring out its subtle delicious taste. Miso paste is high in sodium so no need to add extra salt, but a little sugar offsets the saltiness of the soy paste.

MAKES 4 SERVINGS

2 cups water
3 large fresh mushrooms, sliced
2 cups torn napa cabbage leaves
2 tilapia fillets (about ½ pound total),
  each cut in half

1 tablespoon red (dark) miso paste
¼ teaspoon sugar
1 scallion, including top, thinly sliced

In a 2-quart soup pot, bring 2 cups water to a boil over medium-high heat. Add mushrooms and cabbage, stir briefly, and cook 1 minute, or until soup comes to a boil again. Add fish fillets. Reduce heat to low, cover, and poach 2 minutes, or until fish is just cooked through.

Remove ½ cup of the soup to a soup bowl. Add miso paste and stir until miso dissolves. Return miso mixture to soup. Sprinkle in sugar and stir to dissolve. Sprinkle with scallions. Serve immediately.

Per serving: 64 Calories, 12 g Protein, 0.7 g Total Fat (9.81% of Calories), 0 g Saturated Fat, 3.4 g Carbohydrates, 2 g Dietary Fiber, 34 mg Cholesterol, 226 mg Sodium

Stuffed Cucumber Soup

This satisfying and refreshing soup, a favorite of my cooking class students, has an interesting texture. It is a delicious way to serve your garden-fresh cucumbers. The minced water chestnuts impart a delightful crunchiness to the meat filling in the cucumbers.

MAKES 4 SERVINGS

¼ pound lean ground turkey or chicken
1 Chinese dried mushroom, soaked in hot water 30 minutes, drained, and finely chopped
1 whole small scallion, finely chopped
3 water chestnuts, minced
½ teaspoon reduced-sodium soy sauce
¼ teaspoon salt

1 teaspoon cornstarch
2 long straight cucumbers, peeled, cut crosswise into 16 sections, hollowed, and seeds removed
Cornstarch for dusting
4 cups fat-free, low-sodium chicken broth
1 tablespoon chopped fresh parsley

In a small bowl, combine turkey or chicken, mushroom, scallion, water chestnuts, soy sauce, salt, and cornstarch; mix thoroughly.

Dust cucumber pieces lightly with cornstarch, then stuff with turkey mixture.

In a large pot, bring chicken broth to a boil. Add stuffed cucumbers; cover, reduce heat to medium, and cook 10 minutes, or until cucumbers are tender. Divide soup among 4 soup bowls and garnish with chopped fresh parsley.

Per serving: 72 Calories, 7.6 g Protein, 1.3 g Total Fat (16% of Calories), 0.2 g Saturated Fat, 3 g Carbohydrates, 0 g Dietary Fiber, 20 mg Cholesterol, 217 mg Sodium

Velvety Crab-Corn Soup

This hearty, creamy soup speckled with crabmeat and golden corn has a chowderlike consistency. Its preparation is simple, but you should use an excellent brand of creamed corn. This soup is excellent with Scallion Pancakes (page 264). It is also good with toasted bagels or crisp matzo.

MAKES 6 SERVINGS

1 teaspoon canola oil
2 shallots, finely chopped
1 heaping teaspoon minced fresh ginger
½ pound fresh, frozen, or canned crabmeat, carefully picked over
2 tablespoons dry sherry
2 cups fat-free, low-sodium chicken broth
1 (14-ounce) can good-quality cream-style corn

¼ teaspoon salt or to taste
¼ teaspoon sugar
¼ teaspoon white pepper
1½ tablespoons cornstarch dissolved in 2 tablespoons water
2 egg whites, lightly beaten
Cilantro leaves, for garnish

Heat a 2-quart soup pot over medium heat until hot; add oil and swirl to coat pan. Sprinkle in shallots and ginger and cook, stirring, a few seconds, until aromatic. Stir in crabmeat. Stir in sherry and boil 30 seconds.

Stir in chicken broth, corn, salt, sugar, and pepper until stock and corn are blended. Bring soup to a near-boil. Stir cornstarch mixture; add to pot and cook, stirring gently, about 1 minute, or until soup is glossy and slightly thickened. Bring soup to a low boil. Turn off heat and immediately pour beaten egg whites in a small stream in a wide circle over the surface of soup; stir gently a few times to form egg whites into thin white lacy ribbons.

Ladle soup into heated individual soup bowls, garnish each bowl with cilantro leaves, and serve immediately.

Per serving: 136 Calories, 8 g Protein, 1 g Total Fat (7% of Calories), 0 g Saturated Fat, 18 g Carbohydrates, 1.3 g Dietary Fiber, 27 mg Cholesterol, 623 mg Sodium

Note: Soup must be hot enough for egg to cook or it will not form into thin lacy ribbons.

Watercress and Chicken Soup

Pure white chicken meat contrasted with green watercress and flavored with a hint of fresh young ginger make this soup pleasing to the eye as well as the palate.

MAKES 4 SERVINGS

¼ pound (½ cup) thinly sliced chicken breast
½ teaspoon cornstarch
4 cups fat-free, low-sodium chicken broth
2 Chinese dried mushrooms, soaked in hot water 30 minutes, drained, shredded
1 bunch (6 ounces) fresh watercress, washed and trimmed

Salt and freshly ground black pepper to taste
1 tablespoon finely shredded young spring ginger
1 teaspoon oriental sesame oil

In a small bowl stir together chicken and cornstarch; set aside 15 minutes.

In a heavy 2-quart soup pot, bring chicken broth to a boil over medium-high heat. Add chicken slices and mushrooms, stir to separate the pieces, and cook until chicken turns white, about 1 minute.

Bring soup back to a boil. Add watercress, salt, and pepper. Cover, increase heat to high, and cook 1 minute. Uncover, add ginger and sesame oil, and stir gently a few times. Serve immediately.

Per serving: 77 Calories, 10 g Protein, 2.4 g Total Fat (27% of Calories), 0.3 g Saturated Fat, 2.8 g Carbohydrates, 0.7 g Dietary Fiber, 16 mg Cholesterol, 101 mg Sodium

Hearty Soybean Soup

Soybeans have served as one of the most important sources of protein in Asia. This soup is nutritious and delicious. Accompany it with steamed buns, garlic bread, or brown rice for a light meal.

MAKES 6 SERVINGS

1 cup diced pork tenderloin
2 teaspoons reduced-sodium soy sauce
2 teaspoons cornstarch
2 teaspoons olive oil
2 scallions, including tops, thinly sliced, whites and greens separated
1 stalk celery, diced
2 carrots, peeled and diced
½ teaspoon fennel seeds

1 small potato, peeled and diced
2 cups cooked or canned soybeans, drained
3½ cups fat-free, low-sodium chicken broth
¼ cup green peas
Salt and freshly ground black pepper to taste

Stir together the pork, soy sauce, and cornstarch in a small bowl; set aside.

Heat a 3-quart heavy soup pot over high heat until hot. Add oil and swirl to coat pan. Add white part of scallions and cook, stirring, 20 seconds, or until aromatic. Add celery, carrots, and fennel seeds and cook, stirring, until aromatic, about 1 minute. Add potato and soybeans; cook 2 to 3 minutes, or until heated through.

Add chicken broth and bring to a boil. Reduce heat. Add pork and stir gently to separate the pieces; cook 2 to 3 minutes, or until vegetables are tender. Stir in green part of scallions and green peas. Add salt and freshly ground black pepper to taste. Serve hot.

Per serving: 188 Calories, 17 g Protein, 6.4 g Total Fat (31% of Calories), 1.1 g Saturated Fat, 16 g Carbohydrates, 4.6 g Dietary Fiber, 25 mg Cholesterol, 295 mg Sodium

Chicken and Bean Thread Soup

This is a hearty, warming soup for a cold day. Containing nutritious meats, vegetables, and bean threads, the soup constitutes a meal in itself. In this recipe you can use chicken breast, but the Chinese prefer chicken legs because they are more tender and juicier than breast meat.

MAKES 6 SERVINGS

8 small Chinese dried mushrooms, soaked in 1½ cups hot water 30 minutes
1 (3.5-oz.) package bean threads, soaked in cold water 30 minutes
2 skinless chicken leg quarters, trimmed of all visible fat
3 teaspoons canola oil
1 tablespoon dry sherry
2 scallions, including tops, cut into 1-inch lengths

4 thin slices fresh ginger
5 cups fat-free, low-sodium chicken broth
5 tablespoons reduced-sodium soy sauce
1 teaspoon sugar
½ teaspoon freshly ground white pepper
1 carrot, peeled and cut into thin flower-shaped slices
2 cups coarsely chopped fresh spinach or escarole

Drain and squeeze mushrooms dry; reserve soaking liquid and set aside. Drain bean threads, discarding water. Cut bean threads into 4-inch lengths; set aside. Cut chicken at joints into 4 large pieces.

Heat a heavy 10-inch nonstick frying pan over high heat until hot. Add 2 teaspoons of the oil, swirl to coat pan, and heat 15 seconds. Add chicken and fry until light brown on both sides, about 2 minutes. Add sherry and let it evaporate a few seconds, shaking pan often. Transfer contents to a 4-quart flameproof casserole dish.

Add remaining 1 teaspoon oil to pan, swirl, and heat 15 seconds. Add scallions, ginger, and mushrooms; cook, stirring, until aromatic, about 20 seconds. Add chicken broth, soy sauce, sugar, pepper, and carrot; bring to a boil.

Place the casserole dish containing the chicken on the stove over low heat. Add broth mixture to the chicken. Bring soup to a rapid boil, then cover, reduce heat to low, and simmer gently 20 minutes. Add bean threads and spinach or escarole, cover, and simmer another 5 minutes.

Using a spoon, raise some chicken, mushrooms, carrot, bean threads, and spinach to the surface to make an attractive presentation. Increase heat and bring mixture to a boil, then take it to the table in the casserole dish and serve.

Per serving: 203 Calories, 17 g Protein, 5 g Total Fat (21.47% of Calories), 1 g Saturated Fat, 24 g Carbohydrates, 2 g Dietary Fiber, 40 mg Cholesterol, 655 mg Sodium

Bean Thread and Meatball Soup

This is a delicious satisfying soup. It can be served as a first course or as a light meal by itself. Tianjin preserved cabbage is salt cured and sun dried; it comes in a small brown clay pot and has a unique flavor and delicious taste. Rinse lightly before using to remove excess salt.

MAKES 6 SERVINGS

2 ounces bean threads, soaked in cold water 30 minutes
1/2 pound pork tenderloin
1 tablespoon fish sauce
1 tablespoon dry sherry
1/8 teaspoon ground white pepper
1 egg white
2 teaspoons cornstarch
1/4 cup minced carrot
2 tablespoons minced water chestnuts

1/4 pound firm tofu, drained and mashed
4 cups fat-free, low-sodium chicken broth
2 ounces Tianjin preserved cabbage, rinsed
4 ounces fresh watercress, large stems discarded
1 teaspoon oriental sesame oil
Apple cider vinegar for seasoning (optional)
Chili paste (optional)

Drain bean threads and cut into 3-inch lengths; set aside.

In a food processor fitted with the steel blade, pulse pork until coarsely chopped, about 30 seconds. Add fish sauce, sherry, pepper, egg white, cornstarch, carrot, water chestnuts, and tofu; process until evenly mixed, about 45 seconds. Shape mixture into 24 walnut-size balls and set aside.

Bring chicken broth and preserved cabbage to a rolling boil in a 3-quart heavy soup pot over high heat. Reduce heat until mixture simmers. Add meatballs, cover, and simmer over low heat 8 to 10 minutes, or until cooked through.

Add bean threads, increase heat to high, and cook 3 minutes, or until noodles are al dente. Add watercress and cook 1 minute. Drizzle in sesame oil and serve. Serve vinegar and chili paste on the side, if desired.

TIP

Dried bean threads are very hard to cut. After soaking, they will become soft and easy to cut into desired lengths.

Tofu and Spinach Soup

This soup is rich in protein and calcium, and free of cholesterol. It is an excellent starter or accompany it with Scallion Pancakes (page 264) for a light snack.

MAKES 4 SERVINGS

3 cups fat-free, low-sodium chicken broth
1 tablespoon finely shredded young spring ginger
½ pound regular tofu, cut into ½-inch strips
10 ounces fresh spinach, coarsely chopped

½ teaspoon salt
¼ teaspoon sugar
¼ teaspoon ground white pepper
1 teaspoon oriental sesame oil

In a 3-quart soup pot, bring chicken broth to a boil over high heat. Add ginger and tofu strips, stir gently to separate the pieces, and bring to a boil again. Stir in spinach. Add salt, sugar, and pepper and cook 1 minute. Drizzle in sesame oil. Serve immediately.

Fish Casserole Soup

This is a substantial and heart-warming soup in which whole fish is the superstar, accompanied by plump, silken tofu, flavorful mushrooms, and luscious transparent bean threads in a pot of mouth-watering aromatic broth. It is a delicious main-course dish. Serve it with rice, or serve it with Western crusty bread and a mixed green salad with vinaigrette dressing. You will have a flavorful and satisfying meal.

MAKES 6 SERVINGS

1 (about 2½-lb.) whole white fish or sea bass
6 medium Chinese dried mushrooms, soaked in 1 cup hot water 30 minutes
12 ounces firm tofu, cut into 1 × 2-inch cubes
4 teaspoons canola oil
1 (1-inch) piece fresh ginger, thinly sliced
4 cloves garlic, coarsely chopped
2 tablespoons dry sherry
4 tablespoons reduced-sodium soy sauce

¼ teaspoon freshly ground white pepper
20 Chinese red dates (jujube)
4 cups fat-free, low-sodium chicken broth
3 ounces broad mung bean threads, soaked in cold water 30 minutes, drained, and cut into 4-inch lengths
1 small leek, cut at an angle into thin slices and thoroughly rinsed
Salt and freshly ground white pepper (optional)

Have fish cleaned, scaled, and trimmed but leave head and tail on. Rinse fish thoroughly and pat dry with paper towels. Cut fish crosswise in half; set aside.

Remove mushrooms from soaking liquid; squeeze to remove excess moisture. Reserve soaking liquid. Place tofu cubes in a small pot of hot water and let them soak until ready to use.

Heat a heavy 10-inch nonstick frying pan over high heat until hot. Add 2 teaspoons of the oil, swirl to coat pan, and heat 15 seconds. Add fish and pan-fry until golden brown on both sides, about 2 minutes per side. Transfer fish to a 4-quart casserole dish (being careful to keep the fish skin intact for a beautiful presentation).

Add remaining 2 teaspoons oil to pan, swirl, and heat 15 seconds. Add ginger and garlic and cook, stirring, until aromatic, about 30 seconds. Stir in mushrooms. Add sherry, soy sauce, pepper, dates, chicken broth, and reserved mushroom liquid. Bring to a boil, then transfer to the casserole dish containing the fish. Ladle the broth over the fish several times to season it. Cover and simmer over low heat 15 minutes.

Drain tofu and add it to the casserole, distributing the pieces evenly. Cover and simmer 10 minutes more. Turn and baste tofu a few times. Move tofu to one side and add bean threads to the other side. Cover and simmer 5 minutes more. Increase heat to high and sprinkle in the leek. Boil 30 seconds. Bring the casserole to the table and serve. Add salt and pepper to taste individually, if desired.

Per serving: 181 Calories, 6.5 g Protein, 5.4 g Total Fat (26.7% of Calories), 0.5 g Saturated Fat, 27.6 g Carbohydrates, 1 g Fiber, 0 mg Cholesterol, 493 mg Sodium

Ginseng Cornish Hen Soup

This is a special soup that my mother used to make for me. The broth is more prized than the meat; however, the meat is delicious, too. This soup makes a wonderful starter for a multicourse meal.

MAKES 4 SERVINGS

1 (about 1½-lb.) Cornish game hen, trimmed of all visible fat
16 Chinese red dates (jujube)
1 ounce ginseng slices

4 cups boiling water
Dipping Sauce (opposite page) optional
Salt (optional)

Discard fat from cavity and around neck of hen. Cut off tail. Bring a pot with enough water to cover hen to a boil over high heat and carefully slide in the hen; blanch in boiling water 1 minute to remove excess fat. Drain hen and rinse with water; pat dry with paper towels.

Place hen in a casserole dish or a ceramic bowl large enough to hold it and the boiling water. Add dates and ginseng. Cover tightly with a lid or foil. Place casserole dish in a large pot set on the stovetop. Add enough water to the pot to reach within 1½ inches of top of casserole dish. Cover pot and bring water to a boil. Reduce heat to low to maintain a slow simmer and simmer 2 hours.

When ready to serve, remove chicken with a large slotted spoon. Remove and discard skin and bones. Skim off the fat on the surface of the soup. Discard ginseng pulp. Serve each person a bowl of clear broth with some chicken meat and dates. You do not need to cut the meat; it is so tender that you can tear it apart with a fork or chopsticks. The meat is scrumptious as is or with the dipping sauce. Add some salt to the broth, if desired.

Per serving (without dipping sauce): 116 Calories, 18.3 g Protein, 2.6 g Total Fat (20.51% of Calories), 0.7 g Saturated Fat, 4 g Carbohydrates, 0.5 g Dietary Fiber, 60 mg Cholesterol, 66 mg Sodium

 Dipping Sauce

2 tablespoons reduced-sodium soy
  sauce
2 teaspoons rice vinegar

1 teaspoon sugar
½ teaspoon roasted Sichuan peppercorn
  powder

Combine soy sauce, vinegar, and sugar in a small dish and stir until sugar dissolves. Stir in peppercorn powder and serve.

Per 1 teaspooon: 3 Calories, 0 g Protein, 0 g Total Fat (22% of Calories), 0 g Saturated Fat, 0.7 g Carbohydrates, 0 g Dietary Fiber, 0 mg Cholesterol, 66 mg Sodium

Chinese Fire Pot

Chinese fire pot is a one-course meal of many delights and an impressive way to entertain guests on cold days. To prepare a fire-pot meal, first select a good variety of raw meats, poultry, and seafood. Each must be sliced into large but thin pieces so that they will cook quickly. Arrange them neatly on beautiful platters; and arrange the platters artistically around the pot (see Note) containing the boiling broth in the center of the table. Let your guests do all the cooking. It is great fun with chopsticks, but forks can be used, too. When most of the meats and fish have been consumed, the remaining vegetables, transparent noodles, and contents of the platters are added to the stock, cooked for several minutes, and served in the individual bowls as a delicious soup to top off a delightful meal. This is a spectacular meal to enjoy with family and friends.

MAKES 8 SERVINGS

1 pound boneless, skinless chicken breast, partially frozen
1 pound beef flank steak, trimmed of visible fat, partially frozen
1 pound large fresh shrimp
3 pounds live mussels or littleneck clams, scrubbed
1 pound fillet of sole, flounder, or pike
1 pound squid
Dipping Sauce (see following)
Condiments (see following)
2 pounds napa cabbage, cut diagonally into 1½-inch pieces
2 pounds fresh spinach, washed and drained
1½ pounds soft tofu, cut into ¼-inch-thick slices
2 ounces bean thread noodles, soaked and cut into 4-inch lengths

Garnishes: green leaf lettuce, radish flowers, tomato roses, and parsley sprigs
10 cups or more fat-free low-sodium chicken broth

CONDIMENTS
½ cup premium oyster sauce or soy paste
½ cup hot chili paste
½ cup Hot Mustard Sauce (page 292)
½ cup balsamic vinegar or wine vinegar
½ cup Worcestershire sauce
2 cups cilantro leaves

DIPPING SAUCE (PER PERSON)

1 tablespoon reduced-sodium soy sauce
1 teaspoon oriental sesame oil

Slice the partially frozen chicken and beef diagonally across the grain into large thin slices. Peel and butterfly the shrimp, leaving the tails on. Slice fish into large, thin slices. Arrange chicken, beef, shrimp, and fish attractively, overlapping slices in a circle with garnishes on seperate platters.

Cut tentacles off squid, slit bodies open, discard transparent cartilage, and peel off inner and outer membranes. Using a knife score each squid on inner side in a crisscross pattern and cut it lengthwise into two pieces.

For the dipping sauce, mix soy sauce and sesame oil in individual small dishes for each person.

Put each condiment except for cilantro into separate small dishes, each with a tiny serving spoon in it. Set dishes around the fire pot or on a small tray so each diner can select desired condiments.

Arrange platters, vegetables, tofu, and bean threads attractively on the table around the fire pot. Set out individual bowls, dipping sauce, a Chinese soup spoon, and chopsticks for each person.

Bring the broth in the fire pot to a boil, and begin the meal. Each person picks up meats, fish, or vegetables from the platter, swishes them through the hot broth in the fire pot to cook, and then dips them into the dipping sauce and condiments. When most of the meats and fish have been consumed, the remaining vegetables, tofu, transparent noodles, and contents of the platters are added to the stock, cooked for several minutes, and served in the individual bowls.

Per serving: 496 Calories, 76 g Protein, 11 g Total Fat (20% of Calories), 2.6 g Saturated Fat, 22 g Carbohydrates, 8 g Dietary Fiber, 308 mg Cholesterol, 701 mg Sodium

Notes: Fire pots are available in Asian markets. There are two varieties: One is the traditional copper or bronze funneled pot, which is fueled by charcoal. This traditional kind is not safe to use indoors due to the potential for carbon-monoxide poisoning. The other type is an attractive electric soup pot or skillet with an adjustable temperature control. This type is ideal for indoor use.

The ingredients, and their quantity, depend on your preference and the number of people. Veal, venison, scallops, and oysters are all good choices; plan about ½ pound of meat and fish per person. There should be enough variety, however, to make the meal look exuberant and interesting.

Steamed rice is very good with this and may be served on the side at any time during the meal, if desired.

Salads, Vegetables, and Pickles

During my childhood, on Sunday mornings the happiest thing for me was going to the open market with my mother. There I could smell the scent of fresh fruits, vegetables, and flowers from everywhere. I saw the beautiful colors of the vegetables, the gleaming fish and seafood, and the fresh meats and poultry. The farmers took pride in the products they grew. They strove to bring out the freshest and best-quality produce to display, and all the vendors greeted us with enthusiasm, hoping we would purchase some of their neatly displayed fruits and vegetables. It was a happy feeling just to mingle with the crowds, buying and browsing from one stand to another. Even now, every time I go back to visit Taiwan, top on my list is going to the market every day to purchase fresh fruits and vegetables.

China is essentially an agricultural country. With an overcrowded population and a scarcity of meats, fresh fruits and vegetables are a very important part of the Chinese diet. Because of the scarcity, ingredients such as roots and bulbs, fungi, and seaweed, which contain needed vitamins and minerals, have been developed as sources of nutrition.

The Chinese developed techniques for preserving foods such as black mushrooms, tree ears, lily buds, beans, and nuts by drying them in the sun and air. They also pickled and preserved vegetables such as various types of cabbage, cucumbers, mustard greens, and turnips, which provide a contrast of taste and texture to fresh vegetables. These preserved foods also stimulate the appetite and perk up meals.

In the United States we have a boundless array of fresh greens, vegetables, fruits, and herbs available year-round; thus I have included a large selection of vegetable dishes, main-dish salads, and side-dish salads accented with exciting flavors and textures. Whenever you add good fresh fruits and vegetables to your diet, you add good taste and good health to your life. And remember: To maintain good health, the American Heart Association recommends that we eat five or more servings of vegetables and fruits per day!

Green Papaya Slaw

The large unripened green papaya, cousin of the small yellow sweet papaya, is a cooking papaya. It is as big as a football with a mild flavor and firm crunchy texture. Marinated green papaya makes a wonderful salad that is delicious with meats or seafood, accompanied by rice.

MAKES 8 SERVINGS

4 cloves garlic, crushed

2 to 4 fresh hot green chilies, seeded and sliced (optional)

1/4 cup dried shrimp, soaked in hot water to cover 30 minutes, drained, and finely chopped

1 large tomato, seeded and sliced

2 tablespoons light brown sugar

1 1/2 pounds green papaya, peeled, seeded, and cut into fine shreds (see Tips, opposite page)

3 tablespoons fish sauce

1/4 cup freshly squeezed lime juice

Lettuce leaves

1 cup shredded (as thin as the papaya shreds) carrots

2 cups shredded (as thin as the papaya shreds) green cabbage

2 scallions, including tops, thinly sliced

1/3 cup chopped fresh cilantro

1/2 cup crushed dry-roasted peanuts

Place garlic and chilies in a mortar and pound into a paste. Add chopped shrimp and pound into soft crumbled pieces. Add tomato and brown sugar and lightly pound to release some of the tomato juices and to dissolve the sugar.

In a large bowl, combine crushed ingredients, papaya, fish sauce, and lime juice; mix thoroughly.

Arrange lettuce leaves on a serving platter. Mound papaya mixture in the center and arrange shredded carrots and cabbage around it. Sprinkle scallions, chopped cilantro, and peanuts on top. Cover and refrigerate. Serve cold.

Per serving: 125 Calories, 7.2 g Protein, 4.8 g Total Fat (34.89% of Calories), 0.7 g Saturated Fat, 16.2 g Carbohydrates, 4 g Dietary Fiber, 19 mg Cholesterol, 654 mg Sodium

Use a mandolin (hand slicer/shredder) to shred the papaya to get perfect shreds.

To firm and crisp vegetable shreds, plunge them into a bowl of iced water; drain. Keep them in a plastic bag in the refrigerator 1 hour or longer.

When ripened, the green papaya's flesh turns orange-red, sweet, and flavorful. I use ripened green papaya to make delicious Papaya Beef (page 191).

Mango Salad

*T*his is a colorful exotic salad that complements grilled meats beautifully.

MAKES 6 SERVINGS

2 large firm ripe mangos, peeled and cut into ½-inch-thick strips
1 small cucumber, quartered lengthwise and thinly sliced
1 small red onion, sliced
2 medium scallions, including tops, thinly sliced
½ cup roasted red bell peppers, cut into strips
¼ teaspoon Asian chili sauce, or to taste
⅓ cup raisins
2 tablespoons honey
Freshly squeezed juice of 1 lime
½ tablespoon Dijon mustard
1 tablespoon red wine vinegar
Salt and freshly ground black pepper to taste
⅓ cup chopped fresh cilantro
⅓ cup coarsely chopped roasted peanuts

In a large salad bowl, combine all ingredients except cilantro and peanuts; stir to mix well. Cover and chill in refrigerator until ready to serve. Sprinkle cilantro and chopped peanuts on top just before serving.

Per serving: 146.67 Calories, 6.5 g Protein, 4.5 g Total Fat (27.79% of Calories), 0.6 g Saturated Fat, 26.4 g Carbohydrates, 4.1 g Dietary Fiber, 0 mg Cholesterol, 43 mg Sodium

VARIATION
CHICKEN-MANGO SALAD

Top the mango salad with grilled chicken breast strips.

Tomato, Avocado, and Papaya Salad

Use small yellow sweet papayas for this beautiful exotic salad. It makes an excellent complement to barbecued meats and poultry.

MAKES 4 SERVINGS

3 tablespoons light brown sugar
1 tablespoon fish sauce, or to taste
5 tablespoons fresh lime juice
1/4 cup dried shrimp, minced or ground in a blender or coffee mill
1 ripe Hass avocado, peeled, pitted, and cut into 1/2-inch cubes
1 large tomato, diced

1/2 ripe small yellow sweet papaya, seeded and diced
2 scallions, including tops, thinly sliced
2 tablespoons chopped fresh mint
4 ounces radish sprouts or alfalfa sprouts
Mint leaves, for garnish

Make salad dressing by combining the sugar, fish sauce, and 4 tablespoons of the lime juice in a small dish; stir until sugar dissolves. Stir in minced shrimp; set aside.

In a medium bowl, toss avocado with remaining lime juice. Add tomato, papaya, scallions, and mint. Sprinkle with dressing and toss gently to combine.

Spread radish sprouts as a base on 4 individual salad plates. Scoop 1/4 of the mixed salad on top of sprouts. Garnish with mint leaves and serve.

Per serving: 166 Calories, 7 g Protein, 8.1 g Total Fat (43.6% of Calories), 1.3 g Saturated Fat, 19.3 g Carbohydrates, 3.4 g Dietary Fiber, 38 mg Cholesterol, 570 mg Sodium

Tofu, Tomato, and Eggplant Salad

This is an interesting and delicious salad. If you use globe eggplant, you should peel it because of its tough skin, but you can leave some strips of purple peel intact to add color to this dish. Chinese and Japanese eggplants are very tender; they are never peeled. Serve this dish cold as an appetizer, side dish, or salad.

MAKES 6 SERVINGS

¾ pound firm eggplant, partially peeled and cut into ½-inch cubes
½ teaspoon salt
2 teaspoons oriental sesame oil
1 teaspoon minced fresh ginger
1 tablespoon minced garlic
8 ounces extra-firm tofu, drained and cut into ½-inch cubes

1 teaspoon reduced-sodium soy sauce
¼ teaspoon sugar
5 tablespoons freshly squeezed lime juice
1 ripe tomato, cubed
2 scallions, including tops, thinly sliced
6 to 8 perfect romaine lettuce leaves

Sprinkle eggplant with salt; let stand 30 minutes. Drain thoroughly, squeezing eggplant with your hands to remove excess moisture.

Heat a heavy 10-inch nonstick frying pan over medium heat until hot. Add oil and swirl to coat pan. Add ginger and garlic. Stir and cook until aromatic, about 30 seconds. Add tofu and eggplant; cook, tossing to combine, 30 seconds. Remove pan from heat. Add soy sauce, sugar, and lime juice; stir and toss to season evenly. Add tomato and scallions; toss to combine.

Line a shallow salad bowl with lettuce leaves and mound salad mixture in the center. Cover and refrigerate at least 3 hours or up to 8 hours before serving.

Per serving: 74 Calories, 3.8 g Protein, 3.5 g Total Fat (37.08% of Calories), 0.4 g Saturated Fat, 8.1 g Carbohydrates, 2.2 g Dietary Fiber, 0 mg Cholesterol, 233 mg Sodium

VARIATION
Top this salad with ⅓ cup crumbled Greek feta cheese and ½ teaspoon dried oregano.

Oriental Salad with Miso Dressing

In this refreshing salad, the napa cabbage and bok choy are uncooked, like lettuce in a Western salad. The consistency of this dressing should be creamy and as thick as buttermilk. You can use more flour if you prefer it thicker, or add water by the teaspoonful to thin it out. The dressing is also delicious as a vegetable dip.

MAKES 4 SERVINGS

Miso Dressing (see opposite)
4 cups cut-up napa cabbage leaves
4 cups bok choy, including stalks and
  leaves, thinly sliced diagonally
1 cup hand-torn radicchio
½ cup sliced radishes
1 cup sliced firm mushrooms
2 scallions, including tops, cut diagonally
  into 1½-inch lengths
1 cup fresh bean sprouts

MISO DRESSING

1 tablespoon canola oil
½ teaspoon unbleached flour
1½ tablespoons cider vinegar
2 tablespoons honey
3 tablespoons water
1 tablespoon white miso
1½ teaspoons wasabi

Prepare dressing: Heat a 5-inch saucepan over medium heat until hot. Add oil and swirl to coat pan. Add flour and cook, stirring rapidly, until flour begins to turn light brown, about 45 seconds. Add vinegar and let bubble 30 seconds. Add honey and water; cook, stirring constantly, until mixture is smooth and comes to a boil. Remove pan from heat. Whisk in miso and wasabi until mixture is very smooth. Transfer dressing to a glass bowl, cover, and let stand 30 minutes before serving.

Combine napa cabbage and bok choy in a salad bowl and scatter radicchio, radishes, mushrooms, scallions, and bean sprouts on top. Drizzle with dressing and toss to combine. Or, if you prefer, serve dressing on the side.

Per serving: 97.89 Calories, 7.8 g Protein, 4.2 g Total Fat (39% of Calories), 0.3 g Saturated Fat, 13.4 g Carbohydrates, 5.8 g Dietary Fiber, 0 mg Cholesterol, 263 mg Sodium

Spinach and Grapefruit Salad

*T*oasted sesame seeds lend a wonderful flavor and texture to this refreshing salad. It is great for any occasion.

MAKES 4 SERVINGS

1 tablespoon toasted sesame seeds
1 tablespoon red-wine vinegar
2 tablespoons raspberry or orange juice
   concentrate
1 tablespoon water
Freshly ground black pepper to taste
8 ounces (6 cups) spinach leaves,
   washed and dried

1 large pink or red grapefruit,
   segmented, seeded, and white pith
   removed
4 large white firm mushrooms, cut into
   ⅛-inch-thick slices

In a mortar, pound sesame seeds into a coarse powder; transfer to a small dish. Add vinegar, raspberry or orange juice concentrate, water, and pepper to taste and stir until well mixed; set aside.

Place spinach in a large salad bowl. Add grapefruit segments and mushroom slices and toss to combine. Add dressing just before serving or pass separately.

> Per serving: 61.85 Calories, 3.1 g Protein, 1.5 g Total Fat (21% of Calories), 0.2 g Saturated Fat, 11.2 g Carbohydrates, 3.2 g Dietary Fiber, 0 mg Cholesterol, 47 mg Sodium

Seafood Mesclun Salad

This fast, easy, and healthy salad is a summer delight. Serve it with white wine and Scallion Pancakes (page 264) or Western crusty bread, and enjoy!

MAKES 4 SERVINGS

⅓ pound fresh cod fillet, cut into ¾-inch cubes
1 tablespoon dry sherry
⅛ teaspoon salt
Pinch of sugar
Pinch of white pepper

1 teaspoon cornstarch
⅓ pound squid, cleaned and cut into ¼-inch rings
⅓ pound large bay scallops
¾ pound mesclun greens
Shallot Vinaigrette (page 72) to taste

In a small bowl, combine fish cubes, sherry, salt, sugar, pepper, and cornstarch; set aside to marinate while water comes to a boil.

In a 1-quart pot, bring 2 cups water to a gentle boil; slide in fish and stir gently to keep fish intact. Simmer until fish turns white, about 2 minutes. Using a slotted spoon, transfer fish to a plate and set aside.

Bring water to a boil again. Stir in squid rings; cook until squid turns white, about 1 minute. Using a slotted spoon, immediately remove squid from water. (Do not overcook squid; they shrink and become chewy if cooked too long.) Bring water to a boil again. Stir in scallops; cook until scallops turn white, about 1½ minutes. Immediately drain scallops.

Place greens in a large salad bowl. Distribute fish, squid, and scallops on top. Sprinkle with vinaigrette to taste, toss gently a few times, and serve immediately.

Per serving (without dressing): 112 Calories, 19.8 g Protein, 1.2 g Total Fat (9% of Calories), 0.2 g Saturated Fat, 5.4 g Carbohydrates, 1.3 g Dietary Fiber, 100 mg Cholesterol, 225 mg Sodium

Shallot Vinaigrette

MAKES $^{1}/_{2}$ CUP

2 teaspoons olive oil
2 shallots, minced
3 tablespoons cider vinegar
3 tablespoons sugar

2 tablespoons fish sauce
1 tablespoon freshly squeezed lime juice
$^{1}/_{4}$ teaspoon cayenne pepper

Heat a 6-inch frying pan over medium heat until hot. Add oil and swirl to coat pan. Add shallots and cook, stirring, until aromatic, about 35 seconds. Remove pan from heat. Add remaining ingredients and stir until sugar dissolves.

Per tablespoon: 31 Calories, 0.6 g Protein, 1.2 g Total Fat (34% of Calories), 0.2 g Saturated Fat, 4.9 g Carbohydrates, 0.1 g Dietary Fiber, 0 mg Cholesterol, 355 mg Sodium

Crabmeat-Stuffed Cucumber Salad

Stuffed with crabmeat, this refreshing cucumber salad is amazingly low in calories and fat, and it is perfect as an appetizer or first course.

MAKES 4 SERVINGS

2 medium, firm, straight cucumbers, washed
1 teaspoon salt
12 sprigs watercress, trimmed
6 ounces fresh cooked or canned high-quality crabmeat, carefully picked over

1 cup fresh radish sprouts
Bottled pickled ginger, for garnish
Mint leaves, for garnish
Creamy Tofu-Miso Dressing (page 103), to taste

Cut ½ inch off both ends of cucumbers. Using a fruit zester, partially strip the cucumber peel, leaving decorative pinstripes lengthwise. Cut each cucumber in half crosswise to form 2 short cylinders. With a small spoon, remove the center seeds and soft pulp, leaving a tunnel about 1 inch in diameter. Sprinkle salt over and in the hollowed-out cucumbers; let stand 15 minutes.

Rinse cucumbers under cold water, drain, and pat dry with paper towels. Insert 3 sprigs of watercress into each cucumber half, pressing them against one side. Stuff firmly with crabmeat without disturbing the watercress. Cover and chill in refrigerator until ready to serve.

To serve: Line 4 individual salad plates with radish sprouts. Cut stuffed cucumbers crosswise with a sharp knife into ½-inch-thick slices. Arrange the slices on the radish sprouts and top with a few slices of pickled ginger, arranged vertically. Decorate with mint leaves. Serve dressing on the side.

Per serving (without dressing): 53 Calories, 6.6 g Protein, 0.3 g Total Fat (4.4% of Calories), 0.1 g Saturated Fat, 4.8 g Carbohydrates, 2.6 g Dietary Fiber, 30 mg Cholesterol, 373 mg Sodium

Spicy Calamari Salad

Calamari (squid) is very high in protein and very low in fat. In this salad the calamari is parboiled for just a short time to retain its tenderness. The degree of spiciness can be varied by adjusting the amount of chili used. You can also grill the calamari to make this exotic salad.

MAKES 4 SERVINGS

2½ pounds medium fresh calamari
1 cup thinly sliced small red onion
¼ cup thinly sliced tender lemongrass
1 cup cucumber or celery slices
¼ cup roasted red bell peppers, cut into short strips
Dressing (see opposite)
6 perfect green lettuce leaves
10 fresh mint leaves, shredded

2 tablespoons chopped fresh cilantro

DRESSING

2 tablespoons finely chopped garlic
2 small hot chilies, finely chopped
¼ cup freshly squeezed lime juice
2 tablespoons fish sauce, or to taste
1 teaspoon sugar

Wash calamari and drain; pat dry with paper towels. Hold each calamari by the head just below the eyes and gently pull away from body pouch; discard the soft viscera that come away with head. Carefully remove ink sac and discard. Pull quill-shaped spine from body and discard. Peel skin off body with your fingers. Cut off tentacles just below eyes; discard head. Cut calamari crosswise into about ¼-inch-thick rings.

In a 10-inch skillet, bring 3 cups water to a boil. Add calamari and blanch in the boiling water until they just start to curl and turn opaque, about 1 minute. Drain immediately and transfer to a medium bowl. Add onion, lemongrass, cucumber or celery, and bell peppers; set aside.

In a small bowl, mix dressing ingredients and stir until sugar dissolves. Pour dressing over squid mixture and toss to mix well. Taste and adjust with additional fish sauce or lime juice, if needed.

Arrange lettuce leaves in a circle on a serving dish. Place squid salad in the middle. Sprinkle mint leaves and cilantro on top and serve.

Per serving: 97 Calories, 14.1 g Protein, 0.9g Total Fat (8% of Calories), 0.2 g Saturated Fat, 8.5 g Carbohydrates, 1.1 g Dietary Fiber, 136 mg Cholesterol, 533 mg Sodium

Bean Sprout Salad

The bean sprouts in this salad are supposed to be crisp and crunchy, and they will be if not overcooked.

MAKES 6 SERVINGS

1 pound (about 6 cups packed) fresh mung bean sprouts
½ teaspoon salt
1½ teaspoons sugar
1 tablespoon distilled white vinegar

1 tablespoon oriental sesame oil
Freshly ground black pepper to taste
2 scallions, including tops, thinly sliced diagonally
1 tablespoon toasted sesame seeds

Bring 2 quarts of water to a boil in a 6-quart pot. Turn off heat, dump in bean sprouts, and submerge them in the boiling water 15 seconds. Drain and immediately place bean sprouts in a pot of cold water until they are cold. Drain thoroughly and pat dry with paper towels.

Place bean sprouts in a self-sealing plastic bag. Add salt, sugar, vinegar, sesame oil, and pepper. Seal bag and turn gently to combine. Refrigerate, turning occasionally, until thoroughly cold, about 2 hours.

To serve, place bean sprouts on a serving dish. Sprinkle scallions and sesame seeds on top.

Per serving: 60 Calories, 3.3 g Protein, 2.5 g Total Fat (37% of Calories), 0.3 g Saturated Fat, 6.9 g Carbohydrates, 0.4 g Dietary Fiber, 0 mg Cholesterol, 182 mg Sodium

Sea Scallop Salad with Lemongrass-Lime Dressing

Lemongrass imparts a refreshing gingery lemon essence that enhances many seafood dishes. Use only the tender white stalk for this recipe, save the tougher skin and green stem for seasoning soups.

MAKES 6 SERVINGS

1 pound fresh sea scallops
1 tablespoon reduced-sodium soy sauce
½ teaspoon sugar
1 tablespoon cornstarch
4 cups hand-torn Boston lettuce
1 yellow bell pepper, diced
1 red bell pepper, diced
½ cup fresh spearmint leaves
⅓ cup fresh basil leaves

LEMONGRASS-LIME DRESSING

2 (3-inch) pieces tender lemongrass, finely chopped
1 teaspoon minced fresh garlic
2 tablespoons fish sauce, or to taste
2 tablespoons light brown sugar
½ teaspoon hot chili sauce
⅓ cup freshly squeezed lime juice
2 tablespoons orange juice
1 tablespoon oriental sesame oil

Place scallops in a self-sealing plastic bag. Sprinkle with soy sauce, sugar, and cornstarch; seal and turn to coat well. Refrigerate 1 hour, turning occasionally.

Make the dressing: In a small bowl, combine lemongrass, garlic, fish sauce, brown sugar, chili sauce, lime juice, and orange juice and stir until sugar dissolves. Whisk in sesame oil. Cover and refrigerate until ready to use.

Prepare a charcoal fire or preheat a gas grill. Thread scallops onto skewers. Grill over medium-hot heat until scallops are lightly browned and no longer translucent in the center, about 4 minutes per side.

Remove scallops from skewers and place in a medium bowl. Add 2 tablespoons of dressing and toss to coat well.

In a large shallow salad bowl, toss lettuce, bell peppers, mint, and basil with remaining dressing. Arrange the seasoned scallops on top, serve, and enjoy.

Per serving: 132 Calories, 13.3 g Protein, 3.2 g Total Fat (21.49% of Calories), 0.5 g Saturated Fat, 13.6 g Carbohydrates, 0.9 g Dietary Fiber, 26 mg Cholesterol, 791 mg Sodium

Chinese Long Bean Salad

Long beans, also called yard-long beans or asparagus beans, are actually only half a yard long. They look amazing at full length. This salad is both a culinary and a visual treat. Try it on a sesame bun and accompanied by a light soup for a delicious meal.

MAKES 6 SERVINGS

12 fresh medium unpeeled raw shrimp
1 medium boneless, skinless chicken breast
½ pound Chinese yard-long beans or green beans
½ tablespoon fish sauce, or to taste
1 tablespoon light brown sugar
1 tablespoon Spicy Shrimp Paste (page 301)
¼ cup freshly squeezed lime juice

1 tablespoon oriental sesame oil
3 cloves garlic, minced
1 serrano chili, seeded and thinly sliced
1 cup hand-torn radicchio
1 cup fresh cilantro leaves
16 to 18 Belgian endive leaves
3 tablespoons dry-roasted peanuts, coarsely chopped
Salt and freshly ground pepper to taste

In a 10-inch frying pan, bring 4 cups water to a boil over medium heat. Add shrimp and boil until shrimp turn pink, about 30 seconds. Immediately remove shrimp from water and let cool. Shell shrimp and cut each lengthwise into halves; set aside.

Bring water to a boil again. Add chicken breast. Cover, reduce heat to low, and simmer 10 to 15 minutes. Remove chicken and let cool, then cut into thin shreds; set aside.

Bring water to a boil again. Add long beans and boil, covered, until tender, about 3 minutes. Drain and rinse with cold running water to stop cooking. Cut beans into 2-inch lengths; set aside.

Meanwhile make dressing: In a small bowl, whisk fish sauce, sugar, shrimp paste, lime juice, and sesame oil until sugar dissolves. Stir in garlic and chili.

In a large bowl, combine long beans, chicken, shrimp, radicchio, and cilantro with the dressing. Cover and let the flavors meld, stirring occasionally, 1 hour.

Arrange endive on a platter or individual plates, mound long bean salad in the middle, and sprinkle with chopped peanuts. Season with salt and pepper, if desired.

Per serving: 160 Calories, 16 g Protein, 5 g Total Fat (31% of Calories), 1 g Saturated Fat, 12 g Carbohydrates, 2 g Dietary Fiber, 70 mg Cholesterol, 380 mg Sodium

Snow Peas and Water Chestnuts

Sweet and crunchy, these vegetables pair beautifully with just about any dish.

MAKES 4 SERVINGS

1 tablespoon olive oil
1 pound fresh snow peas, strings
 removed, trimmed, and rinsed
3/4 cup sliced water chestnuts

1 tablespoon dry sherry
1/2 teaspoon salt, or to taste
1/4 teaspoon sugar
1/4 cup water

Heat a heavy 10-inch skillet over medium-high heat until hot. Add oil and swirl to coat pan. Add snow peas and water chestnuts and stir a few times. Quickly add sherry, salt, sugar, and water; cover immediately and cook 1 minute. Reduce heat to low and simmer 15 seconds. Uncover and stir to mix well. Transfer to a hot serving dish and serve.

Per serving: 107 Calories, 3.8g Protein, 4.5 g Total Fat (38% of Calories), 0.5 g Saturated Fat, 15.8 g Carbohydrates, 3.8 g Dietary Fiber, 0 mg Cholesterol, 379 mg Sodium

Minced Chicken in Lettuce Cups

This is a dish that my students invariably received with great enthusiasm. It is unusual, delicious, and great fun to eat.

Traditionally this subtly flavored minced chicken with its bits of delicious Chinese mushrooms and crunchy water chestnuts is wrapped in tender lettuce cups and served as a first course; if accompanied by Hot and Sour Soup (page 44) and steamed rice, it can be a delightful luncheon.

MAKES 8 SERVINGS

1 pound boneless, skinless chicken breast, cut into ¼-inch cubes
1 tablespoon dry sherry
2 teaspoons cornstarch
3 teaspoons oriental sesame oil
1 small onion, chopped
4 large Chinese dried mushrooms, soaked in hot water 30 minutes, drained, and cut into ¼-inch cubes
12 water chestnuts, cut into ¼-inch cubes

1 tablespoon reduced-sodium soy sauce
1 tablespoon hoisin sauce
½ teaspoon salt
¼ teaspoon sugar
¼ teaspoon freshly ground black pepper
½ red bell pepper, diced
2 scallions, including tops, thinly sliced
1 or 2 heads Boston lettuce, leaves separated, washed, and dried
¼ cup pine nuts, toasted

In a medium bowl, combine chicken, sherry, and cornstarch; set aside.

Heat a heavy 10-inch nonstick skillet over medium heat. Add 2 teaspoons of the sesame oil and swirl to coat pan. Add chicken mixture and, using a wooden spoon and chopsticks, stir vigorously to separate the chicken pieces. Shake pan occasionally and continue stirring and turning until chicken is cooked through, about 3 minutes. Transfer to a plate and set aside.

Wipe skillet clean. Add remaining sesame oil and heat a few seconds. Add onion and cook 1 minute, or until aromatic. Add mushrooms and water chestnuts and cook, stirring, until heated through, about 1 minute. Return the chicken to the vegetables and stir to combine.

Add soy sauce, hoisin sauce, salt, sugar, and pepper and stir until evenly distributed and heated through. Fold in bell pepper and scallions.

Arrange a bed of lettuce leaves on a large serving platter. Spoon the chicken mixture over the lettuce in the center and sprinkle pine nuts on top. Arrange extra lettuce leaves around the chicken, or serve them on a separate dish.

To eat, take a lettuce leaf and fill it with 1 or 2 spoonfuls of chicken mixture, wrap it up, and, holding the cup with your fingers, take a big bite.

Per serving: 164 Calories, 16 g Protein, 6 g Total Fat (34% of Calories), 1 g Saturated Fat, 12 g Carbohydrates, 2 g Dietary Fiber, 33 mg Cholesterol, 339 mg Sodium

VARIATION
MINCED SHRIMP IN LETTUCE CUPS

Replace chicken with diced shrimp.

Duck Salad with Dijon Mustard Vinaigrette

Colorful and flavorful, this duck salad makes a beautiful presentation as a first course or cold buffet dish.

MAKES 6 SERVINGS

Dijon Mustard Vinaigrette (see page 293)
2 cups cooked shredded duck meat
  (from ½ roasted or steamed duck)
2 cups fresh bean sprouts
2 ounces wide bean thread noodles,
  soaked in water 15 minutes and
  drained

½ teaspoon oriental sesame oil
2 cups shredded zucchini
2 scallions, including tops, thinly sliced
  diagonally into 2-inch lengths
¼ cup finely shredded carrot
1 tablespoon toasted sesame seeds

Prepare vinaigrette: Whisk all the ingredients in a small bowl until very smooth. Cover and let mellow 30 minutes before using.

Cut duck meat into shreds about 2½ inches long and ¼ inch thick; set aside.

Place bean sprouts in a heatproof bowl. Cover with boiling water and let stand 5 seconds. Drain into a colander and rinse immediately with cold water until completely cold. Drain thoroughly and pat dry with paper towels; set aside.

Cut bean threads into 3-inch lengths. Cook in boiling water 2 minutes, or until al dente; drain well. Toss with sesame oil to prevent sticking.

Mound bean sprouts in the center of a serving platter; scatter duck meat on top of the sprouts. Arrange zucchini in a ring around the base of the sprouts; scatter noodles on top of the zucchini. Scatter scallions on top of the duck; sprinkle carrot on top of the scallions. Finally, scatter sesame seeds on top of the salad.

To serve: Bring salad to the table. Pour vinaigrette in a thin stream in a circle on the salad. Toss gently and serve.

Per serving: 194 Calories, 17 g Protein, 9 g Total Fat (40.7% of Calories), 3 g Saturated Fat, 12 g Carbohydrates, 1 g Dietary Fiber, 50 mg Cholesterol, 439 mg Sodium

Spicy Sichuan Cucumbers

These crisp aromatic pickled cucumbers are a refreshing summer favorite, especially if the cucumbers were picked fresh from your own garden.

MAKES 4 SERVINGS

2 long slender cucumbers, halved lengthwise, and seeded
1 tablespoon canola oil
2 dried red hot chilies, seeded
2 tablespoons Sichuan peppercorns
3 cloves garlic, minced

½ teaspoon salt
¼ cup sugar
1 tablespoon reduced-sodium soy sauce
1 teaspoon oriental sesame oil
¼ cup distilled white vinegar

Cut each half cucumber lengthwise into 4 strips. Gather up the strips and cut crosswise into 4 sections. Pat dry with paper towels; set aside.

Heat a heavy 8-inch frying pan over medium heat until hot. Add canola oil and swirl to coat pan. Add chilies and Sichuan peppercorns and cook until the chilies and peppercorns are fragrant and darkened, about 1 minute. Remove pan from heat. Discard peppercorns and chilies, but reserve the infused oil.

Return pan to heat and increase heat to high. Add garlic and cucumbers; stir and toss to roll them in the hot oil until the cucumber skin is bright green, about 30 seconds. Sprinkle with salt, sugar, and soy sauce; stir briskly to distribute the seasonings. Pour contents of pan immediately into a glass bowl to cool. Cover and refrigerate, stirring occasionally, 1½ hours. Add sesame oil and vinegar and toss to mix well; refrigerate 30 minutes. Stir to mix and serve.

Per serving: 64 Calories, 1.3 g Protein, 2.7 g Total Fat (38% of Calories), 0.3 g Saturated Fat, 9.7 g Carbohydrates, 2.3 g Dietary Fiber, 0 mg Cholesterol, 325 mg Sodium

VARIATION
SWEET AND SOUR CAULIFLOWER

Replace cucumbers with 1 whole head cauliflower. Blanch cauliflower florets in boiling water 2 minutes. Drain and rinse with cold water to stop cooking. Place cauliflower in a large bowl. Heat 1 tablespoon oil in a small frying pan and cook the chilies and peppercorns until darkened. Remove and discard peppercorns and chilies. Add garlic, salt, sugar, soy sauce, sesame oil, and vinegar; stir until sugar dissolves. Pour mixture over the cauliflower and toss to mix well. Cover and refrigerate, stirring occasionally, a few hours before serving.

TIP
Add vinegar to the cucumbers at the last minute so that the acidity will not discolor their vivid green color.

Chicken and Grapefruit Salad

*T*his is a beautiful and delicious salad. The moist chicken blends exquisitely with the sweet, juicy grapefruit. The almond slices add texture to the salad.

MAKES 6 SERVINGS

2 cloves garlic, minced

1 small fresh red hot chili, seeded and chopped

1 tablespoon sugar

1 tablespoon freshly squeezed lime juice

1 tablespoon rice wine vinegar

1½ tablespoons fish sauce, or to taste

1 Basic Steamed Chicken Breast (page 157), shredded

1 pound napa cabbage leaves, hand torn

¼ pound radicchio, hand torn

12 arugula leaves

1 large pink or red grapefruit, segmented, seeded, and white pith removed

⅓ cup shredded fresh mint

¼ cup almond slices

Wonton Chips (page 13) or thin slices of toasted garlic bread

Combine the garlic, chili, sugar, lime juice, vinegar, and fish sauce in a small bowl. Stir to blend well. Set dressing aside.

In a large salad bowl, combine chicken, napa cabbage, radicchio, and arugula. Sprinkle in the dressing and toss briefly. Insert grapefruit segments here and there in the salad. Sprinkle on mint leaves and almond slices. Serve with Wonton Chips or garlic bread.

Per serving: 183 Calories, 19.4 g Protein, 5.6 g Total Fat (28% of Calories), 0.9 g Saturated Fat, 14.7 g Carbohydrates, 4.1 g Dietary Fiber, 53 mg Cholesterol, 779 mg Sodium

Tricolor Stuffed Cabbage

Here the cabbages are stuffed with colorful ham, shiitake mushrooms, and bean sprouts. Cut them in half to serve as appetizers, or serve them whole as part of a multi-course meal. This dish is good at room temperature or chilled.

MAKES 6 ROLLS

1 green cabbage head
2 tablespoons white-wine vinegar
2 tablespoons sugar
1 tablespoon reduced-sodium soy sauce
1 teaspoon fish sauce
1 teaspoon oriental sesame oil
Freshly ground black pepper to taste
¼ pound cooked ham, cut into matchstick shreds

¼ pound fresh shiitake mushrooms, blanched and shredded
¼ pound fresh mung bean sprouts, blanched in boiling water 5 seconds and rinsed
Curly parsley leaves, for garnish

Immerse whole cabbage in a pot of boiling water until leaves are opaque, about 1 minute. Lift out cabbage and detach as many leaves as can be removed easily until you get 6 blanched leaves. Rinse leaves with cold water until cool. Drain and pat dry with paper towels.

Mix together the vinegar, sugar, soy sauce, fish sauce, sesame oil, and pepper to taste in a medium bowl until sugar dissolves; set seasoning sauce aside.

Divide ham, mushrooms, and bean sprouts each into 6 equal portions (these will be the three colors in the tricolored stuffed cabbage). Place 1 portion of ham neatly on each leaf, place 1 portion of bean sprouts next to the ham, and place 1 portion of mushrooms next to the bean sprouts. Roll up leaf and place seam side down. If cabbage leaf is too big, cut it in half before using.

To serve, cut each cabbage roll in half and arrange each, cut side up, on a serving platter. Drizzle seasoning sauce on top and garnish with parsley. Serve at once.

Per ½ roll: 74 Calories, 5.8 g Protein, 2 g Total Fat (24% of Calories), 0.5 g Saturated Fat, 9.1 g Carbohydrates, 2 g Dietary Fiber, 10 mg Cholesterol, 381 mg Sodium

Green Beans with Garlic Sauce

For this dish, usually the green beans are deep-fried in hot oil, then seasoned in the wok. But not in this recipe. Here the green beans are stir-fried in an aromatic garlic sauce. This dish has great taste without all the usual fat, and is good hot or cold.

MAKES 6 SERVINGS

2 pounds fresh green beans, stems removed

2 tablespoons reduced-sodium soy sauce

1 tablespoon dry sherry

¼ teaspoon salt

½ tablespoon sugar

½ tablespoon red-wine vinegar

½ teaspoon hot chili sauce (optional)

2 teaspoons olive oil

1 teaspoon minced fresh ginger

1 tablespoon minced garlic

1 teaspoon oriental sesame oil

2 tablespoons scallion rings, white part only

Bring ½ inch of water to a boil in a heavy 10-inch skillet, over high heat. Add green beans, cover immediately, and cook 2 minutes. Turn off heat and let stand 30 seconds. Drain beans and rinse with cold water to stop the cooking. Drain again and thoroughly pat dry with kitchen towel; set aside.

Mix together soy sauce, sherry, salt, sugar, vinegar, and chili sauce, if using, in a small bowl, until sugar dissolves; set aside.

Heat dry skillet over medium-high heat until hot. Add oil and swirl to coat pan. Add ginger and garlic and cook, stirring, until aromatic, about 30 seconds. Add green beans and soy sauce mixture; stir vigorously and toss until liquid is absorbed. Drizzle in sesame oil, then transfer to a serving dish. Sprinkle scallion rings on top and serve.

Per serving: 81 Calories, 3.6 g Protein, 2.5 g Total Fat (27% of Calories), 0.4 g Saturated Fat, 13.3 g Carbohydrates, 5.3 g Dietary Fiber, 0 mg Cholesterol, 329 mg Sodium

Wild Mushrooms in Oyster Sauce

*T*hese exotic mushrooms are stir-fried in a delicious oyster sauce. Serve them with plenty of steamed rice to soak up the luscious sauce.

MAKES 4 SERVINGS

1 teaspoon olive oil
3 scallions, including tops, cut into 1-inch lengths, whites and greens separated
2 cloves garlic, coarsely chopped
¼ pound fresh oyster mushrooms, wiped clean and cut in half
¼ pound fresh shiitake mushrooms, wiped clean and cut in half
¼ pound fresh crimini mushrooms, wiped clean and cut into ¼-inch-thick slices

1 tablespoon dry sherry
1 tablespoon reduced-sodium soy sauce
1 tablespoon premium oyster sauce
½ teaspoon sugar
Salt and freshly ground pepper to taste (optional)
1 teaspoon cornstarch dissolved in 1 tablespoon water
1 teaspoon oriental sesame oil

Heat a heavy 10-inch skillet over medium-high heat until hot. Add olive oil, swirl to coat skillet, and heat 15 seconds. Add white parts of scallions and garlic; shake pan and cook 15 seconds. Add all the mushrooms; shake pan a few times to even out the contents and cook 30 seconds. Cook, turning mushrooms about every 30 seconds, until mushrooms are slightly wilted, about 2 minutes. Add sherry, soy sauce, oyster sauce, sugar, and green part of scallions and stir to distribute the seasonings. Taste and adjust seasonings with salt and pepper, if desired. Stir cornstarch mixture and stir into contents of skillet. Cook, stirring a few times, until sauce is slightly thickened. Transfer to a serving dish and drizzle sesame oil on top. Serve immediately.

Per serving: 65 Calories, 2.8 g Protein, 2.7 g Total Fat (37% of Calories), 0.7 g Saturated Fat, 8.3 g Carbohydrates, 2.5 g Dietary Fiber, 0 mg Cholesterol, 494 mg Sodium

Broccoli with Garlic Sauce

Here the broccoli is steam-cooked over high heat just briefly to retain its nutrients and preserve its bright color. The garlic and vinegar wake up your taste buds and stimulate your appetite. This dish is good hot or cold.

MAKES 4 SERVINGS

1 teaspoon canola oil
1 teaspoon minced fresh ginger
2 large cloves garlic, minced
1 pound broccoli flowerets, rinsed
1 carrot, peeled and shredded
1/3 cup water
1 tablespoon reduced-sodium soy sauce

1 tablespoon red-wine vinegar
1/2 teaspoon sugar
1/4 teaspoon Chinese chili sauce or
    Chinese hot bean sauce
1/2 teaspoon oriental sesame oil
Steamed rice

Heat a heavy 10-inch skillet over high heat until hot. Add oil, swirl to coat skillet, and heat 5 seconds. Add ginger and garlic; cook, stirring, a few seconds, or until aromatic. Add broccoli with the water clinging to it, the carrot, and the water; cover immediately and cook over high heat 2 minutes.

Uncover pan, stir, and cook to reduce the liquid, about 30 seconds. If too much liquid remains, pour out excess. When all the moisture has evaporated, add soy sauce, vinegar, sugar, and chili sauce or hot bean sauce and stir to season well. Drizzle in sesame oil and transfer to a serving dish. Serve with steamed rice.

Per serving: 64 Calories, 4.2 g Protein, 2.2 g Total Fat (31% of Calories), 0.2 g Saturated Fat, 9.7 g Carbohydrates, 5.1 g Dietary Fiber, 0 mg Cholesterol, 210 mg Sodium

Eggplant with Garlic Sauce

Select slender firm Chinese or Japanese eggplants for this recipe. These eggplants, cooked in a spicy garlic sauce, are simply delicious whether served hot or cold.

MAKES 4 SERVINGS

2 tablespoons reduced-sodium soy
 sauce
2 tablespoons dry sherry
2 tablespoons cider vinegar
1 tablespoon sugar
2 teaspoons olive oil
3 slices fresh ginger, minced
2 large cloves garlic, coarsely chopped

1 tablespoon Chinese hot bean sauce
4 Chinese eggplants (1½ pounds),
 quartered lengthwise, then cut
 crosswise into 3-inch sections
½ cup water
1 teaspoon oriental sesame oil
½ teaspoon toasted Sichuan peppercorn
 powder (optional)

In a small dish, stir together soy sauce, sherry, vinegar, and sugar until sugar dissolves; set aside.

Heat a heavy 10-inch skillet over medium-high heat until hot. Add olive oil, swirl to coat pan, and heat 15 seconds. Add ginger and garlic and stir a few seconds. Add hot bean sauce and cook, stirring, until aromatic, about 15 seconds. Add eggplants; stir and toss to distribute. Add water and cover at once. Increase heat to high and cook 1 minute, or until most of the liquid has evaporated. Add soy sauce mixture. Using a wooden spoon and rubber spatula, gently stir and toss to coat evenly with seasonings. Transfer to a serving dish and drizzle with sesame oil. Sprinkle peppercorn powder on top, if using, and serve.

Per serving: 113 Calories, 3.3 g Protein, 3.6 g Total Fat (29% of Calories), 0.5 g Saturated Fat, 18 g Carbohydrates, 4.6 g Dietary Fiber, 0 mg Cholesterol, 450 mg Sodium

TIP

When cooking eggplant, stir gently without breaking them or they will turn to mush.

Spicy Sweet and Sour Napa

Napa is a long, white (sometimes light green) bulky Chinese cabbage. This dish is an aromatic appetite teaser. It is good hot, at room temperature, or chilled. This dish tastes even better if cooked one day ahead and marinated overnight. It will keep for one week in the refrigerator.

MAKES 6 SERVINGS

2 pounds napa cabbage, leaves
   separated and rinsed
1 tablespoon sesame oil
1½ tablespoons Sichuan peppercorns
3 dried red chilies, seeds removed
1 teaspoon minced garlic

½ teaspoon salt, or to taste
¼ cup water
2 tablespoons sugar
2 tablespoons cider vinegar
2 tablespoons reduced-sodium soy
   sauce

Cut cabbage ribs in half lengthwise, then cut halves into 3-inch lengths. Cut leaves into large pieces.

Heat a wok or heavy 10-inch skillet over medium heat until hot. Add oil and swirl to coat skillet. Add Sichuan peppercorns; stir until peppercorns turn dark and fragrant, about 1 minute. Transfer peppercorns to a square of cheesecloth, tie ends, and reserve, but reserve the oil in pan.

Increase heat to high. Add chilies and garlic and cook, stirring, a few seconds, or until aromatic. Add cabbage; stir and toss 1 minute. Add salt and water and stir briefly. Add sugar, vinegar, and soy sauce and toss a few times; cover and cook over high heat 1 minute. Stir and mix again until cabbage is soft but still has some crunchiness and liquid is reduced. Transfer cabbage to a large bowl, leaving liquid in pan. Add peppercorns in the cheesecloth to the liquid and continue boiling until reduced to 1 cup. Pour liquid over cabbage, stir to mix, and serve.

Per serving: 71 Calories, 2.7 g Protein, 2.7 g Total Fat (34% of Calories), 0.4 g Saturated Fat, 10.8 g Carbohydrates, 4.9 g Dietary Fiber, 0 mg Cholesterol, 412 mg Sodium

Napa in Cream Sauce

Here the napa cabbage is first cooked until tender, then covered with a delicious white sauce. Serve this as a vegetable side dish.

MAKES 4 SERVINGS

2 pounds napa cabbage, leaves
   separated
1 tablespoon canola oil
1 teaspoon salt
½ teaspoon sugar

¾ cup fat-free low-sodium chicken stock
1½ tablespoons cornstarch dissolved in
   ¼ cup low-fat evaporated milk
¼ cup finely chopped cooked Smithfield
   ham (optional)

Rinse cabbage with cold water; drain but do not spin-dry (you need the moisture for cooking). Cut ribs crosswise into 2½-inch sections, then cut sections lengthwise into ¾-inch strips. Tear leaf portion into large pieces.

Heat a heavy 10-inch frying pan over medium-high heat until hot. Add oil, swirl to coat pan, and heat 30 seconds. Add all of the rib pieces and stir-fry 1 minute. Scatter in leaves and add salt and sugar. Cover immediately and cook over high heat about 2 minutes. Reduce heat and simmer 1 minute. Uncover and stir to evenly distribute. Transfer cabbage to a colander to drain liquid.

Add chicken stock to pan and bring to a boil. Stir the cornstarch mixture and stir into broth. Cook, stirring, until sauce thickens. Remove half of this sauce and reserve it. Add cabbage to sauce remaining in pan; stir gently to combine, then transfer it to a hot shallow platter. Pour reserved cream sauce over cabbage and sprinkle with chopped ham, if desired. Serve at once.

Per serving: 72.6 Calories, 3.9 g Protein, 2.1 g Total Fat (26% of Calories), 0.3 g Saturated Fat, 11.3 g Carbohydrates, 6.2 g Dietary Fiber, 0 mg Cholesterol, 579 mg Sodium

Stir-Fried Bean Sprouts

*T*he secret to stir-frying bean sprouts is to have a very hot pan, use a fast flipping and tossing motion, and cook them just until crisp when removed from the pan.

MAKES 4 SERVINGS

1 tablespoon canola oil
3 scallions, including tops, cut into
   1-inch lengths, whites and greens
   separated
1 clove garlic, minced
½ cup shredded yellow bell pepper
   (optional)

¾ pound (about 4 cups) fresh mung
   bean sprouts
¼ teaspoon salt
Freshly ground black pepper to taste

Heat a heavy 10-inch frying pan over high heat until hot. Add oil, swirl to coat pan, and heat 15 seconds. Add white part of scallions and garlic and cook until aromatic, about 15 seconds. Add yellow pepper, if using, bean sprouts, and green part of scallions and stir-fry vigorously about 1 minute, or until bean sprouts are done but still crisp. Season with salt and pepper and stir to combine. Transfer to a serving dish.

Per serving: 40 Calories, 2.9 g Protein, 1.3 g Total Fat (30% of Calories), 0.1 g Saturated Fat, 6 g Carbohydrates, 1.3 g Dietary Fiber, 0 mg Cholesterol, 139 mg Sodium

Stir-Fried Bok Choy

*B*ok choy is a good source of calcium. This juicy vegetable goes very well with rice or any meat dishes.

1½ pounds bok choy, washed   ¼ teaspoon salt
2 teaspoons canola oil   ¼ cup water

Cut white bok choy stalks diagonally into ½-inch-wide pieces and cut greens into large pieces. Place stalks and leaves in separate piles.

Heat a heavy 10-inch skillet over high heat until hot. Add oil, swirl to coat skillet, and heat 15 seconds. Add white stalks; stir-fry 30 seconds. Add greens, salt, and water; cover immediately and cook 1 minute over high heat. Reduce heat to medium and simmer 1 minute. Uncover and stir. Transfer to a serving dish.

Per serving: 42 Calories, 2.55 g Protein, 2.6 g Total Fat (57% of Calories), 0.2 g Saturated Fat, 3.7 g Carbohydrates, 5.3 g Dietary Fiber, 0 mg Cholesterol, 244 mg Sodium

VARIATION
The same technique can be used to cook fresh spinach or cabbage.

TIP
When stir-frying vegetables, start with high heat to heat the pan, and have a well-fitting lid ready. When the water contacts the hot pan it creates very hot steam. You should cover immediately to enclose the hot steam to cook the vegetables quickly in a very short time and still keep them bright and crisp.

Stir-Fried Parsley

Do not underestimate parsley! More people should take advantage of this vitamin A-, vitamin C-, and iron-packed vegetable. Food would not look fresh and vivid without a parsley sprig or a sprinkling of chopped parsley. Parsley is one of the main ingredients in the bouquet garni used in flavoring stocks. And parsley blends harmoniously with any dish and any cuisine. Serve stir-fried parsley as a vegetable and accompany it with steamed rice. You will be pleasantly surprised.

MAKES 4 SERVINGS

1 pound parsley, thoroughly washed and
  drained
1 teaspoon olive oil

2 cloves garlic, minced
½ teaspoon salt
¼ cup water

Hold parsley in bunches and cut them into 1-inch sections.

Heat a heavy 10-inch frying pan over high heat until hot. Add oil, swirl to coat pan, and heat 15 seconds. Add garlic and shake pan. Add parsley and stir and toss a few times. Sprinkle with salt and add water; cover immediately and cook over high heat 1 minute. Turn off heat and wait 45 seconds. Uncover and stir a few times until stems and leaves are evenly mixed. Transfer to a serving dish.

Per serving: 50 Calories, 2.6 g Protein, 1.5 g Total Fat (27% of Calories), 0.2 g Saturated Fat, 8.3 g Carbohydrates, 4 g Dietary Fiber, 0 mg Cholesterol, 311 mg Sodium

Celery with Soybean Cake

This refreshing celery is speckled with tasty shrimp and protein-rich bean cake. It is an aromatic dish, and is well balanced nutritionally. Serve it with steamed rice.

MAKES 4 SERVINGS

2 tablespoons dried shrimp
2 tablespoons dry sherry
1 teaspoon olive oil
1 medium onion, cut into ½-inch wedges
6 inner stalks celery, cut diagonally into thin 2-inch-long shreds
4 ounces thinly shredded soybean cake
2 tablespoons reduced-sodium soy sauce, or to taste

½ teaspoon sugar
Freshly ground white pepper to taste
½ cup fat-free, low-sodium chicken stock
1 teaspoon cornstarch dissolved in 1 tablespoon water
1 teaspoon oriental sesame oil

In a small dish, soak dried shrimp with sherry and 2 tablespoons hot water 30 minutes. Drain shrimp, reserving soaking liquid.

Heat a heavy 10-inch frying pan over high heat until hot. Add oil, swirl to coat pan, and heat 10 seconds. Add onion; stir-fry until aromatic, about 30 seconds. Add celery; stir-fry 1 minute. Add shrimp, bean cake, soy sauce, sugar, pepper, chicken stock, and the soaking liquid; stir to distribute evenly and bring to a boil. Cover and steam vigorously 1 minute. Stir cornstarch mixture and add to pan. Cook, stirring, until sauce is slightly thickened. Drizzle in sesame oil and serve immediately.

Per serving: 110 Calories, 8.2 g Protein, 4.8 g Total Fat (38% of Calories), 0.8 g Saturated Fat, 7.6 g Carbohydrates, 2.9 g Dietary Fiber, 19 mg Cholesterol, 621 mg Sodium

Vegetarian's Delight

This dish combines a variety of vegetables, protein, and carbohydrates all in one pot. In Asia this dish is important in the diet of monks and priests, but it's perfectly nutritious for us, too.

MAKES 6 SERVINGS

8 small Chinese dried mushrooms, soaked in hot water 30 minutes, drained, and 1 cup soaking liquid reserved

12 small button mushrooms, wiped clean with damp towel

1 bean curd stick, presoaked in hot water, drained, and cut into 2-inch lengths (optional)

12 pieces canned wheat gluten

1 small cucumber, partially peeled, halved, seeded, and sliced

½ carrot, peeled and sliced

¼ pound cauliflowerets

8 whole baby corn

½ cup sliced winter bamboo shoots

½ cup sliced water chestnuts

1 tablespoon peanut oil

3 tablespoons reduced-sodium soy sauce

1 teaspoon sugar

2 ounces bean thread noodles, soaked, drained, and cut into 4-inch lengths

12 snow peas

Salt and freshly ground black pepper to taste

1 teaspoon oriental sesame oil

Place all vegetables in separate piles on a large working platter.

Heat a heavy 10-inch frying pan over high heat until hot. Add peanut oil, swirl to coat pan, and heat 15 seconds. Add both kinds of mushrooms and cook, stirring a few times, until mushrooms are heated through, about 1 minute. Add remaining vegetables; stir and toss until vegetables are heated through. Add soy sauce, sugar, and mushroom soaking liquid. Stir to distribute evenly, cover and bring to a boil. Sprinkle noodles over the vegetables and add snow peas, cover and cook 2 minutes. Stir to distribute evenly. Adjust seasoning with salt and pepper, if desired. Drizzle in sesame oil and serve.

Per serving: 150 Calories, 6.6 g Protein, 3.8 g Total Fat (23% of Calories), 0.5 g Saturated Fat, 26 g Carbohydrates, 4 g Dietary Fiber, 0 mg Cholesterol, 453 mg Sodium

Mu Shu Vegetarian

Every vegetable in this dish is thinly shredded. It contains an interesting contrast of colors and textures as well as good amounts of protein and fiber. Serve it with Chinese Thin Pancakes (page 266) and a Tofu and Spinach Soup (page 55) for a satisfying meal.

MAKES 4 SERVINGS

3 teaspoons canola oil

½ pound cabbage, thinly shredded and rinsed

3 thin slices fresh ginger, finely shredded

¼ cup dried cloud ear mushrooms, soaked in warm water 30 minutes, drained, and shredded

4 Chinese dried mushrooms, soaked in warm water 30 minutes, drained, and shredded

30 dried tiger lily buds, soaked in cool water 30 minutes, drained, and each cut in half

4 ounces thinly shredded soybean cake

1 small carrot, peeled and thinly shredded

1 tablespoon hoisin sauce

2 tablespoons reduced-sodium soy sauce

½ teaspoon sugar

4 scallions, including tops, cut diagonally into thin 2-inch lengths

1 teaspoon oriental sesame oil

Salt and freshly ground black pepper to taste

Heat a heavy 10-inch skillet over high heat until hot. Add 1 teaspoon of the canola oil, swirl to coat pan, and heat 15 seconds. Add rinsed cabbage and stir-fry about 1 minute, or until cabbage is heated through. Transfer cabbage to a serving platter; discard liquid.

Rinse skillet and wipe dry. Heat skillet over high heat. Add remaining 2 teaspoons oil, swirl to coat pan, and heat 15 seconds. Add ginger, stir a few seconds. Add both kinds of mushrooms and lily buds and stir-fry 30 seconds. Add bean cake shreds and carrot; stir-fry 1 minute. Add hoisin sauce, soy sauce, and sugar and stir to distribute. Return cabbage to pan and stir to mix well; cook until heated through, about 30 seconds. Add scallions and drizzle in sesame oil. Adjust seasoning with salt and pepper, if desired. Serve immediately.

Per serving: 271 Calories, 19 g Protein, 7 g Total Fat (24% of Calories), 1 g Saturated Fat, 71 g Carbohydrates, 12 g Dietary Fiber, 0 mg Cholesterol, 616 mg Sodium

Oven-Dried Soybeans

*B*esides being nutritious, high in protein, and low in fat, these soybean morsels are great munchies. They are also used as a nutritious condiment for rice porridge or salads.

MAKES 3 CUPS

1 cup dried soybeans, rinsed, soaked overnight, and drained
4 cups water

2 tablespoons reduced-sodium soy sauce
2 tablespoons plus 1 teaspoon sugar

Rinse soybeans thoroughly again and drain. In a heavy 2-quart pot, combine soybeans and water; cover and bring to a boil over high heat. Reduce heat to the lowest setting and simmer slowly until beans are tender, about 2 hours. Drain off all liquid except ¼ cup.

Add soy sauce and sugar to soybeans and stir gently without breaking their skins. Cook, stirring, over medium heat until liquid is absorbed but not completely dry, about 10 minutes; set aside.

Preheat oven to 250F (120C). Coat a baking sheet with cooking spray. Spread soybeans on prepared baking sheet in a single layer. Bake about 30 minutes, or until their skins are slightly wrinkled. Remove beans from oven. Serve them hot or cold as snacks, or add them to salads.

Per ¼ cup: 65 Calories, 4.9 g Protein, 2.4 g Total Fat (32% of Calories), 0.3 g Saturated Fat, 7 g Carbohydrates, 2 g Dietary Fiber, 0 mg Cholesterol, 111 mg Sodium

Tofu

 Tofu is bland by itself, but because of its blandness, it can take on the flavors of other ingredients during cooking. Tofu is versatile: It can be stir-fried, pan-fried, deep-fried, braised, baked, broiled, grilled, marinated, or smoked.

Tofu (soybean curd) originated in China more than two thousand years ago and is one of the most important sources of protein in China, Japan, and most Southeast Asian countries.

In China there is a lack of grazing land, so cows are very scarce, and cow's milk was not available until recently, when importers started to introduce powdered milk from Western countries. Fresh cow's milk is rare and very expensive. Most people are raised with soybean milk, and tofu is the baby's first solid food because tofu is easy to digest and rich in protein and calcium.

Soybeans are an integral part of Asian cuisine. They have been transformed into many different products, such as soybean milk, soybean curd (tofu), soybean cake, soybean sheets, soybean sticks, fermented bean curd, fermented soybean sauce, and fermented soybean paste (miso).

Soy protein is one of the few plant proteins considered to be complete, which means that it contains all the essential amino acids. It is rich in B vitamins and calcium. It is also rich in omega-3 fatty acids, believed to decrease the risk of strokes and heart attacks. Current research also indicates that at least 30 grams of soy protein a day may help reduce the risk of osteoporosis and breast cancer, and may help reduce the symptoms of menopause. So include soy foods in your diet regularly to reap their benefits.

Creamy Tofu-Miso Dressing

Tofu makes a perfect full-bodied smooth dressing for salads, a spread for sandwiches, or a nondairy dip for veggie trays. This dressing has just 14 calories and 0.9 gram fat per tablespoon.

MAKES 1½ CUPS

1 tablespoon white (light) miso
3 tablespoons rice wine vinegar
½ teaspoon honey
2 teaspoons grated fresh ginger
½ teaspoon minced garlic

2 teaspoons Coleman's dry mustard
  powder
½ pound (1 cup) soft or silken tofu,
  rinsed and cut into cubes
1 tablespoon extra-virgin olive oil

In a food processor fitted with the metal blade, combine miso, vinegar, honey, ginger, garlic, and mustard and pulse to blend. Add tofu and process until very smooth. Drizzle in olive oil through the feedtube in a steady thin stream while motor is running. Process until mixture is smooth and thick, about 1 minute. Transfer to a glass jar, seal, and refrigerate 1 hour or longer for the flavor to develop.

Per tablespoon: 14 Calories, 0.6 g Protein, 0.9 g Total Fat (61% of Calories), 0.1 g Saturated Fat, 0.7 g Carbohydrates, 0 g Dietary Fiber, 0 mg Cholesterol, 34 mg Sodium

VARIATION
Serve this dressing on romaine lettuce with garlic croutons and grated Parmesan cheese for a Caesar salad.

Note: The consistency of soft tofu varies from manufacturer to manufacturer, The Japanese and Korean ones, which are extremely smooth and soft like custard, make a smooth salad dressing. The American companies make soft tofu that is a little firmer and makes a good tofu mayonnaise.

Sichuan Spicy Tofu

This is a simple yet magnificent dish—spicy, fragrant, and delicious. The hot bean sauce and Sichuan peppercorns provide the signature flavors of this Sichuan specialty. Serve it with plenty of steamed rice.

MAKES 6 SERVINGS

1½ pounds firm tofu, rinsed and drained
1 teaspoon olive oil
1 cup fresh ground turkey
3 cloves garlic, finely chopped
3 scallions, including tops, sliced into thin rings
1 tablespoon Chinese hot bean sauce

2 tablespoons reduced-sodium soy sauce
⅔ cup fat-free, low-sodium chicken broth
1 tablespoon cornstarch dissolved in 1 tablespoon water
½ teaspoon ground Sichuan peppercorns
1 teaspoon oriental sesame oil

Cut tofu into ½-inch cubes. Place in a bowl, add hot water to cover, and soak until ready to use.

Heat a heavy 10-inch nonstick frying pan over medium-high heat. Add oil, swirl to coat pan, and heat 15 seconds. Add turkey and cook, stirring to separate turkey, until no longer pink. Push turkey to one side of pan. Add garlic and 2 of the scallions and stir-fry until aromatic. Stir in hot bean sauce. Drain tofu and gently stir into turkey mixture. Add soy sauce and chicken broth and bring to a boil. Cover, reduce heat to low, and simmer 3 minutes, or until tofu is heated through. Stir cornstarch mixture and stir into tofu mixture. Cook, stirring gently, until sauce is thickened.

Transfer tofu and turkey mixture to a heated serving dish. Sprinkle Sichuan peppercorn powder and remaining scallion rings on top. Drizzle with sesame oil and serve.

Per serving: 150 Calories, 17 g Protein, 6 g Total Fat (36% of Calories), 0.7 g Saturated Fat, 7 g Carbohydrates, 1 g Dietary Fiber, 16 mg Cholesterol, 649 mg Sodium

Homestyle Tofu

Here the tofu is pan-fried first to add a satisfying chewiness to its surface, while keeping the inside tender and delicious. A touch of hoisin sauce gives this dish its characteristic flavor.

MAKES 4 SERVINGS

1½ pounds firm tofu, rinsed and drained
1 tablespoon canola oil
1 clove garlic, coarsely chopped
3 Chinese dried mushrooms, soaked 30 minutes, drained, and quartered
1 green bell pepper, cut into large squares
1 red bell pepper, cut into large squares
¾ cup fat-free, low-sodium chicken broth

1½ tablespoons hoisin sauce
2 tablespoons reduced-sodium soy sauce
1 tablespoon dark soy sauce (optional)
1 tablespoon cornstarch dissolved in 1 tablespoon water
1 scallion, including top, cut into 1½-inch lengths
1 teaspoon oriental sesame oil

Cut tofu into ½-inch-thick small triangles and pat dry with paper towels.

Heat a heavy 10-inch nonstick frying pan over high heat. Add ½ tablespoon of the oil, add tofu, and pan-fry on both sides until golden brown, about 2 minutes per side. Transfer tofu to a plate.

Add remaining ½ tablespoon oil to pan and heat a few seconds. Add garlic, mushrooms, and bell peppers; stir-fry about 1 minute, or until peppers are slightly charred. Transfer pepper mixture to a separate plate.

Add chicken broth, hoisin sauce, reduced-sodium soy sauce, and dark soy, if using, to pan and bring to a boil. Reduce heat to medium. Return tofu to pan, cover, and simmer 2 minutes. Stir cornstarch mixture and stir into tofu mixture. Cook, stirring, until sauce is slightly thickened. Add reserved pepper mixture to tofu. Add scallion and drizzle in sesame oil. Stir to combine and transfer to a heated serving dish.

Per serving: 197 Calories, 13 g Protein, 10 g Total Fat (44% of Calories), 1 g Saturated Fat, 15 g Carbohydrates, 1 g Dietary Fiber, 0 mg Cholesterol, 576 mg Sodium

Shrimp-Stuffed Tofu

Here a delightful shrimp mixture is stuffed into each block of tender tofu and then smothered by a delicious wine sauce. This is a magnificent dish for special occasions.

½ recipe Basic Shrimp Paste (page 24)
1 pound firm tofu, rinsed
¼ cup cornstarch, for dusting
1 cup fat-free, low-sodium chicken broth
1 tablespoon dry sherry
1 tablespoon reduced-sodium soy sauce
1 teaspoon premium oyster sauce

¼ teaspoon sugar
Freshly ground black pepper to taste
2 teaspoons cornstarch dissolved in
    1 tablespoon water and 1 teaspoon
    sesame oil
2 scallions, including tops, sliced
    diagonally into thin 2-inch shreds

Prepare Basic Shrimp Paste and chill for 2 hours or longer.

Cut tofu in half lengthwise, then cut each half crosswise into thirds. Pat tofu dry with paper towels. Using a small spoon, scoop out some tofu from each piece to make a hole about ½ inch deep and 1 inch in diameter, without going through the sides. Dust interior of holes with cornstarch. Stuff 1 portion of shrimp mixture in each hole and smooth edges with a knife or with your finger.

Place tofu on a heatproof plate coated with cooking spray. Place in steamer over boiling water and steam over medium heat 10 minutes, or until shrimp mixture is cooked. Drain off liquid on plate and transfer tofu to a heated serving platter.

Meanwhile, bring chicken broth, sherry, soy sauce, oyster sauce, sugar, and black pepper to a boil in a small pot over medium heat. Stir cornstarch mixture and stir into broth mixture. Cook, stirring, until sauce is slightly thickened. Spoon sauce over tofu and sprinkle shredded scallions on top. Serve at once.

Per piece: 194 Calories, 13 g Protein, 4 g Total Fat (19% of Calories), 0.6 g Saturated Fat, 25 g Carbohydrates, 0 g Dietary Fiber, 57 mg Cholesterol, 417 mg Sodium

When steaming or simmering tofu, use medium heat to ensure a tender, smooth tofu. High heat toughens the tofu and shrinks the shrimp mixture.

Aromatic Braised Tofu

This meaty-tasting, richly flavored tofu is saturated with an aromatic sauce. The Chinese mushrooms add contrasting texture and flavor. The dish is easy to make and can be prepared one or two days in advance and refrigerated. Serve as an entree or as part of a buffet. It is delicious with rice.

MAKES 4 SERVINGS

1 pound fresh firm tofu, rinsed
8 Chinese dried mushrooms, soaked in
    1 cup hot water 30 minutes
2 teaspoons oriental sesame oil
1 (¼-inch-thick) slice fresh ginger, lightly
    crushed
2 scallions, including tops, cut into
    4-inch lengths

1 dried hot chili (optional), seeds
    removed
1 tablespoon dry sherry
2½ tablespoons reduced-sodium soy
    sauce
2 tablespoons light brown sugar
1 cup fat-free, low-sodium chicken broth
1 star anise

Cut tofu into ½-inch-thick small triangles and pat dry with paper towels. Drain mushrooms, reserving soaking liquid.

Heat a heavy 10-inch nonstick skillet over medium-high heat; coat pan with cooking spray. Arrange tofu slices in pan and pan-fry until light brown on all sides, about 2 minutes per side. Transfer tofu to a plate.

Return pan to heat. Add sesame oil, ginger, scallions, chili, if using, and mushrooms; stir-fry until aromatic, about 1 minute. Add tofu, sherry, soy sauce, sugar, chicken broth, reserved soaking liquid, and star anise. Simmer, partially covered, over low heat, stirring occasionally, 15 minutes, or until sauce is reduced by half. Transfer to a serving dish.

Per serving: 144 Calories, 10 g Protein, 5.5 g Total Fat (34% of Calories), 0.8 g Saturated Fat, 15 g Carbohydrates, 1 g Dietary Fiber, 0 mg Cholesterol, 453 mg Sodium

Tofu and Broccoli

*B*roccoli is a member of the cruciferous group of vegetables, said to offer some protection against cancer. Together with tofu, which is rich in protein and calcium, this dish is a winner. Serve it with steamed rice.

MAKES 4 SERVINGS

1 pound broccoli flowerets
2 teaspoons olive oil
1 teaspoon minced fresh ginger
1 teaspoon minced garlic
½ cup fat-free, low-sodium chicken broth
1 tablespoon premium oyster sauce
1 tablespoon reduced-sodium soy sauce
1 tablespoon dry sherry

¼ teaspoon salt
¼ teaspoon sugar
Freshly ground black pepper to taste
1 pound firm tofu, rinsed and cut into thin slices
4 teaspoons cornstarch dissolved in 2 tablespoons water
1 teaspoon oriental sesame oil

Cook broccoli in a pot of boiling water 2 minutes. Drain and set aside.

Heat a heavy 10-inch nonstick frying pan over medium heat until hot. Add olive oil and swirl to coat pan. Add ginger and garlic; cook, stirring, a few seconds, or until garlic is light brown and aromatic. Add chicken broth, oyster sauce, soy sauce, sherry, salt, sugar, and black pepper; stir to combine and bring to a boil.

Add tofu slices; cover, and simmer over low heat 3 minutes. Stir cornstarch mixture and stir into tofu mixture. Cook, stirring, until sauce is slightly thickened. Scatter reserved broccoli evenly over the tofu; cover and simmer 1 minute, or until heated through. Stir and mix gently without breaking tofu. Drizzle in sesame oil and serve.

Per serving: 159 Calories, 12 g Protein, 7 g Total Fat (39% of Calories), 1 g Saturated Fat, 14 g Carbohydrates, 4 g Dietary Fiber, 0 mg Cholesterol, 693 mg Sodium

Note: You can use soft, firm, or extra-firm tofu for this recipe. The difference between firm tofu and soft tofu is that the firm tofu is pressed longer and more water is extracted, which explains why it is firm. The soft tofu is pressed less and contains more water. So if you compare the two kinds, for the same weight the firm tofu contains more soy protein than the soft tofu does.

Tofu with Mushrooms and Vegetables

Here is an easy and healthy dish. You can use any kind of mushroom to suit your taste. Serve this saucy dish with steamed rice.

MAKES 4 SERVINGS

1 pound firm tofu, rinsed

1 tablespoon olive oil

3 scallions, including tops, cut into 1-inch lengths, white and green parts separated

1 clove garlic, minced

5 Chinese dried mushrooms, soaked in hot water 30 minutes, drained, and each cut in half

1 carrot, peeled and cut diagonally into $\frac{1}{16}$-inch-thick slices

$\frac{1}{2}$ winter bamboo shoot, sliced

2 tablespoons reduced-sodium soy sauce

1 tablespoon premium oyster sauce

$\frac{1}{2}$ teaspoon sugar

Freshly ground black pepper to taste

$\frac{3}{4}$ cup fat-free, low-sodium chicken broth

16 snow peas, strings removed

1 tablespoon cornstarch dissolved in 1 tablespoon water

1 teaspoon oriental sesame oil

Cut tofu lengthwise into thirds, then cut crosswise into $\frac{1}{4}$-inch-thick slices; set aside.

Heat a heavy 10-inch frying pan over high heat until hot. Add oil and swirl to coat pan. Add white parts of scallions and garlic; cook, stirring, 15 seconds, or until aromatic. Add mushrooms, carrot, and bamboo shoot; stir-fry until heated through, about 1 minute. Stir in soy sauce, oyster sauce, sugar, and black pepper. Add chicken broth and tofu slices and bring to a boil. Cover, reduce heat to medium, and simmer 2 minutes.

Add snow peas and green parts of scallions. Stir cornstarch mixture and stir into tofu mixture. Cook, stirring gently, until snow peas are bright green and sauce is slightly thickened. Drizzle in sesame oil. Transfer to a serving dish and serve.

Per serving: 171 Calories, 10 g Protein, 7.8 g Total Fat (41% of Calories), 1.1 g Saturated Fat, 16 g Carbohydrates, 2 g Dietary Fiber, 0 mg Cholesterol, 717 mg Sodium

Tofu with Chili and Garlic

This is a velvety peppery dish that goes well with plenty of steamed rice. Chilies are high in vitamin C and contain capsiacinoids—natural substances that produce a burning sensation in the mouth. Capsiacinoids have been found to work as an anticoagulant, possibly helping to prevent blood clots that cause heart attacks or strokes.

MAKES 4 SERVINGS

1 pound soft tofu, preferably Nasoya brand
2 teaspoons canola oil
1 tablespoon minced fresh ginger
2 teaspoons minced garlic
2 red chilies, seeded and sliced
1 tablespoon Chinese hot bean sauce
1/4 cup tree ear mushrooms, soaked in hot water 30 minutes, drained, and rinsed

1 tablespoon reduced-sodium soy sauce
1 tablespoon premium oyster sauce
1/2 teaspoon sugar
3/4 cup fat-free, low-sodium chicken broth
4 ounces snow peas, strings removed
1 ripe medium tomato, cut into wedges
2 teaspoons cornstarch dissolved in 1 tablespoon water
1 teaspoon oriental sesame oil

Cut tofu lengthwise into thirds, then cut crosswise into 3/8-inch-thick slices. Drain off excess water and pat dry with paper towels.

Heat a heavy 10-inch nonstick frying pan over medium heat until hot. Add oil and swirl to coat pan. Add ginger, garlic, and chilies and cook, stirring, 30 seconds, or until aromatic. Add hot bean sauce and mushrooms and stir-fry until heated through. Add tofu slices, soy sauce, oyster sauce, sugar, and chicken broth; stir gently and bring to a boil. Carefully baste tofu a few times. Cover, reduce heat, and simmer slowly 2 minutes.

Scatter in snow peas and tomato, cover, and simmer 2 more minutes, until vegetables are heated through. Stir cornstarch mixture and stir into tofu mixture. Cook, stirring carefully with a wooden spoon until sauce is slightly thickened. Transfer mixture to a heated serving platter. Drizzle in sesame oil and serve immediately.

Per serving: 135 Calories, 8 g Protein, 6.8 g Total Fat (51% of Calories), 0.8 g Saturated Fat, 13 g Carbohydrates, 2 g Dietary Fiber, 0 mg Cholesterol, 647 mg Sodium

Tofu and Shrimp

In this dish, the tofu is soft and smooth; the shrimp is succulent; and the black mushrooms, ham, and sweet peas add a medley of subtle flavors.

½ pound small shrimp, peeled
1 tablespoon egg white, lightly beaten
1 teaspoon cornstarch
1 pound firm tofu, cut into ½-inch cubes
1 teaspoon olive oil
2 slices fresh ginger, lightly smashed
1 scallion, including top, cut into
   1-inch lengths
3 Chinese dried mushrooms, soaked in
   hot water 30 minutes, drained, and
   cubed
2 tablespoons dry sherry

1 tablespoon reduced-sodium soy sauce
¼ teaspoon white pepper
Pinch of sugar
1 cup fat-free, low-sodium chicken broth
2 teaspoons cornstarch dissolved in
   1 tablespoon water
1 (⅛-inch-thick) slice honey ham,
   chopped
⅓ cup fresh or frozen green peas
1 teaspoons oriental sesame oil
Salt (optional)

Mix together shrimp, egg white, and cornstarch; set aside 30 minutes. Cover tofu cubes with hot water; set aside 15 minutes or until ready to cook, then drain.

Heat a heavy 10-inch nonstick frying pan over medium-high heat until hot. Add oil and swirl to coat pan. Add ginger and scallion and cook, stirring, a few seconds. Add mushrooms and cook, stirring, until aromatic, about 30 seconds. Add drained tofu cubes, sherry, soy sauce, pepper, sugar, and chicken broth; stir gently and bring to a boil.

Stir shrimp mixture and spread evenly over the tofu. Cover, reduce heat, and simmer 1 minute, or until shrimp turn pink. Stir cornstarch mixture and stir into tofu mixture. Cook, stirring, until sauce is creamy and slightly thickened. Add ham and peas and stir to combine. Drizzle in sesame oil and transfer to a heated serving dish. Add salt to taste, if desired.

Per serving: 140 Calories, 16 g Protein, 4.7 g Total Fat (30% of Calories), 0.9 g Saturated Fat, 7 g Carbohydrates, 0.6 g Dietary Fiber, 63 mg Cholesterol, 460 mg Sodium

Tofu and Turkey in Spicy Tomato Sauce

The tender tofu cubes blend deliciously with the flavorful turkey meat in a robust tomato sauce. This is a delicious way to eat leftover turkey. Serve with plenty of steamed rice to soak up the sauce, and accompany with Stir-Fried Bok Choy (page 95) to offset the spiciness.

MAKES 6 SERVINGS

1 teaspoon olive oil
3 large cloves garlic, coarsely chopped
2½ cups (about ¾ pound) ¾-inch-cubes cooked turkey breast
2 tablespoons Chinese hot bean sauce
2 tablespoons reduced-sodium soy sauce
1 tablespoon dry sherry

1 cup fat-free, low-sodium chicken broth
1½ pounds regular tofu, cut into ¾-inch cubes
½ cup canned, no-salt-added chopped tomatoes, drained
2 tablespoons cornstarch dissolved in ¼ cup water
1 teaspoon oriental sesame oil

Heat a heavy 10-inch nonstick frying pan over high heat until hot. Add oil and swirl to coat pan. Add garlic and cook, stirring, a few seconds. Add turkey and stir-fry until aromatic. Add hot bean sauce and stir-fry 1 minute. Add soy sauce and sherry and stir-fry 30 seconds. Add chicken broth and bring to a boil.

Scatter tofu cubes over turkey, and scatter tomatoes over tofu. Cover, reduce heat to low, and simmer gently 3 minutes. Stir contents to combine ingredients evenly, being careful not to break up the tofu. Stir cornstarch mixture and stir into tofu mixture. Cook, stirring gently, until sauce is slightly thickened. Cover and simmer 1 minute. Drizzle in sesame oil and transfer to a heated serving dish.

Per serving: 189 Calories, 21 g Protein, 7.6 g Total Fat (36% of Calories), 0.7 g Saturated Fat, 10 g Carbohydrates, 0.7 g Dietary Fiber, 18 mg Cholesterol, 789 mg Sodium

TIP

Simmering the tofu and turkey slowly on low heat keeps them tender and moist. Harsh boiling toughens the tofu and meat.

# Tofu Patties

Here the tofu is mashed and mixed with chopped mushrooms, sesame seeds, and jasmine rice to form delicious aromatic meatless patties. Tofu patties are versatile. Serve them warm with brown sauce as an entree, or serve them as a hamburger substitute in buns with ketchup. Make them petite and serve them as appetizers with sweet and sour sauce.

MAKES 8 PATTIES

3 teaspoons olive oil
3 scallions, including tops, thinly sliced,
    white and green parts separated
2 teaspoons minced fresh garlic
1 cup chopped fresh mushrooms
12 ounces extra-firm tofu, squeezed to
    remove excess moisture

2 teaspoons curry powder
1 tablespoon reduced-sodium soy sauce
2 egg whites, lightly beaten
1 cup cooked jasmine rice
2 tablespoons toasted sesame seeds
¼ cup dry bread crumbs
Cilantro sprigs, for garnish

Heat a heavy 10-inch nonstick frying pan over medium heat until hot. Add 1 teaspoon of the oil and swirl to coat pan. Add white parts of scallions and garlic and cook, stirring, until aromatic, about 30 seconds. Add mushrooms and cook, stirring, over high heat until mushrooms are slightly softened and are about to release their juices, about 45 seconds. Immediately transfer mixture to a plate.

In a food processor fitted with the metal blade, pulse tofu a few times. Add curry powder, soy sauce, egg whites, rice, sesame seeds, green parts of scallions, and mushroom mixture. Process a few seconds until just blended. Add bread crumbs and pulse a few times to combine. Form mixture into 8 patties about ½ inch thick and 3 inches in diameter.

Heat the frying pan over medium heat until hot. Add another 1 teaspoon of the oil and swirl to coat pan. Pan-fry 4 patties at a time until crisp and browned, 4 to 5 minutes per side. Transfer to a plate. Add remaining teaspoon of oil to pan and fry remaining 4 patties. Place cooked patties on a warm serving plate. Garnish with cilantro and serve.

Per patty: 95 Calories, 6 g Protein, 3.4 g Total Fat (32% of Calories), 0.5 g Saturated Fat, 10 g Carbohydrates, 1 g Dietary Fiber, 0 mg Cholesterol, 146 mg Sodium

VARIATION

Serve tofu patties with radish sprouts, lettuce, and tomato slices and Creamy Tofu-Miso Dressing (page 103) in pita bread.

Tofu Cutlets with Mushroom Sauce

Pan-fried tofu cutlets have a chewy texture on the outside but are smooth and tender on the inside. The mushroom sauce gives these meatlike tofu cutlets an outstanding flavor. Serve with plenty of steamed jasmine rice.

MAKES 4 SERVINGS

2 teaspoons canola oil
1 pound firm tofu, rinsed and cut into 4 slices lengthwise
2 scallions, including tops, cut into 1-inch lengths
4 ounces fresh enoki mushrooms, with 1 inch trimmed from root ends and rinsed
1 cup peeled straw mushrooms

1 cup hot fat-free, low-sodium chicken broth
1 tablespoon reduced-sodium soy sauce
1 tablespoon cornstarch dissolved in 1 tablespoon water
1 teaspoon oriental sesame oil
Cilantro sprigs, for garnish
Salt and freshly ground black pepper (optional)

Heat a heavy 10-inch nonstick frying pan over high heat until hot. Add oil and swirl to coat pan. Add tofu slices and pan-fry until light brown on both sides, about 2 minutes per side. Transfer to a serving platter and arrange them with slices overlapping; set aside.

Add scallions to pan and cook, stirring, 30 seconds, or until aromatic. Add enoki and straw mushrooms, chicken broth, and soy sauce; bring to a boil. Stir cornstarch mixture and stir into mushroom mixture. Cook, stirring, until sauce is slightly thickened. Spoon sauce over tofu slices. Drizzle with sesame oil and garnish with cilantro sprigs. Season with salt and black pepper, if desired. Serve immediately.

Per serving: 140 Calories, 12 g Protein, 6.5 g Total Fat (30% of Calories), 0.8 g Saturated Fat, 10 g Carbohydrates, 2 g Dietary Fiber, 0 mg Cholesterol, 257 mg Sodium

Grilled Teriyaki Tofu and Vegetables

The tofu is pan-seared first to acquire a meatlike texture, then marinated in a sweet soy sauce mixture and grilled to perfection. After eating this delicious, satisfying dish filled with soy protein, you won't miss the meat anymore.

MAKES 4 SERVINGS

2 teaspoons canola oil
1½ pounds extra-firm tofu, cut into
    2 × 1-inches pieces
½ cup Teriyaki Sauce (page 289)
1 large onion, cut into 1-inch squares
2 summer squash, cut into ½-inch-thick
    rounds

1 large red bell pepper, cut into 1-inch
    squares
8 fresh firm mushrooms, wiped clean
Steamed rice

Heat a heavy 10-inch nonstick frying pan over medium-high heat until hot. Add oil, swirl to coat pan, and heat 10 seconds. Add tofu pieces and pan-fry until light brown on all sides, about 7 minutes. Transfer tofu to a 9-inch pie plate. Pour Teriyaki Sauce over tofu and refrigerate, turning frequently, 2 hours, to ensure even coating.

Prepare grill. Drain tofu, reserving marinade. Thread tofu lengthwise onto 4 skewers. Thread vegetables onto another 4 skewers and brush with the reserved marinade.

Grill skewers over medium-high heat, basting occasionally, until deep brown and crusty, 1 to 2 minutes per side for tofu and about 4 minutes per side for the vegetables. Serve hot with rice.

Per serving: 179 Calories, 15 g Protein, 7.3 g Total Fat (37% of Calories), 0.9 g Saturated Fat, 14 g Carbohydrates, 2 g Dietary Fiber, 0 mg Cholesterol, 234 mg Sodium

Fish and Shellfish

China's huge eastern coast and those of many Asian countries border on the Yellow and South China seas, providing access to an enormous variety of fish and shellfish year-round. Seafood dishes are included in family meals every day. Usually a simple preparation of whole fish, such as steamed whole fish, pan-fried trout, or braised sea bass, is served and shared by the whole family. Fish fillets, a Western influence, were not seen in markets until recent years. In this book I have adapted Chinese recipes to use fish fillets and have developed some mouthwatering dishes such as Stir-Fried Flounder with Vegetables and Crispy Fish Rolls. I have modified many deep-fried dishes using broiling and grilling techniques, thereby reducing their fat content and making them healthier yet delightful to eat. Most fresh white-fleshed fish are healthy choices, and all types of fresh shellfish are low in fat. All fresh seafood contains some omega-3 fatty acids, but salmon, tuna, and mackerel are especially high. Studies have shown that diets rich in omega-3 acids help lower cholesterol, blood pressure, and the risk of heart disease. So it's important to include seafood in your regular diet.

Steamed Fish with Ginger and Scallions

Steaming is an excellent way to preserve the flavor and texture of a fish.

MAKES 4 SERVINGS

1 (about 2½-pound) yellow snapper, whitefish, or sea bass
2 tablespoons dry sherry
½ teaspoon sugar
Freshly ground black pepper to taste
2 cloves garlic, finely chopped
1 heaping tablespoon finely shredded fresh ginger

2 tablespoons Chinese fermented black beans
2 to 3 scallions, including tops, cut diagonally into 2-inch fine shreds
1 tablespoon reduced-sodium soy sauce mixed with 2 teaspoons red wine vinegar and ¼ teaspoon sugar (optional)

Have fish cleaned, scaled, and trimmed but leave head and tail on. Sprinkle salt on both sides of the fish skin. Cover and refrigerate 1 hour. Rinse off salt with cold water, and pat dry with paper towels. Cut diagonal slashes 1 inch apart on each side of the fish to facilitate even cooking.

Spray a heatproof plate large enough to hold the fish and 1 inch smaller than the diameter of the steamer with cooking spray. Place fish on plate. Sprinkle sherry, sugar, black pepper, garlic, ginger, and black beans all over fish.

Place plate with fish in steamer, tightly cover, and steam fish over boiling water 8 minutes. Remove from heat and let fish remain covered another 10 minutes. Uncover and carefully slide fish and its steaming juices onto a heated serving plate. Scatter shredded scallions evenly on top of fish. Serve immediately with the soy sauce and vinegar mixture on the side, if desired.

Per serving: 334 Calories, 56 g Protein, 8 g Total Fat (22% of Calories), 2 g Saturated Fat, 4 g Carbohydrates, 0 g Dietary Fiber, 156 mg Cholesterol, 562 mg Sodium

VARIATION

Replace the whole fish with 4 (about 8-oz.) salmon steaks. Reduce steaming time to 4 minutes.

Stir-Fried Flounder with Vegetables

The egg-white and cornstarch coating keeps the fish fillets moist and tender. The crisp vegetables contrast with the succulent fish fillet. Simmered in a subtly sweet and tart sauce, this is an excellent dish. Serve it with Curried Fried Rice (page 223).

MAKES 4 SERVINGS

1 pound (about 6 large fillets) flounder
   fillets
2 teaspoons cornstarch
1 tablespoon egg white, beaten
1 teaspoon oriental sesame oil (optional)
3 tablespoons balsamic vinegar
2 tablespoons sugar
1 tablespoon reduced-sodium soy sauce
1/8 teaspoon salt or to taste
Freshly ground black pepper
2 teaspoons tapioca starch dissolved in
   3/4 cup fat-free, low-sodium chicken
   broth

1 teaspoon olive oil
1 clove garlic, minced
1 carrot, cut diagonally into 1/8-inch-thick
   slices
1/4 cup dried tree ear mushrooms,
   soaked in warm water 30 minutes,
   drained, and thoroughly rinsed
1/4 cup water
4 ounces snow peas, strings removed

Cut each fillet lengthwise in half, then cut each half crosswise into 3 pieces. Place fish slices on a plate. Sift cornstarch all over the fish and toss a few times with a rubber spatula. Add beaten egg white and toss again. Refrigerate 30 minutes or longer. Add sesame oil, if using, and toss gently just before cooking.

In a small bowl, combine vinegar, sugar, soy sauce, salt, black pepper, and tapioca starch mixture. Stir until sugar dissolves; set aside.

Heat a heavy 10-inch nonstick skillet over medium heat until hot. Add olive oil and swirl to coat pan. Add garlic and cook, stirring, a few seconds. Add carrot and mushrooms and stir-fry about 30 seconds. Add water, cover, and cook 1 minute, or until vegetables are heated through. Add snow peas, replace cover, and cook 1 minute, or until snow peas are bright green. Transfer contents of pan to a plate.

Stir vinegar mixture, add to pan, and bring to a gentle boil. Distribute fish slices evenly in a single layer in pan, cover, and simmer 2 minutes, or until fish turns white. Return vegetables to pan. Using rubber spatula turn and baste gently until mixture is saturated with the sauce. Transfer to a heated serving platter and serve.

Per serving: 177 Calories, 21 g Protein, 3.3 g Total Fat (17% of Calories), 0.6 g Saturated Fat, 17 g Carbohydrates, 2 g Dietary Fiber, 57 mg Cholesterol, 369 mg Sodium

Note: The flounder fillets are very delicate. Carefully turn the fish with a rubber spatula or wooden spoon to avoid breaking them.

Crispy Whole Fish in Sweet and Sour Sauce

A centerpiece banquet dish, this fish traditionally was deep-fried, which required more work and added a lot of fat. With my cooking method, you can enjoy this delicious fish often, without excessive fat calories.

MAKES 4 SERVINGS

1 (2½- to 3-lb.) fresh whole fish, such as haddock, sea bass, or scrod
2 scallions, including tops, lightly smashed
4 slices fresh ginger, lightly smashed
½ teaspoon salt
2 tablespoons dry sherry
1 tablespoon reduced-sodium soy sauce
4 tablespoons sugar
4 tablespoons cider vinegar
3 tablespoons ketchup
1 tablespoon cornstarch dissolved in ¾ cup fat-free, low-sodium chicken broth

3 teaspoons peanut oil
¼ cup all-purpose flour, for dusting
3 tablespoons finely shredded fresh ginger
1 clove garlic, minced
4 Chinese dried mushrooms, soaked in warm water 30 minutes, drained, and shredded
½ cup shredded red bell pepper
½ cup shredded tender celery
2 scallions, including tops, cut diagonally into 2-inch thin shreds

Have fish cleaned, scaled, and trimmed but leave head and tail on. Rinse fish well and pat dry with paper towels. Holding the knife at an angle, cut diagonal slashes, almost to the bone, 1 inch apart on each side of fish.

In a small bowl, combine scallions, smashed ginger, salt, and sherry. Rub this mixture all over the fish, including inside the slashes. Cover fish and refrigerate 1 hour. Discard marinade and pat fish dry with paper towels.

Preheat oven to 500F (260C) for 15 minutes. Coat a 13 × 9-inch baking pan with cooking spray.

In a small bowl, combine the soy sauce, sugar, vinegar, ketchup, and cornstarch mixture and stir until sugar dissolves; set aside.

Brush fish evenly all over, including inside the slashes, with 2 teaspoons of peanut oil. Dust whole fish, including inside the slashes, with flour; shake off excess flour. Place fish on its stomach and pull out the cut sides to prop up the fish in the baking pan, keeping the slashes open. Arrange fish to curve naturally with its head turned one way and its tail the other, as if it were swimming. Bake 15 minutes, or until the fish flakes easily. Remove fish and let it stand 10 minutes.

Meanwhile, heat a heavy 8-inch frying pan over medium heat until hot. Add remaining 1 teaspoon oil, swirl to coat pan, and heat 15 seconds. Sprinkle in ginger and garlic and cook, stirring, 15 seconds. Add mushrooms, bell pepper, and celery and stir-fry until aromatic and heated through, about 1 minute. Stir soy sauce mixture and add to pan. Bring to a boil and cook, stirring, until sauce is slightly thickened. Remove pan from heat.

Using 2 spatulas, slide them under the fish and transfer it carefully to a heated large serving platter, propped in the swimming position, stomach side down. Spoon sauce and vegetables over fish and sprinkle shredded scallions on top. Serve immediately.

Per serving: 410 Calories, 60 g Protein, 6 g Total Fat (13% of Calories), 1 g Saturated Fat, 31 g Carbohydrates, 2 g Dietary Fiber, 187 mg Cholesterol, 610 mg Sodium

TIP

If the fish will not remain upright in the baking pan, secure it with one or two 12-inch-long skewers threaded through the back of the fish, and prop the skewers on the edges of the baking pan.

Pan-Fried Ginger Trout

Ginger and scallions are seared in hot oil to release their enticing aroma, then they are used to garnish the dish. The simple seasoning sauce complements the fish without overpowering its natural delicate flavor. This aromatic fish is quick, easy, and delicious. Serve it with steamed jasmine rice.

MAKES 4 SERVINGS

4 (about 6-oz.) trout, dressed and
    cleaned
½ teaspoon salt
3 tablespoons all-purpose flour
2 tablespoons reduced-sodium soy sauce
2 tablespoons red wine vinegar
2 tablespoons dry sherry
2 teaspoons sugar

Freshly ground black pepper to taste
1 tablespoon canola oil
2 tablespoons finely shredded fresh
    young ginger
3 scallions, including tops, cut into
    1-inch lengths, white and green parts
    separated
Cilantro sprigs, for garnish

Sprinkle trout with salt and let stand 30 minutes. Rinse with cold water and pat dry with paper towels. Make 3 shallow cuts on each side of each trout; dredge trout in flour and shake off any excess.

In a small dish, combine soy sauce, vinegar, sherry, sugar, and black pepper. Stir until sugar dissolves; set aside.

Heat a heavy 10-inch nonstick frying pan over medium heat until hot. Add oil and swirl to coat pan. Add ginger and white parts of scallions and cook, stirring rapidly, 30 seconds, or until aromatic. Add green parts of scallions and cook, stirring, 30 seconds, or until the color brightens. Transfer ginger and scallions to a plate, reserving the oil in pan.

Add trout to pan and pan-fry 5 minutes, or until bottom is lightly browned. Turn trout over and cook the other side 3 minutes, or until bottom is slightly browned. Pour soy sauce mixture over trout and boil 1 minute. Carefully transfer trout to a warm serving platter. Sprinkle reserved ginger and scallions over trout and garnish with cilantro. Serve immediately.

Per serving: 408 Calories, 38 g Protein, 23 g Total Fat (51% of Calories), 5 g Saturated Fat, 9 g Carbohydrates, 0 g Dietary Fiber, 0 mg Cholesterol, 536 mg Sodium

Poached Salmon with Creamy Tofu-Miso Dressing

The salmon can be made a day in advance and kept chilled. Serve the salmon and mixed greens with Vegetarian Fried Rice (page 222) for a satisfying, elegant light meal.

MAKES 4 SERVINGS

3 slices fresh ginger, lightly smashed
1 thin stalk fresh lemongrass, lightly smashed
1 teaspoon black peppercorns
2/3 cup dry sherry or dry white wine
1/3 cup water

1½ pounds fresh salmon fillets
3/4 pound mixed salad greens
Creamy Tofu-Miso Dressing (page 103)
½ cup cucumber slices
¼ cup lightly packed fresh cilantro leaves

In a heavy 10-inch skillet, combine ginger, lemongrass, peppercorns, sherry or wine, and water and bring to a boil. Reduce heat so that mixture simmers. Gently add salmon fillets; cover, and simmer 4 to 5 minutes for each ½ inch of thickness. Remove pans from heat and let stand 5 minutes. Uncover and carefully transfer fish to a plate. Cover and set aside.

To serve, divide salad greens among 4 individual plates. Place a salmon fillet on each salad. Spoon dressing over salmon and garnish with cucumber slices and cilantro leaves.

Per serving: 290 Calories, 37 g Protein, 9 g Total Fat (29% of Calories), 2 g Saturated Fat, 6 g Carbohydrates, 2 g Dietary Fiber, 60 mg Cholesterol, 221 mg Sodium

Broiled Salmon with Teriyaki Sauce

This is a quick, easy, yet delicious dish. Serve the salmon with a spinach salad and steamed rice for a wholesome healthy meal.

MAKES 4 SERVINGS

1 (1-lb.) salmon fillet
2 teaspoons cornstarch

2 tablespoons Teriyaki Sauce (page 289)

Place salmon, skin side down, on a 12 × 8-inch piece of foil coated with cooking spray. Sift cornstarch evenly over salmon. Fold up sides of foil snugly around salmon, leaving the top open. Spoon Teriyaki Sauce evenly over salmon and marinate 30 minutes.

Preheat broiler. Place salmon with foil on broiler pan and broil 7 to 8 minutes, or until salmon flakes easily and sauce is bubbling. Remove salmon and foil from oven and place on a serving platter. Serve immediately.

Per serving: 146 Calories, 23 g Protein, 4.2 g Total Fat (26% of Calories), 0.8 g Saturated Fat, 2 g Carbohydrates. 0 g Dietary Fiber, 40 mg Cholesterol, 199 mg Sodium

VARIATION
Replace salmon with swordfish steak to make Broiled Swordfish with Teriyaki Sauce.

Almond-Crusted Haddock with Hot Bean Sauce

*T*empting haddock is served with hot bean sauce, which brings a lively spiciness to this delicate fish. The sauce can be made ahead of time and reheated just before serving. Pair this dish with steamed asparagus and Scallion Pancakes (page 264) or steamed rice.

MAKES 4 SERVINGS

1 (1-lb.) fresh haddock fillet
2 tablespoons dry sherry
2 teaspoons cornstarch
1 tablespoon egg white, lightly beaten
⅓ cup chopped almonds
1 tablespoon chopped fresh tarragon
1 teaspoon olive oil
1 teaspoon minced fresh ginger

2 cloves garlic, coarsely chopped
1 tablespoon Chinese hot bean sauce
1 tablespoon reduced-sodium soy sauce
1 teaspoon sugar
1½ teaspoons cornstarch dissolved in
   ¾ cup fat-free, low-sodium chicken broth
1 tablespoon thinly sliced scallion rings,
   for garnish

Preheat oven to 400F (205C). Combine fish with 1 tablespoon of the sherry, cornstarch, and egg white in a shallow bowl and let stand 15 minutes.

Place fish on a 12 × 10-inch piece of foil coated with cooking spray. Sprinkle almonds and tarragon evenly over fish. Bake 15 minutes, or until fish flakes easily. (Do not overbake it.) Transfer fish to a heated serving platter.

Meanwhile, heat a 1-quart heavy saucepan over medium heat until hot. Add oil and heat 15 seconds. Add ginger and garlic and cook, stirring rapidly, 30 seconds, or until garlic starts to turn golden. Add hot bean sauce and cook, stirring, 30 seconds. Add remaining 1 tablespoon sherry, soy sauce, sugar, and cornstarch mixture. Cook, stirring, until mixture boils and thickens slightly.

Pour sauce around the fish on the platter and sprinkle the scallion rings on the sauce. Serve immediately.

Per serving: 203 Calories, 25 g Protein, 8 g Total Fat (37% of Calories), 1 g Saturated Fat, 8 g Carbohydrates, 1 g Dietary Fiber, 68 mg Cholesterol, 355 mg Sodium

Swordfish Kabobs

Swordfish kabobs are excellent for a light summer meal. The Teriyaki Sauce provides flavor and the cornstarch coating seals in the juices. A rice pilaf and tossed tender greens served with the fish will make a delicious meal.

MAKES 4 SERVINGS

1½ pounds swordfish, cut into 2-inch chunks

¼ cup Teriyaki Sauce (page 289)

1 teaspoon cornstarch

10 ounces equal-size firm mushrooms

8 large scallions, white part only, cut into 2-inch lengths

2 summer squash, cut into ½-inch-thick rounds

8 cherry tomatoes

Place swordfish chunks in a self-sealing plastic bag. Add Teriyaki Sauce and sprinkle with cornstarch. Seal bag and let stand, turning several times, 30 minutes.

Divide fish and vegetables into 4 equal portions. Thread fish and vegetables alternately on 4 long metal skewers. Brush the vegetables with marinade from plastic bag.

Preheat broiler or grill to hot. Spray broiler pan or grill rack with cooking spray to prevent sticking. Broil fish kabobs 6 to 8 minutes, or until fish is slightly brown. Remove skewers and serve the fish and vegetables immediately.

Per serving: 252 Calories, 36 g Protein, 7 g Total Fat (26% of Calories), 2 g Saturated Fat, 10 g Carbohydrates, 4 g Dietary Fiber, 94 mg Cholesterol, 366 mg Sodium

Grilled Prawns with Mango Relish

Prawns are jumbo shrimp. Here they are marinated with aromatic herbs and carefully grilled without overcooking them. These are wonderful as appetizers or as an entree.

MAKES 4 SERVINGS

1 pound unpeeled large shrimp
2 teaspoons minced garlic
¼ cup chopped fresh cilantro
¼ teaspoon salt
½ teaspoon curry powder
1 tablespoon olive oil or coconut cream

1 tablespoon cornstarch
1 tablespoon Garlic-Chili Dipping Sauce
  (page 29)
¾ pound mesclun greens
1 recipe Mango Relish (page 295)

Soak 4 (10-inch) bamboo skewers in warm water 1 hour or longer.

Peel and devein shrimp, but keep the last segment of shell and tail intact. In a medium bowl, combine shrimp, garlic, cilantro, salt, curry powder, oil or coconut cream, and cornstarch; toss to coat evenly. Cover and refrigerate 30 minutes.

Preheat grill to medium-hot. Stir shrimp mixture and thread shrimp lengthwise onto the skewers without crowding.

Spray grill rack with cooking spray. Arrange skewers on grill and cook about 3 minutes. Turn skewers over and grill the other side 2 minutes. Remove from heat. Brush shrimp with dipping sauce.

Divide salad greens among 4 salad plates and top each salad with 1 shrimp skewer. Serve with relish.

Per serving: 176 Calories, 17 g Protein, 4.5 g Total Fat (23% of Calories), 0.6 g Saturated Fat, 18 g Carbohydrates, 3 g Dietary Fiber, 128 mg Cholesterol, 348 mg Sodium

Seafood Stir-Fry

Seafood and vegetables are a delicious combination. Here the scrumptious lobster, plump shrimp, and succulent scallops are accented by aromatic herbs and mingled with fresh crisp vegetables. Serve this dish with steamed rice preceeded by Tofu and Spinach Soup (page 55) and you will have a superb meal!

MAKES 6 SERVINGS

1 tablespoon olive oil
2 cloves garlic, minced
1 small red chili, seeded and sliced (optional)
2 Maine lobster tails, shelled and cut in half lengthwise
½ pound large shrimp, peeled and deveined
½ pound sea scallops, cut crosswise into ¼-inch rounds
4 large fresh firm mushrooms, cut into ⅛-inch-thick slices
2 tablespoons dry sherry
1 small red bell pepper, cut into ¼-inch-thick strips

½ pound asparagus, trimmed and cut diagonally into 2-inch lengths
6 baby corn
½ cup fat-free, low-sodium chicken broth
1 tablespoon reduced-sodium soy sauce
1 tablespoon premium oyster sauce
½ teaspoon sugar
1 teaspoon cornstarch dissolved in 1 tablespoon water
½ cup lightly packed fresh basil leaves
Salt and freshly ground black pepper to taste

Heat a heavy 10-inch nonstick frying pan over medium-high heat until hot. Add oil and swirl to coat pan. Add garlic and chili, if using. Cook, stirring, a few seconds or until aromatic. Add lobster, shrimp, scallops, and mushrooms and cook, shaking pan a few times, 30 seconds. Add sherry and stir-fry until shrimp turn pink on the edges and are almost cooked through, about 1 minute. Transfer contents of pan to a plate.

Add bell pepper, asparagus, baby corn, and chicken broth to pan and bring to a boil over high heat. Cover, reduce heat, and simmer about 1 minute. Add soy sauce, oyster sauce, and sugar. Stir cornstarch mixture and stir into vegetable mixture. Cook, stirring, until sauce is bubbling and slightly thickened. Reduce heat and return seafood mixture to pan. Add basil and cook, stirring, until seafood is heated through, about 1 minute. Season with salt and pepper. Transfer to a heated serving platter and serve at once.

Per serving: 156 Calories, 22 g Protein, 3.6 g Total Fat (21% of Calories), 0.5 g Saturated Fat, 8 g Carbohydrates, 1 g Dietary Fiber, 102 mg Cholesterol, 558 mg Sodium

Shrimp Duet

This is a delicious and colorful shrimp dish, half with white sauce and the other half with red sauce, separated by a bar of bright green broccoli flowerets. It is an artistic creation that delights both the eye and the palate, and is easy to prepare.

MAKES 6 SERVINGS

1½ pounds unpeeled medium shrimp
½ teaspoon salt
1 egg white, well beaten
1 tablespoon cornstarch
½ pound broccoli flowerets
1 tablespoon olive oil
4 slices fresh ginger, minced

4 small scallions, including tops, thinly sliced
1 tablespoon dry sherry
1 tablespoon hoisin sauce
1 tablespoon ketchup
¼ teaspoon Asian hot chili sauce

Peel and devein shrimp. In a medium bowl, mix shrimp, salt, egg white, and cornstarch. Cover and refrigerate at least 1 hour for coating to adhere to shrimp.

Cook broccoli, covered, in ½ inch of boiling water over high heat 2 minutes, until bright green. Drain broccoli and place crosswise in the middle of a serving platter as the divider.

Heat a heavy 10-inch nonstick skillet over medium-high heat until hot. Add oil and swirl to coat pan. Add ginger and scallions and cook, stirring, a few seconds. Add shrimp, shake pan, and cook, stirring, 1 minute. Add sherry and stir-fry until shrimp turn pink. Scoop out half of the shrimp and arrange on one side of the broccoli on the serving dish.

Add hoisin sauce, ketchup, and chili sauce to shrimp remaining in pan. Stir until shrimp are coated evenly. Transfer shrimp to the other side of the broccoli and serve at once.

Per serving: 157 Calories, 23 g Protein, 3.4 g Total Fat (19% of Calories), 0.5 g Saturated Fat, 8 g Carbohydrates, 2 g Dietary Fiber, 170 mg Cholesterol, 480 mg Sodium

Shrimp with Asparagus

This is a simple and elegant dish. The succulent pink shrimp contrast with the bright-green asparagus in white-wine sauce. Take care not to overcook the shrimp or the asparagus.

MAKES 4 SERVINGS

1 pound unpeeled large shrimp
¼ teaspoon sugar
1½ tablespoons lightly beaten egg white
1 tablespoon cornstarch
3 teaspoons olive oil
1 pound medium-thick asparagus, cut diagonally into 2-inch lengths

½ cup water
1 (¼-inch-thick) slice fresh ginger, smashed
3 tablespoons dry sherry
½ teaspoon salt or to taste
¼ teaspoon cornstarch dissolved in 1 tablespoon water
1 teaspoon white-wine vinegar

Peel and devein shrimp. In a medium bowl, mix shrimp, sugar, and egg white until evenly coated. Sift cornstarch evenly over the shrimp; toss a few times to mix well. Cover and refrigerate at least 1 hour for coating to adhere to the shrimp. Bring it to room temperature and stir before cooking.

Heat a heavy 10-inch nonstick skillet over high heat until hot. Add 1 teaspoon of the oil and swirl to coat pan. Add asparagus and ½ cup water, cover, and boil vigorously over high heat 1 minute. Reduce heat and simmer 30 seconds, or until asparagus are bright green and crisp-tender. Transfer asparagus and cooking liquid to a bowl; set aside.

Wipe pan with paper towels and heat over medium-high heat until pan is hot. Add remaining 2 teaspoons oil, swirl to coat pan, and heat 15 seconds. Add ginger and cook, pressing lightly a few times. Add shrimp and cook, stirring and shaking pan often to prevent sticking, until shrimp turn pink, about 1 minute. Add sherry and cover at once; steam-cook over medium-high heat 30 seconds. Return asparagus and their liquid to pan. Sprinkle with salt and cook, stirring, a few seconds to season evenly. Stir cornstarch mixture and stir into asparagus mixture. Cook, stirring, until mixture is slightly thickened. Sprinkle in vinegar and cook, stirring, about 30 seconds. Transfer to a large serving dish and serve.

Per serving: 193 Calories, 25 g Protein, 5 g Total Fat (21% of Calories), 1 g Saturated Fat, 12 g Carbohydrates, 2 g Dietary Fiber, 170 mg Cholesterol, 437 mg Sodium

Shrimp Rose

I created this dish for my cooking class students. Everybody loved it, and they named it "Shrimp Rose." Grapefruit is a good source of fiber and vitamin C. In addition, the pink or red varieties contain beta carotene, an antioxidant that may help prevent cancer. Serve this fruity, luscious shrimp dish with steamed jasmine rice.

MAKES 4 SERVINGS

1 pound unpeeled jumbo shrimp
3 tablespoons dry sherry
¼ teaspoon salt
½ teaspoon sugar
1 small egg white, lightly beaten
1 tablespoon cornstarch
¼ cup thawed frozen pineapple juice concentrate
1 tablespoon reduced-sodium soy sauce
2 tablespoons ketchup
⅛ teaspoon cayenne pepper

1 tablespoon cornstarch dissolved in ½ cup water
1 tablespoon olive oil
2 tablespoons minced shallots
1 tablespoon minced fresh ginger
1 large ruby-red grapefruit, segmented, with pith and seeds removed, and juice reserved
1 scallion, including top, finely sliced, for garnish

Peel and devein shrimp. In a medium bowl, combine shrimp, 1 tablespoon of the sherry, salt, sugar, egg white, and cornstarch and mix gently. Cover and refrigerate 1 hour.

In a small bowl, combine pineapple juice concentrate, soy sauce, remaining 2 tablespoons sherry, ketchup, cayenne pepper, and cornstarch mixture and stir until thoroughly mixed; set aside.

Heat a heavy 10-inch nonstick frying pan over medium-high heat until hot. Add oil and swirl to coat pan. Add shallots and ginger and cook, stirring, until aromatic, about 45 seconds. Add shrimp and cook, shaking pan occasionally, 1 minute. Turn shrimp over and cook another 30 seconds, until they turn pink.

Stir pineapple juice mixture and stir into shrimp with reserved grapefruit juice. Spoon sauce over shrimp, cover, and steam-cook 1 minute, or until sauce is slightly thickened. (Do not overcook shrimp.) Carefully fold in the grapefruit segments without breaking them. Transfer to a heated serving dish and sprinkle the scallion on top. Serve immediately.

Per serving: 236 Calories, 23 g Protein, 4 g Total Fat (17% of Calories), 1 g Saturated Fat, 24 g Carbohydrates, 0 g Dietary Fiber, 170 mg Cholesterol, 573 mg Sodium

Shrimp in Spicy Sichuan Sauce

This fiery shrimp dish gets its spiciness from the hot bean sauce. A touch of tomato ketchup modifies the flavor and blends beautifully with the sauce. Serve it with a cool, soothing green salad and steamed brown rice to soak up the delicious sauce.

MAKES 4 SERVINGS

1 pound unpeeled large shrimp
3 tablespoons dry sherry
2½ teaspoons sugar
1 small egg white, lightly beaten but not frothy
5 teaspoons cornstarch
1 tablespoon reduced-sodium soy sauce
2 teaspoons cider vinegar
¾ cup fat-free, low-sodium chicken broth
1 tablespoon olive oil

4 large scallions, including tops, cut into 1-inch lengths, white and green parts separated
2 teaspoons minced garlic
1 medium red bell pepper, cut into 2-inch strips
¼ cup snow peas, strings removed
2 teaspoons Chinese hot bean sauce
2 tablespoons ketchup

Peel and devein shrimp. Combine shrimp, 1 tablespoon of the sherry, ½ teaspoon of the sugar, and the egg white in a medium bowl and mix well. Sprinkle in 3 teaspoons of the cornstarch and mix evenly. Cover and refrigerate 1 hour. Bring to room temperature and stir before cooking.

In a medium bowl, combine soy sauce, cider vinegar, remaining 2 teaspoons sugar, remaining 2 teaspoons cornstarch, the chicken broth and stir until sugar dissolves; set aside.

Heat a heavy 10-inch nonstick frying pan over medium-high heat until hot. Add oil and swirl to coat pan. Add white parts of scallions, garlic, bell pepper, and snow peas; stir-fry 45 seconds, or until aromatic. Transfer vegetables to a plate, reserving oil in pan.

Add hot bean sauce and ketchup to pan and cook, stirring rapidly, 15 seconds. Add shrimp and stir-fry 45 seconds, or until shrimp turn pink on the edges. Add remaining 2 tablespoons sherry and swirl pan a few times. Stir soy sauce mixture and add to pan. Add green parts of scallions. Cover and bring to a boil; cook 30 seconds. Return vegetables to shrimp and cook, stirring gently, until sauce is evenly thickened. Remove pan from heat and transfer contents to a serving platter. Serve at once.

Per serving: 223 Calories, 25 g Protein, 4.5 g Total Fat (18% of Calories), 0.6 g Saturated Fat, 20 g Carbohydrates, 3 g Dietary Fiber, 170 mg Cholesterol, 627 mg Sodium

T I P

If you do not have a nonstick frying pan, use a regular heavy frying pan but spray the bottom with cooking spray first, then add the required amount of oil. This will help to prevent food from sticking to the pan.

Crispy Shrimp

Usually the shrimp are deep-fried. Here they are coated with water chestnut flour, broiled just long enough to crisp the coating while the shrimp remain tender, and then tossed in a sweet and sour sauce. Serve this scrumptious dish with Vegetarian Fried Rice (page 222).

MAKES 4 SERVINGS

¾ pound unpeeled large shrimp
4¼ teaspoons sugar
2 tablespoons dry sherry
1 large egg white, lightly beaten
¾ cup water chestnut flour (see Note, opposite page)
1 tablespoon plus 1 teaspoon peanut oil
2 tablespoons reduced-sodium soy sauce
2 tablespoons ketchup
1 tablespoon red-wine vinegar

¼ teaspoon hot chili sauce or to taste
1 teaspoon minced fresh ginger
2 teaspoons minced garlic
6 Chinese dried mushrooms, soaked in warm water 30 minutes, drained, and cut into ½-inch cubes
1 small carrot, thinly sliced
6 water chestnuts, cut into ½-inch cubes
2 teaspoons cornstarch dissolved in ¾ cup fat-free, low-sodium chicken broth
½ cup frozen green peas, thawed

Peel and devein shrimp. Cut each shrimp lengthwise in half. In a medium bowl, combine shrimp, ¼ teaspoon of the sugar, 1 tablespoon of the sherry, and egg white and stir to coat well; set aside 30 minutes.

Into a small bowl, measure water chestnut flour. Using a fork, stir in 1 tablespoon of the peanut oil and mix well to distribute it evenly (or use your fingers to squeeze and mix the flour mixture evenly); set aside.

In another small bowl, combine soy sauce, ketchup, vinegar, remaining 4 teaspoons sugar, chili sauce, and remaining 1 tablespoon sherry and stir until sugar dissolves; set aside.

Preheat broiler for 15 minutes. Coat a 13 × 12-inch piece of foil with cooking spray. Dredge each shrimp in the water chestnut flour mixture and place on the prepared foil; set aside.

Meanwhile, heat a heavy 10-inch nonstick skillet over medium-high heat until hot. Add remaining 1 teaspoon oil and swirl to coat pan. Add ginger and garlic and cook, stirring, until fragrant, about 15 seconds. Add mushrooms, carrot, and water chestnuts and cook, stirring, 1 minute. Add soy sauce mixture to pan and cook, stirring, until boiling. Stir cornstarch mixture and stir into mushroom mixture. Cook, stirring constantly, until sauce is slightly thickened and glossy. Turn off the heat. Cover and keep warm.

Transfer shrimp with the foil to the broiler and broil 4 inches from heat source 2 minutes, Turn shrimp over and broil the other side 1 minute, or until light brown.

Add shrimp to vegetable sauce and stir to coat well. Sprinkle in peas and cook, stirring, until heated through. Transfer to a heated serving platter and serve immediately.

Per serving: 326 Calories, 19 g Protein, 6 g Total Fat (17% of Calories), 1 g Saturated Fat, 48 g Carbohydrates, 3 g Dietary Fiber, 128 mg Cholesterol, 682 mg Sodium

Note: Some brands of water chestnut flour are fine and some are coarse. If the brand you bought is too coarse, put it in a plastic bag and roll over it several times with a rolling pin to break up clumps and obtain an even consistency.

Wok-Seared Prawns

Here the large shrimp, in their shells, are rolled in cornstarch and pan-seared until crusty outside but extremely tender and moist inside. Covered with a flavorful sweet-and-sour red sauce, these shrimp are absolutely delicious. Serve with steamed rice and light stir-fried vegetables such as broccoli or cauliflower.

MAKES 6 SERVINGS

1½ pounds unpeeled jumbo shrimp
½ cup cornstarch
3 tablespoons ketchup
1 tablespoon reduced-sodium soy sauce
2 tablespoons dry sherry
1½ tablespoons Worcestershire sauce
¼ teaspoon salt
1 tablespoon sugar
1 tablespoon cornstarch dissolved in 1 cup fat-free, low-sodium chicken broth

4 teaspoons olive oil
2 teaspoons minced fresh ginger
2 teaspoons minced garlic
2 large scallions, including tops, finely sliced
Salt and freshly ground black pepper to taste
1 teaspoon oriental sesame oil (optional)
2 heaping tablespoons coarsely chopped fresh cilantro, for garnish

Remove feet and sharp-pointed tails from shrimp. Using a pair of kitchen shears, cut each shrimp down the back without cutting it all the way through and devein if necessary. Place cornstarch on a plate and roll shrimp in it until evenly coated, shaking off any excess.

In a small bowl, mix the ketchup, soy sauce, sherry, Worcestershire sauce, salt, sugar, and cornstarch mixture and stir until sugar dissolves; set aside.

Heat a nonstick wok or heavy 10-inch nonstick skillet over medium heat until hot. Add 2 teaspoons of the oil and swirl to coat pan. Add shrimp in a single layer and brown slowly, shaking pan occasionally to prevent sticking, about 2 minutes. Turn shrimp over, drizzle in 1 teaspoon oil from the sides, and pan-fry 2 minutes more. Transfer shrimp to a plate and set aside.

Wash and dry wok. Add remaining 1 teaspoon oil to wok and heat over medium heat until hot. Add ginger, garlic, and scallions and stir-fry a few seconds. Stir the seasoning mixture and stir into ginger mixture. Cook, stirring, until the sauce is slightly thickened. Return shrimp to wok and stir until they are coated with sauce and heated through. Taste for seasoning and add more salt and pepper, if needed. Transfer to a warm serving platter. Drizzle in sesame oil, if using, and garnish with cilantro leaves. Serve at once.

Per serving: 202 Calories, 22 g Protein, 4 g Total Fat (18% of Calories), 1 g Saturated Fat, 17 g Carbohydrates, 1 g Dietary Fiber, 170 mg Cholesterol, 500 mg Sodium

Shrimp with Lobster Sauce

*A*lthough the sauce for this popular dish is called lobster sauce, there is no lobster in it. It is usually made with whole egg and pork, but here I use egg white and ground turkey, which reduces fat and cholesterol while keeping the original taste and texture. Serve it with plenty of steamed rice. A spinach salad will go well with this dish.

MAKES 4 SERVINGS

¾ pound unpeeled large shrimp
1 teaspoon cornstarch
2 teaspoons olive oil
¼ pound (½ cup) lean ground turkey
1 tablespoon Chinese fermented black beans
1 large clove garlic, coarsely chopped
1 tablespoon dry sherry
1 tablespoon reduced-sodium soy sauce

½ teaspoon sugar
¾ cup fat-free, low-sodium chicken broth
1 tablespoon cornstarch dissolved in 2 tablespoons water
2 egg whites, lightly beaten
3 scallions, including tops, cut into thin rings
Salt and freshly ground pepper to taste

Peel and devein shrimp. Using a small strainer or sifter, dust shrimp evenly with cornstarch; set aside.

Heat a heavy 10-inch nonstick skillet over medium-high heat until hot. Add oil and swirl to coat pan. Add turkey and cook, stirring to break up meat, until no longer pink, about 1 minute. Push turkey to one side of pan. Add black beans and garlic to pan and cook, stirring rapidly, 30 seconds. Stir in sherry, soy sauce, and sugar. Add chicken broth and scatter shrimp evenly in pan. Cover, bring to a boil.

Reduce heat to medium and cook 1 minute. Stir cornstarch mixture and stir into shrimp mixture. Cook, stirring, until sauce slightly thickens. Remove pan from heat and pour egg whites in a wide circle over the surface. Let stand 30 seconds to let egg white set but not harden. Stir shrimp mixture briefly and transfer to a heated serving dish. Scatter scallions on top. Season with salt and pepper and serve immediately.

Per serving: 171 Calories, 25 g Protein, 4 g Total Fat (21% of Calories), 0.7 g Saturated Fat, 7 g Carbohydrates, 1 g Dietary Fiber, 146 mg Cholesterol, 455 mg Sodium

Curried Shrimp with Fresh Pineapple

The colors are beautiful in this dish. Red curry paste gives this dish tang and flavor while blending smoothly with the coconut milk. Serve this luscious curried dish with steamed jasmine rice.

MAKES 4 SERVINGS

1 pound unpeeled large shrimp
1½ tablespoons lightly beaten egg white
1 tablespoon cornstarch
3 teaspoons canola oil
1 tablespoon red curry paste
3 cups fresh pineapple chunks
1 zucchini, cut crosswise into ⅜-inch rounds

1 teaspoon minced fresh ginger
2 shallots, thinly sliced
¾ cup reduced-fat coconut milk
1 tablespoon fish sauce
2 teaspoons sugar
1 teaspoon tapioca starch dissolved in 1 tablespoon water
1 tablespoon cilantro leaves, for garnish

Peel and devein shrimp, leaving tails intact. In a medium bowl, mix shrimp with egg white and stir until evenly coated. Sift cornstarch over shrimp and stir until evenly coated. Cover and refrigerate 1 hour. Bring shrimp to room temperature and stir before cooking.

Heat a heavy 10-inch nonstick frying pan over medium high heat until hot. Add 2 teaspoons of the oil, swirl to coat pan, and heat 15 seconds. Add shrimp and cook, using a wooden spatula to stir or push the shrimp and shaking the pan frequently to prevent sticking, until shrimp turn pink on the edges, about 1 minute. Transfer to a plate and set aside.

Add remaining 1 teaspoon oil to pan over medium heat. Add red curry paste and cook, stirring, 30 seconds. Add pineapple chunks and zucchini, then add ginger and shallots; stir-fry 15 seconds. Add coconut milk and bring to a boil; cook 5 minutes. Stir in fish sauce and sugar and cook, stirring a few times to combine the mixture. Stir tapioca mixture and stir into pineapple mixture. Cook, stirring gently, until sauce is slightly thickened. Return shrimp to pan and stir into sauce. Cover and simmer 1 minute, until heated through. Transfer to a large heated serving platter, garnish with cilantro leaves, and serve at once.

Per serving: 285 Calories, 22 g Protein, 11 g Total Fat (35% of Calories), 6 g Saturated Fat, 27 g Carbohydrates, 2 g Dietary Fiber, 170 mg Cholesterol, 530 mg Sodium

Lobster with Ginger and Scallion

This is a simple and delicious way to prepare a lobster. It will serve four people as part of a multicourse meal. Accompany it with steamed rice.

MAKES 4 SERVINGS

1 2-pound live lobster
1 tablespoon cornstarch
1 tablespoon olive oil
1 tablespoon thinly shredded peeled
   fresh ginger
6 scallions, including tops, cut into
   2-inch lengths
1 tablespoon Chinese fermented black
   beans

2 tablespoons dry sherry
1 tablespoon reduced-sodium soy sauce
1 tablespoon dark soy sauce (optional)
½ teaspoon sugar
½ cup hot fat-free, low-sodium chicken
   broth
1 teaspoon cornstarch dissolved in
   2 teaspoons water

Wearing a pair of kitchen gloves, rinse lobster well under cold running water. Place lobster, stomach side down, on a work surface without removing the rubber bands on its claws. To kill the lobster, plunge the tip of a sharp knife into the lobster where the tail and body join to sever the spinal cord. Break off claws, then remove and discard the rubber bands. Remove and discard legs. Twist to disjoint body and tail. Using a cleaver, chop off and discard tip of head where eyes and antennae are located. Split lobster in half lengthwise; remove and discard stomach sac (in the head) and feathery tissue but keep intact the greenish tomalley and any roe. Split tail in half lengthwise, then crosswise into 4 pieces. Chop each claw into 2 pieces and crack shells slightly with the blunt edge of a cleaver so that the sauce can permeate the meat inside the shells. Dust lobster pieces with cornstarch, especially the tail meat. Set aside.

Heat a heavy nonstick 10-inch frying-pan over high heat until hot. Add oil and swirl to coat pan. Add ginger, scallions, and black beans and stir-fry 30 seconds, or until aromatic. Transfer to a plate, reserving the oil in pan.

Add lobster pieces and cook, tossing occasionally, about 30 seconds. Add sherry and let it evaporate for a few seconds. Add soy sauce and sugar and cook, stirring, about 30 seconds. Add hot chicken broth and shake pan to even out the lobster pieces. Cover and steam-cook 2 to 3 minutes. Stir cornstarch mixture and stir into lobster mixture. Cook, stirring, until sauce is slightly thickened. Stir in reserved ginger and scallion mixture. Transfer to a heated serving dish and serve at once.

To eat, taste the sauce on the shells and suck out the delicious meat.

Per serving: 276 Calories, 40 g Protein, 8 g Total Fat (27% of Calories), 1 g Saturated Fat, 7 g Carbohydrates, 1 g Dietary Fiber, 175 mg Cholesterol, 752 mg Sodium

Lobster Chinese Style

A one and one half–pound lobster served Western style barely satisfies one lobster lover. By serving it Chinese style, cooked with a little minced pork, you can use one lobster to serve four people. Serve it with plenty of steamed rice to soak up this delicious sauce.

MAKES 4 SERVINGS

1 1½-pound live lobster
1 tablespoon cornstarch
2 teaspoons olive oil
1 clove garlic, minced
1 tablespoon Chinese fermented black beans
¼ pound extra-lean ground pork or turkey
2 tablespoons dry sherry

1 tablespoon reduced-sodium soy sauce
½ teaspoon sugar
¼ teaspoon freshly ground pepper
¾ cup fat-free, low-sodium chicken broth
1 tablespoon cornstarch dissolved in 2 tablespoon water
2 egg whites, lightly beaten
1 teaspoon oriental sesame oil
3 scallions, including tops, finely sliced

Wearing a pair of kitchen gloves, kill and prepare lobster as described on page 144. Dust lobster pieces with cornstarch, especially the tail meat; set aside.

Heat a large heavy nonstick frying-pan over medium-high heat until hot. Add oil and swirl to coat pan. Scatter in garlic and black beans and cook, stirring, 15 seconds, or until garlic turns light brown. Add pork or turkey and cook, stirring to break up the meat, until no longer pink.

Add lobster pieces and sherry to pan and cook, stirring, a few seconds. Stir in soy sauce, sugar, and pepper. Add broth, cover, and steam-cook over medium heat 1½ minutes. Stir cornstarch mixture and stir into lobster mixture. Cook, stirring, until sauce thickens. Pour beaten egg whites over lobster in a wide circle and remove pan from heat immediately. Stir once or twice so that egg has a flowing consistency. Drizzle in sesame oil and scatter in scallions. Transfer lobster mixture to a heated serving dish and serve at once.

Per serving: 274 Calories, 38 g Protein, 9 g Total Fat (30% of Calories), 2 g Saturated Fat, 6 g Carbohydrates, 0 g Dietary Fiber, 148 mg Cholesterol, 680 mg Sodium

Clams with Black Bean Sauce

Clams and mussels are a good source of vitamin B_{12}. They are easy and quick to prepare. Cook them just until their shells open; discard any that do not open. Serve them in their shells either as appetizers or as part of a multicourse meal. The black bean–flavored sauce is delicious with rice.

MAKES 6 SERVINGS

1 tablespoon canola oil
3 slices fresh ginger, minced
2 large cloves garlic, coarsely chopped
1 tablespoon Chinese fermented black beans, coarsely chopped
24 live littleneck clams or mussels, scrubbed clean
2 tablespoons dry sherry

2 teaspoons reduced-sodium soy sauce
1 tablespoon premium oyster sauce
½ teaspoon sugar
½ cup water
2 teaspoons cornstarch dissolved in 1 tablespoon water
2 tablespoons thinly sliced scallion rings
2 tablespoons chopped red bell pepper

Heat a heavy 10-inch skillet over medium-high heat until hot. Add oil, swirl to coat pan, and heat 15 seconds. Add ginger, garlic, and black beans and cook, stirring rapidly, until aromatic, about 30 seconds. Add clams and shake pan a few times. Add sherry, soy sauce, oyster sauce, sugar, and water. Cover immediately and steam-cook over high heat 3 to 4 minutes, or until all the clams have opened. Reduce heat to medium-low.

Using a slotted spoon, transfer clams to a serving dish, leaving the liquid in the pan. Stir cornstarch mixture and stir into liquid. Cook, stirring constantly, until slightly thickened. Spoon sauce over each clam, garnish with scallions and bell pepper, and serve immediately.

Per serving: 81 Calories, 6 g Protein, 2.8 g Total Fat (32% of Calories), 0.3 g Saturated Fat, 7 g Carbohydrates, 0 g Dietary Fiber, 37 mg Cholesterol, 513 mg Sodium

Scallops with Garlic Sauce

This is a high-spirited production that features a medley of stars: succulent white scallops, red and orange peppers, yellow squash, deep green broccoli, and moist black mushrooms, all in a delicious garlic sauce. Serve it with steamed brown or white rice.

MAKES 4 SERVINGS

¾ pound sea scallops
2 teaspoons cornstarch
1 tablespoon reduced-sodium soy sauce
1 tablespoon dry sherry
2 tablespoons balsamic vinegar
1 tablespoon sugar
1 teaspoon premium oyster sauce
¾ cup fat-free, low-sodium chicken broth
2 teaspoons canola oil
½ small red bell pepper, cut into
    1½-inch cubes
½ small orange bell pepper, cut into
    1½-inch cubes

1 yellow summer squash, cut crosswise
    into ¼-inch rounds
2 cups broccoli flowerets, blanched
6 Chinese dried mushrooms, soaked in
    warm water 30 minutes and each cut
    in half
1 teaspoon minced fresh ginger
2 teaspoons minced garlic
1 tablespoon Chinese hot bean sauce
1½ teaspoons cornstarch dissolved in
    1 tablespoon water

Cut scallops crosswise into even ⅜-inch-thick slices. Sprinkle with cornstarch and toss to mix evenly; set aside.

In a small bowl, combine soy sauce, sherry, vinegar, sugar, oyster sauce, and chicken broth and stir until sugar dissolves; set aside.

Heat a heavy 10-inch nonstick frying pan over high heat until hot. Add 1 teaspoon of the oil and swirl to coat pan. Add bell peppers and stir-fry over high heat until peppers are slightly charred, about 1 minute. Add squash, broccoli flowerets, and mushrooms and stir-fry 1 minute. Transfer vegetables to a plate.

Add remaining 1 teaspoon oil to pan over medium heat and swirl to coat pan. Add ginger and garlic and cook, stirring rapidly to prevent sticking, about 15 seconds. Add hot bean sauce and cook, stirring, 30 seconds. Add broth mixture and bring to a boil. Scatter scallops evenly in pan. Reduce heat, cover, and steam-cook until scallops turn white and are heated through, 1 to 2 minutes. (Do not overcook scallops.) Stir cornstarch mixture and stir into scallop mixture. Cook, stirring gently, until sauce is glossy. Return vegetables to pan and cook, stirring, until heated through. Transfer to a serving dish and serve immediately.

Per serving: 160 Calories, 16 g Protein, 3.5 g Total Fat (19% of Calories), 0.3 g Saturated Fat, 18 g Carbohydrates, 3 g Dietary Fiber, 30 mg Cholesterol, 624 mg Sodium

TIP

Choose fresh no-water-added sea scallops for the best results.

Crab with Spicy Black Bean Sauce

Although preparing crab requires some work, this dish is extraordinarily delicious. Serve it with steamed rice.

MAKES 4 SERVINGS

2 large live crabs
2 teaspoons canola oil
2 cloves garlic, minced
2 teaspoons finely minced fresh ginger
1 tablespoon Chinese fermented black beans, coarsely chopped
2 tablespoons dry sherry
1/4 teaspoon hot chili sauce

1 tablespoon reduced-sodium soy sauce
1/2 teaspoon sugar
1/2 cup fat-free, low-sodium chicken broth
2 teaspoons cornstarch dissolved in 1 tablespoon water
1 teaspoon oriental sesame oil
2 whole large scallions, cut diagonally into thin slices

Clean and prepare crab before cooking: Plunge crabs into a large pot of boiling water for about 2 minutes to kill crabs but not cook them. Remove crabs, rinse under cold running water, and scrub away any mossy patches on the shell. Remove hard top shell by inserting a knife at back seam and twisting off; lift apron with the tip of a knife and twist off, together with the dark vein. Remove and discard both sets of feathery gills. Leave shell with its tomalley and any roe intact but remove and discard the stomach sac, which is located between and attached to the eyes. Twist off the large claws and chop each claw in half at the joint. Crack shell with blunt edge of a cleaver so that the sauce can penetrate. Chop bodies in half down the middle, then cut each half crosswise in two again. Leave legs attached but chop off the pointed tips. Place all pieces on a large plate; discard any liquid from the crabs.

Heat a heavy 10-inch skillet over high heat until hot. Add oil and swirl to coat pan. Add garlic, ginger, and black beans and cook, stirring rapidly, a few seconds. Add crab pieces and cook, stirring, a few seconds. Add sherry and stir to combine. Add chili sauce, soy sauce, sugar, and chicken broth. Spread out crab evenly, cover, and steam-cook 2 minutes. Uncover and stir several times. Reduce heat. Stir cornstarch mixture and stir into crab mixture. Cook, stirring, until sauce thickens. Drizzle in sesame oil. Transfer to a serving dish, sprinkle scallions on top, and serve immediately.

Per serving: 94 Calories, 7 g Protein, 4.5 g Total Fat (43% of Calories), 0.4 g Saturated Fat, 5 g Carbohydrates, 0 g Dietary Fiber, 31 mg Cholesterol, 354 mg Sodium

Asian Crab Cakes

Here the delicate lumps of crabmeat are mixed with shredded potatoes, which add a pleasing texture and bind the crabmeat together. The tangy lime juice and aromatic herbs make this crab cake outstanding. You can make small patties for appetizers or large patties for a main dish. For a great meal, accompany them with a green salad and Vegetarian Fried Rice (page 222).

MAKES 10 PATTIES

2 small potatoes, boiled 10 minutes, peeled, and grated
8 ounces crabmeat, preferably backfin, carefully picked over
2 tablespoons dried bread crumbs
1 teaspoon grated lime zest
1 teaspoon lime juice
2 small scallions, including tops, finely sliced

1 tablespoon chopped fresh cilantro
1/4 teaspoon salt
1/4 teaspoon sugar
Freshly ground black pepper to taste
1 tablespoon olive oil
Ginger Sauce I (page 288), (optional)

In a medium bowl, combine shredded potatoes, crabmeat, bread crumbs, lime zest, lime juice, scallions, cilantro, salt, sugar, and black pepper. Mix gently, being careful not to break up the crabmeat. Using an ice cream scoop, form the mixture into 10 patties, each 1/2 inch thick. Place patties on a large plate, cover, and refrigerate at least 2 hours.

Heat a heavy 10-inch nonstick frying pan over medium heat until hot. Add oil and swirl to coat pan. Add patties and pan-fry until light brown on both sides, about 4 minutes per side. Serve with sauce, if desired.

Per patty: 50 Calories, 3 g Protein, 1.4 g Total Fat (26% of Calories), 0.2 g Saturated Fat, 5 g Carbohydrates, 1 g Dietary Fiber, 16 mg Cholesterol, 215 mg Sodium

VARIATION
You can replace the crabmeat with cooked salmon or other firm white fish to make fish cakes.

Stuffed Calamari in Tomato Sauce

Serve these stuffed calamari as part of a meal, or serve them as finger foods without the tomato sauce. This is a nutritious dish for adults and children.

MAKES 8 STUFFED CALAMARI

8 small calamari (about 1 pound total weight)
1 teaspoon olive oil
3 shallots, finely chopped
½ cup lean ground turkey
¼ cup chopped mushrooms
½ cup cooked rice
1 tablespoon fish sauce
¼ teaspoon sugar

¼ teaspoon freshly ground black pepper
1 tablespoon chopped fresh basil
1 tablespoon chopped fresh cilantro
2 ripe tomatoes, diced
⅛ teaspoon sugar
Salt and freshly ground black pepper to taste
¼ cup chopped chives, for garnish

Wash calamari and drain; pat dry with paper towels. Hold each calamari by the head just below the eyes and gently pull away from body pouch; discard the soft viscera that come away with it. Carefully remove ink sac and discard. Pull quill-shaped spine from body and discard. Peel skin off the body with your fingers. Cut off tentacles just below eyes; reserve head and tentacles for garnish.

Heat a heavy 10-inch nonstick frying pan over medium heat until hot. Add oil and swirl to coat pan. Add shallots and cook, stirring, until aromatic, about 1 minute. Add turkey and mushrooms and cook, stirring to break up meat, until no longer pink, about 1 minute. Add the rice, fish sauce, sugar, and pepper and stir to mix well. Remove pan from heat and stir in basil and cilantro. Stuff calamari two-thirds full with rice mixture, packing firmly to eliminate air pockets; set aside.

Heat an 8-inch frying pan over medium heat. Add tomatoes, sugar, salt, and pepper and bring to a boil. Reduce heat and simmer 1 minute. Add stuffed calamari and reserved heads and tentacles, cover, and simmer 3 to 4 minutes, or until calamari are firm to the touch. (Do not overcook the calamari or they will shrink and become too chewy.) Transfer calamari to a serving dish, placing them neatly in one row, and arrange heads and tentacles on each calamari.

Spoon tomato sauce in a wide band across the calamari and garnish with chives. Serve immediately.

Per stuffed calamari: 95 Calories, 13 g Protein, 1.8 g Total Fat (17% of Calories), 0.3 g Saturated Fat, 6 g Carbohydrates, 1 g Dietary Fiber, 111 mg Cholesterol, 236 mg Sodium

Calamari Cakes

Calamari (squid) is very low in fat and high in protein. Calamari cakes make good appetizers, or they can be served as an entree or in sandwiches.

MAKES 12 PATTIES

8 small or 4 large calamari, cleaned
3 shallots, thinly sliced
2 cloves garlic, crushed
1 teaspoon sugar
4 water chestnuts, diced into
    peppercorn-size cubes

1 teaspoon fish sauce
1 small egg white, lightly beaten
1 tablespoon chopped chives
¼ teaspoon freshly ground white pepper
2 teaspoons canola oil

Rinse calamari and wipe dry thoroughly with paper towels. (It is crucial that they be completely free of moisture in order to form the paste.) Cut calamari into 1-inch pieces.

Combine calamari, shallots, garlic, and sugar in a food processor fitted with the metal blade and process until very smooth and sticky, stopping as necessary to scrape down the sides of the bowl. Add water chestnuts, fish sauce, egg white, chives, and pepper; pulse briefly to combine. Transfer mixture to a medium bowl, cover, and refrigerate at least 1 hour to firm up mixture. Form mixture into 12 patties.

Heat a heavy 10-inch nonstick frying pan over medium heat until hot. Add oil and swirl to coat pan. Arrange patties in pan and pan-fry until golden brown on both sides, about 4 minutes per side. Serve immediately.

Per patty: 39 Calories, 5 g Protein, 1.2 g Total Fat (28% of Calories), 0.1 g Saturated Fat, 2 g Carbohydrates, 0 g Dietary Fiber, 51 mg Cholesterol, 71 mg Sodium

VARIATION
CALAMARI BALL SOUP

Shape the calamari mixture into walnut-size balls and poach in boiling water until they rise to the surface. Serve them in hot chicken broth. Garnish with flower-shaped carrot slices, 1 tablespoon chopped celery, watercress sprigs, and a few drops of oriental sesame oil.

 Soy Sauce-Seasoned Anchovies

In China these tiny dried calcium-rich anchovies are an important condiment. A small amount provides a lot of taste. Use as a side dish with rice or rice porridge or add some to salads. They are good hot, at room temperature, or chilled.

MAKES 24 SERVINGS (ABOUT 4 ANCHOVIES EACH)

1 cup (2-inch-long) dried anchovies, soaked in 1 cup water 45 minutes and drained

1½ tablespoons reduced-sodium soy sauce

1 tablespoon dry sherry

1 tablespoon sugar

¼ teaspoon hot chili sauce or hot pepper sauce (optional)

1 teaspoon oriental sesame oil

½ teaspoon toasted white sesame seeds

In a 1-quart saucepan, combine anchovies, soy sauce, sherry, sugar, and chili sauce, if using, and simmer over low heat about 5 minutes, stirring until all anchovies are coated with soy sauce mixture and most of the liquid has evaporated but not completely dried out. Drizzle in sesame oil and remove pan from heat.

With a rubber spatula, stir anchovies gently a few more turns, then transfer them to a small serving dish. Sprinkle with sesame seeds and serve.

Per serving: 9 Calories, 1 g Protein, 0.2 g Total Fat (23% of Calories), 0 g Saturated Fat, 1 g Carbohydrates, 0 g Dietary Fiber, 2 mg Cholesterol, 47 mg Sodium

TIP

Save the anchovy soaking liquid; it can be used as fish stock for cooking.

Poultry

Chicken, duck, and squab are all prized in Chinese cuisine. Today chicken is almost everybody's favorite. Its meat is nutritious and low in fat; it browns beautifully; and it cooks quickly. I have included extensive chicken recipes using many different cooking techniques.

Duck is also delicious and nutritious. For too long, many people have had the misconception that all duck dishes have a high fat content. The truth is that if duck is prepared without the skin, it is considered to be lean meat. According to the U.S. Department of Agriculture's Handbook 8, a 3.5-ounce serving of skinless duckling breast contains 2 grams of fat and 132 calories. On the other hand, the same size serving of a skinless chicken breast contains 3.6 grams of fat and 165 calories. Ounce for ounce, skinless duckling breast has less fat and calories than chicken.

I have included many traditional classic recipes as well as some trendy contemporary preparations. All are delicious.

Basic Steamed Chicken Breast

Steaming makes this chicken wonderfully tender, juicy, and flavorful. You may cook and chill the chicken a day in advance, but seal it airtight so that no part becomes dried or discolored. It can be used in any recipes calling for cooked chicken.

MAKES 4 SERVINGS

1 (2-inch) piece fresh ginger, crushed
2 scallions, including tops, lightly
 smashed
1 tablespoon dry sherry
1 teaspoon salt

Freshly ground white pepper to taste
1 large whole bone-in chicken breast
 (about 1½ pounds), trimmed of all
 visible fat

Combine ginger, scallions, sherry, salt, and white pepper in an 8-inch glass pie plate and mix evenly. Rub chicken breast with ginger mixture. Place chicken, skin side up, in plate over remaining ginger mixture.

Bring water in a steamer to a boil over high heat. Transfer plate with chicken to steamer, cover, and steam 15 minutes. Remove from heat and let stand 5 minutes without uncovering to retain heat. Uncover and plunge chicken immediately into a pot of iced water to cool. (The ice and water should cover the chicken to stop the cooking and jell its natural juice within.)

Transfer chicken to a cutting board, discard bone and skin, and cut into bite-size pieces. Serve with your choice of dipping sauce or in a recipe calling for cooked chicken.

Per serving: 139 Calories, 24 g Protein, 3.5 g Total Fat (23% of Calories), 0.9 g Saturated Fat, 1 g Carbohydrates, 0 g Dietary Fiber, 79 mg Cholesterol, 621 mg Sodium

Note: The quick cooling process with ice cubes is crucial. It performs the important task of instantly jelling the juices, which makes the meat more tender and juicy. Otherwise the meat will be dry and hard.

Strain the chicken steaming juices from the plate into a clean bowl and chill in the refrigerator until the fat solidifies on the surface and can be removed. Use the clarified juices in soups or other dishes.

Master Soy Sauce Chicken

Making soy sauce–flavored chicken is a traditional practice in every Chinese kitchen. The preparation requires almost no work, but at the end of one or two hours of perfumed simmering, you are left with a supremely flavorful chicken and a wonderfully scented sauce. You can serve some sauce with the chicken and freeze the remainder as a starter for making more master sauce, by adding more water, spices, and seasonings to achieve the taste you like. But try to keep to the original proportions given in the recipe and follow the same cooking procedure. The flavor of the sauce gets richer each time. Some claim that their master soy sauce has been passed down for generations. The master soy sauce can be used to cook chicken, duck, beef, or pork.

MAKES 6 SERVINGS

1 (about 3-lb.) roasting chicken
1/3 cup dry sherry
1 cup reduced-sodium soy sauce
1/4 cup dark soy sauce or 2 teaspoons thick soy sauce
2 tablespoons sugar
1 (1-inch) piece fresh ginger, crushed
2 scallions, including tops, lightly smashed

1 cinnamon stick
2 whole star anise
1 teaspoon fennel seeds
Orange zest from half of 1 small orange
5 cups water or fat-free, low-sodium chicken broth

Fill an 8-quart pot with enough water to cover chicken and bring to a rolling boil over high heat. Add chicken and bring water to a boil again; cook 2 minutes. Drain and rinse chicken under warm water. Discard water and wash pot.

To the clean pot, add sherry, soy sauces, sugar, ginger, scallions, cinnamon, star anise, fennel seeds, orange zest, and water or chicken broth and bring to a boil over high heat. Add chicken, breast side down, and bring to a boil. Reduce heat to medium-low to maintain a strong simmer, cover, and simmer 15 minutes. Turn chicken breast side up, cover, and cook another 10 minutes. Turn chicken breast down again. Reduce heat to low, cover, and simmer 20 minutes. Remove pot from heat and let chicken steep, without removing cover, for 30 minutes.

Carefully transfer chicken to a plate, let it cool and firm up, then cut it into bite-sizes. Sprinkle a few tablespoons of sauce over the chicken and serve. Remove skin and any visible fat before eating.

Strain remaining sauce into a container, seal airtight, and freeze for future use.

Per serving (meat only): 241 Calories, 35 g Protein, 4 g Total Fat (15% of Calories), 1 g Saturated Fat, 12 g Carbohydrates, 0 g Dietary Fiber, 93 mg Cholesterol, 540 mg Sodium

Basic Poached Chicken Breast

This is a quick way to cook flavorful chicken. Poached chicken can be shredded and used in various recipes, such as soups, salads, lo mein noodles, or fried rice. It will keep in the refrigerator for two days.

MAKES 4 SERVINGS

2 cups water
1 (1-inch) piece fresh ginger, crushed
1 scallion, including top, lightly smashed
1 teaspoon Sichuan peppercorns
2 tablespoons dry sherry

1 pound boneless, skinless whole chicken breast, trimmed of all visible fat
Salt and freshly ground pepper to taste (optional)

Bring the water, ginger, scallion, peppercorns, and sherry to a boil in a heavy 3-quart pot. Carefully add chicken and bring to a boil again. Reduce heat to low, cover, and simmer 6 minutes. Remove pot from heat and let stand 10 minutes without uncovering to retain heat.

Transfer chicken to a plate. Season with salt and pepper, if desired, cover, and let breast cool and firm before cutting. Strain cooking liquid for chicken broth.

Per serving: 133 Calories, 26 g Protein, 1.4 g Total Fat (10% of Calories), 0.4 g Saturated Fat, 1 g Carbohydrates, 0 g Dietary Fiber, 66 mg Cholesterol, 75 mg Sodium

Drunken Chicken

This is a marvelous recipe. You can make the chicken a day in advance and serve it cold or you can warm it to room temperature just before serving. The wine-flavored chicken makes a great appetizer for buffets and parties.

MAKES 8 APPETIZER SERVINGS

Basic Steamed Chicken Breast (page 157)

2 cups Chinese Shaoxing (rice) wine or pale dry sherry

1 to 2 tablespoons reduced-sodium soy sauce (optional)

Cilantro sprigs, for garnish

Steam chicken and cool. Chop the chicken in half lengthwise, then chop each half crosswise into 4 to 6 pieces, keeping chicken pieces in place without separating them so that they resemble the original shape. Using the side of a cleaver, scoop up chicken and place it, skin side down, in a bowl that will hold the chicken snugly. (You can place the neatest large pieces at the very bottom, and any uneven pieces on the sides or in the center.)

Set bowl on a plate, then pour enough wine over chicken to cover. Add soy sauce and steamed chicken liquid from the plate, if desired. Compress chicken by placing a heavy bowl on top. Refrigerate 5 to 6 hours or overnight.

Remove chicken from refrigerator 1 hour before serving. Drain wine into another bowl and keep refrigerated up to 2 days for later use in cooking. Select a beautiful serving plate and invert chicken quickly onto the plate. Sprinkle a few tablespoons of the wine liquid over chicken, garnish with cilantro, and serve. Discard the skin when eating.

Per serving: 110 Calories, 12 g Protein, 1.8 g Total Fat (14% of Calories), 0.5 g Saturated Fat, 1 g Carbohydrates, 0 g Dietary Fiber, 40 mg Cholesterol, 314 mg Sodium

Lemon Chicken

This tender chicken is glazed by a refreshing lemon sauce. It is fruity and delicious.

2 whole boneless, skinless chicken
    breasts (about 1 pound), trimmed of
    all visible fat
1 tablespoon dry sherry
¼ teaspoon garlic salt
1 tablespoon egg white, lightly beaten

1 cup Lemon Sauce (page 290)
1 cup dry bread crumbs
2 tablespoons sesame seeds
1 tablespoon chopped fresh cilantro
1 tablespoon peanut oil
Lemon and cucumber slices, for garnish

Cut each chicken breast in half lengthwise to make 4 chicken breast halves. Put each half between 2 sheets of waxed paper. Lightly pound with the broad side of a cleaver or a rolling pin into an even ½-inch thickness.

In a medium bowl, combine sherry, garlic salt, and egg white. Add chicken and mix well. Let stand 30 minutes.

Prepare Lemon Sauce, cover, and keep warm.

Preheat oven to 450F (230C). Coat a baking sheet with cooking spray.

In a medium bowl, combine bread crumbs, sesame seeds, cilantro, and peanut oil and stir until evenly mixed. Dredge each chicken piece in bread crumb mixture and place on prepared baking sheet. Bake 15 minutes, or until crumbs are crisp and light brown.

Cut each chicken piece diagonally crosswise into 1-inch-thick slices. Arrange slices on a serving platter. Ladle Lemon Sauce across chicken and decorate with cucumber and lemon slices. Serve immediately.

Per serving: 390 Calories, 32 g Protein, 7 g Total Fat (16% of Calories), 1 g Saturated Fat, 45 g Carbohydrates, 0 g Dietary Fiber, 66 mg Cholesterol, 564 mg Sodium

Chicken and Wild Mushrooms

Here tender chicken and exotic mushrooms sautéed in a delicate white-wine sauce are contrasted by crunchy water chestnuts and snow peas. Serve this dish with steamed jasmine rice.

MAKES 4 SERVINGS

¾ pound boneless, skinless chicken breasts, cut into thin slices
3 tablespoons dry sherry
2 teaspoons cornstarch
½ teaspoon salt
¼ teaspoon sugar
¼ teaspoon white pepper
2 teaspoons cornstarch dissolved in ½ cup fat-free, low-sodium chicken broth

3 teaspoons olive oil
1 cup shiitake mushrooms, each cut in half
1 cup porcini mushrooms, each cut in half
1 cup crimini mushrooms, sliced
1 teaspoon minced garlic
⅓ cup sliced water chestnuts
12 fresh snow peas, strings removed

In a medium bowl, combine chicken, 1 tablespoon of the sherry, and cornstarch and stir to coat well. Let stand 30 minutes.

In a small bowl, combine salt, sugar, pepper, remaining 2 tablespoons sherry, and the cornstarch mixture and stir until sugar dissolves. Set aside.

Heat a 10-inch nonstick frying pan over high heat until hot. Add 1 teaspoon of the oil and swirl to coat pan. Add all the mushrooms and cook, stirring, 1 minute, or until mushrooms are just about to give out their juices. Transfer to a plate and set aside.

Return pan to medium heat. Add remaining 2 teaspoons oil, swirl to coat pan, and heat 15 seconds. Add garlic and cook, stirring, a few seconds. Add the chicken slices and stir to separate the pieces; cook 2 minutes, or until chicken is cooked through. Stir sherry mixture and stir into chicken mixture. Cook, stirring constantly, until sauce comes to a boil and is slightly thickened. Add water chestnuts, snow peas, and reserved mushrooms to pan. Stir gently until vegetables are heated through and coated with sauce. Transfer to a hot serving dish.

Per serving: 164 Calories, 21 g Protein, 4.8 g Total Fat (26% of Calories), 0.8 g Saturated Fat, 7 g Carbohydrates, 2 g Dietary Fiber, 49 mg Cholesterol, 346 mg Sodium

Spicy Chicken with Peanuts

This is a tangy palate-pleasing dish. The crunchiness of the peanuts contrasts with the flavorful chicken for a satisfying combination of flavor and texture. It is very popular in restaurants. You can adjust the degree of spiciness according to your taste. Serve it with steamed jasmine rice and Stir-Fried Bok Choy (page 95).

MAKES 4 SERVINGS

¾ pound boneless, skinless chicken breasts, cut into ⅜-inch cubes
2 tablespoons dry sherry
1 tablespoon egg white, lightly beaten
2 teaspoons cornstarch
2 tablespoons reduced-sodium soy sauce
1 tablespoon dark soy sauce or ½ teaspoon thick soy sauce (optional)
1 tablespoon balsamic vinegar or red wine vinegar

1 tablespoon sugar
½ tablespoon cornstarch dissolved in ¼ cup fat-free, low-sodium chicken broth
3 teaspoons canola oil
1 cup cubed red bell peppers
1 cup cubed celery
4 to 6 small dried red chilies, broken in half and seeds removed
1 teaspoon minced fresh ginger
½ cup dry-roasted peanuts
1 teaspoon oriental sesame oil (optional)

In a medium bowl, combine chicken, 1 tablespoon sherry, egg white, and cornstarch and stir to mix well. Cover and refrigerate 30 minutes or longer.

In a small bowl, combine reduced-sodium soy sauce, dark soy sauce, if using, remaining sherry, vinegar, sugar, and the cornstarch mixture and stir until sugar dissolves; set aside.

Heat a heavy 10-inch nonstick skillet over high heat until hot. Add 1 teaspoon of the canola oil, swirl to coat pan, and heat 15 seconds. Add bell peppers and stir-fry over high heat 1 minute. Add celery and stir-fry until the color brightens, about 1 minute. Transfer vegetables to a plate.

Add remaining 2 teaspoons oil to pan over medium heat and swirl to coat pan. Add chilies and ginger and cook, stirring rapidly, until chilies turn dark and become aromatic but are not burned. Add chicken and gently stir-fry about 1 minute, or until chicken turns white and is cooked through. Stir soy sauce mixture and stir into chicken. Cook, stirring, until sauce thickens slightly and thoroughly coats chicken. Return vegetables to chicken and stir briefly to blend. Transfer to a serving dish and sprinkle peanuts on top. Drizzle with sesame oil, if desired, and serve immediately.

Per serving: 280 Calories, 27 g Protein, 14 g Total Fat (42% of Calories), 2 g Saturated Fat, 13 g Carbohydrates, 3 g Dietary Fiber, 49 mg Cholesterol, 699 mg Sodium

Note: Some facilities where I taught cooking classes had no exhaust fan, and although my students loved this dish, we all coughed when the room filled with the fumes from the aromatic chilies. Be sure to turn on the exhaust fan when you prepare this dish or the fumes from the chilies will make you cough and sneeze, too.

Chicken with Hoisin Sauce

Coated by a rich brown hoisin and bean sauce, this chicken has a bold delicious flavor. It goes very well with steamed rice or plain white noodles. Accompany it with a light cool vegetable such as stir-fried cabbage.

MAKES 4 SERVINGS

¾ pound boneless, skinless chicken breast, cut into ¾-inch cubes
2 tablespoons dry sherry
1 tablespoon lightly beaten egg white
2 teaspoons cornstarch
1 tablespoon hoisin sauce
1 tablespoon Chinese hot bean sauce
2 tablespoons reduced-sodium soy sauce
2 teaspoons sugar
3 teaspoons safflower oil

1 orange bell pepper, cut into ¾-inch squares
1 yellow bell pepper, cut into ¾-inch squares
1 teaspoon minced fresh ginger
1 large clove garlic, minced
1 teaspoon cornstarch dissolved in 1 tablespoon water
2 scallions, including tops, cut into 1-inch lengths
⅓ cup toasted cashews (optional)

In a medium bowl, combine chicken, 1 tablespoon of the sherry, egg white, and cornstarch and stir until meat is evenly coated. Cover and refrigerate 30 minutes.

In a small bowl, combine hoisin sauce, hot bean sauce, soy sauce, remaining 1 tablespoon sherry, and sugar and stir until sugar dissolves; set aside.

Heat a heavy 10-inch nonstick skillet over high heat until hot. Add 1 teaspoon of the oil, swirl to coat pan, and heat 15 seconds. Add bell peppers and stir-fry over high heat 2 minutes, or until slightly blistered and their color brightens. Transfer peppers to a plate.

Add remaining 2 teaspoons oil, swirl to coat pan, and heat over medium heat. Add ginger and garlic and cook, stirring, a few seconds. Add chicken pieces and stir-fry until chicken turns white and cooks through, about 2 minutes. Add hoisin sauce mixture and cook, stirring rapidly, about 30 seconds. Increase heat to high; return vegetables to pan and stir a few times.

Stir cornstarch mixture and stir into chicken mixture. Cook, stirring rapidly to coat chicken evenly. Add scallions and cashews, if using, Transfer to a hot serving dish.

Per serving: 181 Calories, 22 g Protein, 4.8 g Total Fat (24% of Calories), 0.6 g Saturated Fat, 10 g Carbohydrates, 1 g Dietary Fiber, 49 mg Cholesterol, 630 mg Sodium

Five-Spiced Chicken Drumsticks

These aromatic flavorful chicken drumsticks are good hot or cold. They are ideal for a picnic accompanied by a fruit salad and Scallion Pancakes (page 264).

MAKES 6 DRUMSTICKS

6 boneless, skinless chicken drumsticks (about 1½ pounds)
2 tablespoons reduced-sodium soy sauce
2 tablespoons dry sherry
2 tablespoons ketchup
1½ teaspoons sugar

Salt and freshly ground black pepper
⅛ teaspoon cayenne pepper
½ teaspoon five-spice powder
1 scallion, including top, finely chopped
2 teaspoons finely minced fresh ginger
2 tablespoons chopped fresh cilantro
Mango Sauce (page 297), (optional)

Combine the chicken drumsticks with all the ingredients, except Mango Sauce, in a self-sealing plastic bag. Refrigerate 2 hours, turning frequently.

Preheat oven to 400F (205C). Transfer drumsticks to a baking pan sprayed with nonstick cooking spray and bake 35 minutes, basting once with marinade halfway through the cooking. Serve drumsticks with Mango Sauce, if desired.

Per drumstick: 203 Calories, 23 g Protein, 10 g Total Fat (44% of Calories), 3 g Saturated Fat, 4 g Carbohydrates, 0 g Dietary Fiber, 92 mg Cholesterol, 386 mg Sodium

Chicken with Black Bean Sauce

Chinese fermented black beans have a delicious and wonderfully intense flavor. The juicy pineapples provide a pleasing contrast in this dish, transforming ordinary chicken into a gourmet treat.

MAKES 4 SERVINGS

1 pound boneless, skinless chicken breasts, trimmed of all visible fat and cut into thin strips
1 tablespoon dry sherry
2 teaspoons premium oyster sauce
1 tablespoon cornstarch
3 teaspoons canola oil
1 medium onion, cubed
1 large red bell pepper, chopped
2 cloves garlic, coarsely chopped
1 tablespoon Chinese fermented black beans
1/2 cup fat-free, low-sodium chicken broth

1 teaspoon sugar
1 tablespoon reduced-sodium soy sauce
Freshly ground black pepper to taste
2 cups fresh pineapple chunks, preferably Del Monte Gold extra-sweet pineapple
1 cup straw mushrooms
2 scallions, including tops, cut into 2-inch lengths
2 teaspoons cornstarch dissolved in 1 tablespoon water
1/2 cup toasted cashews

In a medium bowl, combine chicken, sherry, oyster sauce, and cornstarch and stir to blend well; set aside.

Heat a heavy 10-inch nonstick frying pan over high heat until hot. Add 1 teaspoon of the oil, onion, and bell pepper and stir-fry until fragrant, about 1 minute. Transfer to a plate.

Add remaining 2 teaspoons oil to pan, swirl to coat pan, and heat 15 seconds. Add garlic and black beans and cook, stirring rapidly, 15 seconds. Add chicken pieces and stir to prevent sticking. Cook, stirring, until chicken is white and cooked through, about 2 minutes. Transfer to a plate and set aside.

Add chicken broth, sugar, soy sauce, and black pepper to pan, stir, and bring to a boil. Add pineapple and mushrooms and cook, stirring, until heated through. Add scallions. Stir cornstarch mixture and stir into pineapple mixture. Cook, stirring, until sauce is slightly thickened. Return chicken, onion, and bell pepper to pan and stir to blend. Stir in cashews and serve immediately.

Per serving: 354 Calories, 32 g Protein, 14 g Total Fat (35% of Calories), 2 g Saturated Fat, 26 g Carbohydrates, 3 g Dietary Fiber, 66 mg Cholesterol, 686 mg Sodium

Chicken with Chili and Sichuan Peppercorns

*T*his is a Sichuan specialty full of flavor and aroma. The brown Sichuan peppercorns impart a distinctive sweet fragrance that sets them apart from all other peppercorns. It is that special touch that makes this dish outstanding. Serve it with steamed brown rice and a green salad.

MAKES 4 SERVINGS

1 pound skinless, boneless chicken breasts or leg meat, trimmed of all visible fat
1 tablespoon lightly beaten egg white
2 teaspoons cornstarch
2 teaspoons safflower oil
1 green bell pepper, chopped
1 red bell pepper, chopped
2 teaspoons minced fresh ginger
½ tablespoon minced garlic

2 dried Chinese red chilies
1 tablespoon Chinese hot bean sauce
1 tablespoon dry sherry
1 tablespoon reduced-sodium soy sauce
1 tablespoon red wine vinegar
1 teaspoon sugar
1 tablespoon cornstarch dissolved in ½ cup fat-free, low-sodium chicken broth
1 teaspoon oriental sesame oil
1 teaspoon ground Sichuan peppercorns

Give chicken breasts a few firm but light smashes with the broad side of a cleaver and score the smooth side. Or pound leg meat from inside with the back of a cleaver or heavy knife, and score outside of the leg meat lightly with crisscross hatching. Then cut meat into 1-inch squares.

Place chicken in a medium bowl. Add egg white and stir lightly. Stir in cornstarch until chicken is coated. Cover and refrigerate 30 minutes.

Heat a heavy 10-inch nonstick frying pan over high heat until hot. Add 1 teaspoon of the oil, swirl to coat pan, and heat 15 seconds. Add bell peppers and stir-fry until they are fragrant and brighter in color, about 2 minutes. Transfer peppers to a plate; set aside.

Add remaining 1 teaspoon oil to pan over medium-high heat and heat 10 seconds. Add ginger, garlic, and chilies and cook, stirring, a few seconds. Reduce heat. Add hot bean sauce and cook, stirring, until aromatic. Add chicken and stir-fry until chicken is white and cooked through, about 2 minutes.

Add sherry, soy sauce, vinegar, and sugar and stir gently until chicken is well coated. Stir cornstarch mixture and stir into chicken mixture. Boil, stirring constantly, until sauce is slightly thickened. Stir in bell peppers, then transfer to a hot serving dish. Drizzle in sesame oil and sprinkle with Sichuan peppercorn powder. Serve immediately.

Per serving: 197 Calories, 28 g Protein, 5 g Total Fat (23% of Calories), 0.8 g Saturated Fat, 8 g Carbohydrates, 1 g Dietary Fiber, 66 mg Cholesterol, 360 mg Sodium

General Zuo's Chicken

This is a very popular dish served in all Chinese restaurants. In all the restaurant dishes that I have sampled, the chicken is deep-fried until crispy, then coated with a luscious red sauce. I have not used deep-frying here, so you can enjoy this delicious dish without the extra fat content.

MAKES 4 SERVINGS

¾ pound boneless, skinless chicken leg meat or thigh meat, trimmed of all visible fat and cut into 1½-inch chunks

3 tablespoons reduced-sodium soy sauce

1 tablespoon dry sherry

¼ teaspoon freshly ground white pepper

2 teaspoons cornstarch

1 egg white, lightly beaten

2 tablespoons ketchup

¼ cup cider vinegar

5 tablespoons light brown sugar

1 tablespoon plus 1 teaspoon peanut oil

¾ cup water chestnut flour (see Note, page 139)

4 dried Chinese red chilies

3 slices fresh ginger, lightly smashed

2 scallions, white part only, cut into 1-inch lengths

5 teaspoons cornstarch dissolved in 1 cup fat-free, low-sodium chicken broth

¾ pound broccoli flowerets, blanched

Place chicken in a medium bowl. Add 1 tablespoon of the soy sauce, sherry, white pepper, cornstarch, and egg white and stir to coat evenly. Cover and marinate in refrigerator 1 hour or longer.

In a measuring cup, combine remaining 2 tablespoons soy sauce, ketchup, vinegar, and brown sugar and stir until sugar dissolves; set aside.

Preheat oven to 450F (230C) for 15 minutes. Coat a baking sheet with cooking spray; set aside.

In a small bowl, combine 1 tablespoon of the peanut oil and water chestnut flour and stir until evenly mixed. Dredge each chicken piece in the water chestnut flour mixture, then place on the prepared baking sheet without touching. Bake chicken in hot oven 12 to 15 minutes, or until coating is light brown and crisp.

Meanwhile, heat a wok or heavy 10-inch nonstick frying pan over medium heat until hot. Add remaining 1 teaspoon peanut oil and swirl to coat pan. Add chilies, ginger, and scallions and cook, stirring, a few seconds, or until aromatic. Add soy sauce mixture, stir, and bring to a boil. Stir cornstarch mixture and stir into scallions. Cook, stirring constantly, until sauce thickens.

Add chicken pieces to sauce and stir gently, turning until chicken is glistening and coated with sauce. Mound chicken and sauce in the middle of a hot serving platter and surround it with the broccoli. Serve immediately.

Per serving: 388 Calories, 27 g Protein, 11 g Total Fat (25% of Calories), 2 g Saturated Fat, 46 g Carbohydrates, 4 g Dietary Fiber, 92 mg Cholesterol, 582 mg Sodium

Note: In the United States, some Chinese restaurants call this dish General Gao's Chicken; others call it General Tso's Chicken; and I have seen some call it Jordan's Chicken. But the correct Beijing name is General Zuo's Chicken.

Spicy Chicken Curry

*T*his aromatic full-flavored chicken curry is lighter than the Indian or Thai versions, which contain saturated fat–coconut milk. Serve this fragrant dish over steamed rice for a very satisfying one-dish meal, and accompany it with a soothing green salad.

MAKES 6 SERVINGS

1 pound boneless, skinless chicken breasts, cut into 1½-inch chunks
1 tablespoon cornstarch
3 teaspoons safflower oil
1 medium onion, cut into 1-inch squares
2 cloves garlic, minced
1½ tablespoons curry powder
2 cups fat-free, low-sodium chicken broth
3 tablespoons reduced-sodium soy sauce
1 tablespoon sugar

2 medium red potatoes, cut into ¾-inch cubes
1 cup peeled baby carrots
¼ cup golden raisins
1 Granny Smith apple, peeled, cored, and cut into 1-inch cubes
1 large firm banana, cut crosswise into ½-inch-thick slices
Salt and freshly ground black pepper (optional)

In a medium bowl, combine chicken and cornstarch and set aside 30 minutes.

Heat a large 10-inch nonstick frying-pan over medium high heat until hot. Add 2 teaspoons of the safflower oil and swirl to coat pan. Distribute chicken pieces evenly in pan and stir-fry until chicken is white and cooked through, 2 to 3 minutes. Transfer chicken to a dish and set aside.

Return pan to heat, add remaining 1 teaspoon oil, and swirl to coat pan. Add onion and stir-fry a few seconds. Add garlic and curry powder and stir-fry until aromatic. Add chicken broth, soy sauce, sugar, potatoes, carrots, and raisins and bring to a boil. Reduce heat to medium, cover, and simmer 10 minutes, stirring once after 6 minutes.

Spread apple and banana evenly over potato mixture and return chicken chunks to pan, spreading them evenly over the fruit. Cover and simmer 5 minutes longer, or until vegetables are tender and chicken is heated through. Stir mixture carefully without breaking the bananas, making sure each ingredient is coated with curry sauce. Taste and adjust the seasoning with salt and pepper, if desired. Serve immediately.

Per serving: 236 Calories, 21 g Protein, 4 g Total Fat (16% of Calories), 1 g Saturated Fat, 30 g Carbohydrates, 4 g Dietary Fiber, 44 mg Cholesterol, 418 mg Sodium

VARIATION

For a thicker sauce drizzle in 2 teaspoons cornstarch dissolved in 1 tablespoon water during the last 2 minutes of cooking and stir gently until sauce thickens.

Strange-Flavored Chicken

This is a classic Chinese dish, and a favorite. No one knows how the name came about, but those who have tried it know that the seasonings and spices in this recipe are sophisticated. It combines sweet, sour, salty, tangy, spicy, and aromatic flavors all in one dish to produce a unique outstanding taste. Perhaps that's why they call it strange flavored. This dish can be served hot, at room temperature, or cold. Accompany it with a cucumber salad and steamed rice or cooked white noodles.

MAKES 6 SERVINGS

2 cups shredded iceberg lettuce
Basic Steamed Chicken Breast (page 157), skin and bone removed
1 tablespoon oriental sesame paste
2 tablespoons hot water
2 tablespoons reduced-sodium soy sauce
1 tablespoon sugar
1 tablespoon balsamic or red wine vinegar

1 tablespoon oriental sesame oil
1 scallion, including top, thinly sliced
2 teaspoons minced fresh ginger
2 teaspoons minced garlic
½ teaspoon ground Sichuan peppercorns
1 tablespoon Chinese hot bean sauce
Cilantro sprigs, for garnish

Spread shredded lettuce on a serving platter as a bed for the chicken; set aside.

Cut chicken in half lengthwise, then neatly cut each half crosswise into 1-inch-thick pieces. As you are cutting it, keep the pieces in position. Then using the broad side of a cleaver, scoop up and transfer the sliced chicken to the lettuce in its original shape.

In a small bowl, dissolve the sesame paste in the hot water, stirring with the back of a spoon until smooth. Add soy sauce, sugar, and vinegar and stir until sugar dissolves; set seasoning sauce aside.

Heat a small saucepan over medium heat until hot but not smoking. Add sesame oil and swirl to coat pan. Add scallion, ginger, garlic, and Sichuan peppercorn powder and cook, stirring, about 30 seconds. Add hot bean sauce and cook, stirring rapidly, 10 seconds, or until aromatic.

Add seasoning sauce and stir to mix evenly. Pour mixture over the chicken and garnish with cilantro. Serve immediately.

Per serving: 160 Calories, 18 g Protein, 6.9 g Total Fat (39% of Calories), 1.2 g Saturated Fat, 5 g Carbohydrates, 1 g Dietary Fiber, 60 mg Cholesterol, 715 mg Sodium

VARIATIONS

Try this sauce on 1 pound of steamed Chinese eggplant or on 1 pound of pan-seared sea scallops.

Thanksgiving Turkey

Although there is no Thanksgiving holiday in Asia, the Asian people in America are learning to celebrate this important feast holiday. As a tradition I make this turkey in a brown paper bag every year. The turkey comes out tender and moist, and a beautiful golden brown. After the turkey is removed, you can wrap up the sack and throw it away with no mess to scrub and wash. I use this technique to cook turkey when I cater for parties, and I teach it in cooking classes, too. My students all requested that this recipe be included in my cookbook, so here it is.

MAKES 24 OR MORE SERVINGS

1 (13- to 16-lb.) turkey
Salt and freshly ground black pepper
 (optional)

6 tablespoons or more reduced-sodium
 soy sauce
1 cup peanut oil (no substitute)

The day before cooking, rinse turkey thoroughly inside and out with cold running water. Drain thoroughly and pat dry with paper towels. Sprinkle salt and pepper inside the cavity, if desired. Place turkey on a rack in a roasting pan and refrigerate overnight to dry the skin.

The next day, brush soy sauce over turkey breast, legs, thighs, and wings; let dry 1 hour. Then brush entire turkey, except back, with some of the peanut oil.

Preheat oven to 325F (165C). Select a clean, large, heavy brown supermarket paper bag with no holes. Brush inside and outside of the whole bag generously with remaining peanut oil.

Carefully transfer turkey, breast side up, into the paper bag, with someone holding the bag open for you. Close open end of bag, fold over twice, and staple in 6 to 8 places to seal it securely. Carefully place turkey with the bag in a roasting pan. Bake about 10 minutes per pound. When turkey is done, let it sit 15 minutes before opening the bag. Since the bag is air-tight, there will be live steam; therefore, be careful, opening end furthest from you first. Enjoy!

Per serving: 188 Calories, 27 g Protein, 8.5 g Total Fat (41% of Calories), 2.8 g Saturated Fat, 1 g Carbohydrates, 0 g Dietary Fiber, 64 mg Cholesterol, 77 mg Sodium

Duck with Bean Sprouts

This is a delicious way to eat duck, and you can make it with leftover duck meat. Serve it with steamed long-grain rice.

MAKES 4 SERVINGS

2 teaspoons safflower oil
¾ pound fresh bean sprouts
2 scallions, including tops, cut into 1½-inch lengths, white and green parts separated
1 tablespoon Chinese hot bean sauce
¾ pound cooked duck meat, shredded
1 tablespoon dry sherry

2 tablespoons reduced-sodium soy sauce
1½ teaspoons sugar
1 tablespoon balsamic vinegar
1 teaspoon cornstarch dissolved in ½ cup fat-free, low-sodium chicken broth
Salt and freshly ground black pepper to taste

Heat a heavy 10-inch nonstick skillet over high heat until hot. Add 1 teaspoon of the oil, swirl to coat pan, and heat 15 seconds. Add bean sprouts and stir-fry over high heat until they are just about to turn opaque, about 1 minute. Transfer sprouts to a plate.

Wipe skillet clean and return to heat. Add remaining 1 teaspoon oil, swirl to coat skillet, and heat 15 seconds. Add white parts of scallions and cook, stirring, a few seconds. Add hot bean sauce and duck meat and cook, stirring, 1 minute. Add sherry, soy sauce, sugar, and vinegar; stir-fry until heated through, about 1 minute. Add green parts of scallions. Stir cornstarch mixture and stir into duck mixture. Cook, stirring, until sauce thickens and duck is lightly glazed. Return bean sprouts to skillet and heat through, stirring. Season with salt and pepper. Transfer to a hot serving platter and serve immediately.

Per serving: 247 Calories, 25 g Protein, 12 g Total Fat (45% of Calories), 4 g Saturated Fat, 10 g Carbohydrates, 1 g Dietary Fiber, 76 mg Cholesterol, 510 mg Sodium

VARIATION

You can substitute shredded bok choy or tender celery for the bean sprouts, if desired.

Aromatic Fire Duck

This duck dish is a marvelous Cantonese specialty. The luscious amber duck is crisp on the outside and moist, aromatic, and delicious on the inside. Originally this duck was fired in a kiln since ovens were not available in China. You can roast this duck in a hot oven or on a rotisserie over a grill. It is good hot or cold, served with steamed rice. It is also a delicious addition to rice porridge or noodle soup.

MAKES 6 SERVINGS

1 (5-lb.) duck, all visible fat removed, rinsed, and patted dry thoroughly outside and inside
1 teaspoon peanut oil
2 scallions, including tops, finely sliced
2 thin slices fresh ginger, minced
1 large clove garlic, minced
2 tablespoons chopped fresh cilantro
1 tablespoon Chinese hot bean sauce
1/4 teaspoon Sichuan peppercorns
1/2 teaspoon ground cinnamon

1 tablespoon grated orange zest
1 tablespoon dry sherry
5 tablespoons reduced-sodium soy sauce
1/2 teaspoon salt
3 tablespoons honey
1 cup fat-free, low-sodium chicken broth
1 cup boiling water
1 tablespoon distilled white vinegar
Cilantro sprigs, for garnish

Close neck cavity of duck securely with skewers, or sew it closed with needle and thread. Place duck in a bowl. With a skewer or a fork, prick holes in the skin, being careful not to pierce the flesh.

Preheat oven to 450F (230C). Heat a 7-inch skillet over medium heat until hot. Add oil and heat 15 seconds. Add the scallions, ginger, garlic, and cilantro and cook, stirring rapidly, until fragrant, about 30 seconds. Add hot bean sauce, peppercorns, cinnamon, orange zest, sherry, 3 tablespoons of the soy sauce, salt, 1 tablespoon of the honey, and chicken broth and bring to a boil. Reduce heat, cover, and simmer 2 to 3 minutes. Remove from heat and let cool 5 minutes.

Put duck, neck down, in a deep 4-quart pot just big enough in diameter to hold the duck upright. Pour warm marinade into the body cavity and close the opening securely.

Fill a roasting pan with about ½ inch of hot water and place on the bottom rack of the oven as a drip pan. Spray another oven rack with cooking spray and place above the pan in the center of the oven.

Place duck directly on the center rack, breast side up, and roast 30 minutes. Reduce oven temperature to 350F (175C).

Meanwhile, in a small bowl, combine remaining 2 tablespoons honey, remaining 2 tablespoons soy sauce, boiling water, and vinegar. Baste duck with honey mixture and continue roasting 1½ hours, basting every 15 minutes, or until skin is waxy and deep brown.

Transfer duck to a chopping board and let cool 30 minutes. Remove trussing strings. Strain marinade liquid from duck cavity into a small bowl. Chop duck through the bones into 2-inch pieces or carve it Western style. Arrange duck pieces on a serving platter and drizzle the marinade over the duck. Garnish with sprigs of cilantro and serve. Remove the skin and any visible fat before eating.

Per serving: 208 Calories, 27 g Protein, 9 g Total Fat (38% of Calories), 3 g Saturated Fat, 4 g Carbohydrates, 0 g Dietary Fiber, 102 mg Cholesterol, 694 mg Sodium

Shanghai Braised Duck

*B*raised slowly in a rich sweet soy sauce until the meat is very tender, this is another delicious duck dish. It is full of flavor, and the skin is a reddish-brown color. This dish can be prepared one or two days ahead and refrigerated. Remove any fat that solidifies on the surface before reheating. To serve, heat over low heat for 15 minutes or until hot. Served with plenty of steamed rice and accompanied by a stir-fried vegetable, this makes a wonderful meal.

MAKES 6 SERVINGS

1 (5-lb.) duck, all visible fat removed, rinsed, and patted dry thoroughly outside and inside

2 tablespoons dark soy sauce

4 medium scallions, lightly smashed

3 (¼-inch-thick) slices fresh ginger, lightly smashed

2 whole star anise

½ stick cinnamon

5 tablespoons dry sherry

4 tablespoons reduced-sodium soy sauce

Salt and freshly ground black pepper to taste

2 cups boiling water

3 tablespoons crushed rock sugar or brown sugar

2 pounds Stir-Fried Bok Choy (page 95) or broccoli rabe

Trim off excess neck skin from duck and cut off tail. Brush entire duck with dark soy sauce. Place duck in a colander and let it dry in the refrigerator for 2 to 3 hours or longer, until soy sauce has dried on the skin. This can be done a day in advance.

Heat a heavy 8-quart pot over high heat until hot. Spray lightly with cooking spray. Add duck and cook, turning it from side to side, until skin is slightly browned. Transfer duck to a plate; discard any fat in pot and wipe pot clean.

Return pot to heat. Place a piece of parchment paper or 2 chopsticks on bottom of pot to prevent duck from scorching. Place duck, breast side down, on paper or chopsticks. Add scallions, ginger, star anise, cinnamon, sherry, reduced-sodium soy sauce, salt, and pepper. Bring to a boil and quickly baste the duck a few times. Add boiling water and bring to a boil again. Reduce heat to low to maintain a steady gentle simmer. Cover and simmer, basting and turning duck occasionally, 1 hour. Turn duck breast up. Add crushed rock sugar or brown sugar and simmer, basting and turning occasionally, 45 minutes, or until duck is tender.

Increase heat to medium-high and baste duck constantly 2 to 3 minutes, or until duck is glistening and sauce has reduced to about 1 cup.

Transfer duck to a large serving platter. Surround duck with bok choy or broccoli rabe. Strain sauce through a fat separator. Discard fat and pour sauce into a gravy boat. Serve duck with sauce on the side. The tender duck can be torn apart with a fork or chopsticks. Remove skin and any visible fat before eating.

Per serving: 334 Calories, 35 g Protein, 15 g Total Fat (41% of Calories), 6 g Saturated Fat, 11 g Carbohydrates, 5 g Dietary Fiber, 118 mg Cholesterol, 994 mg Sodium (see Note)

Note: The high sodium per serving is based on consuming all of the gravy, so use the gravy sparingly.

Stir-fried Duck and Vegetables

Use steamed duck meat or leftover roast duck for this dish, and save the duck carcass for stock. Serve this savory stir-fry with steamed jasmine rice or on Asian noodles.

MAKES 4 SERVINGS

2 teaspoons olive oil
2 cups sliced tender celery
½ cup shredded carrot
4 cups shredded bok choy
1 tablespoon finely shredded fresh
   ginger
2 teaspoons minced garlic
1 cup shredded fresh shiitake
   mushrooms

1 tablespoon Chinese hot bean sauce
2 cups shredded cooked duck meat
2 tablespoons reduced-sodium soy
   sauce
1 tablespoon balsamic vinegar
½ teaspoon honey
1 teaspoon cornstarch dissolved in
   ½ cup defatted duck stock

Heat a heavy 10-inch nonstick skillet over high heat until hot. Add 1 teaspoon of the oil and heat 15 seconds. Add celery and carrot and stir-fry a few seconds. Add bok choy and stir-fry until the leaves are bright green, about 2 minutes. Transfer vegetables to a plate and set aside.

Wipe skillet clean and return to heat. Add remaining 1 teaspoon oil, swirl to coat skillet, and heat 15 seconds. Add ginger and garlic and cook, stirring, a few seconds. Add mushrooms and hot bean sauce and cook, stirring, 1 minute. Add duck meat and cook, stirring, until heated through, about 1 minute. Return the vegetables to duck mixture. Add soy sauce, vinegar, and honey and mix well. Stir cornstarch mixture and stir into duck mixture. Cook, stirring, until slightly thickened. Transfer contents of pan to a heated serving dish. Serve immediately.

Per serving: 243 Calories, 24 g Protein, 12 g Total Fat (38% of Calories), 4 g Saturated Fat, 10 g Carbohydrates, 4 g Dietary Fiber, 76 mg Cholesterol, 611 mg Sodium

Chinese Roast Duck

Pricking the duck skin before roasting will let most of the fat cook off. Place a pan of hot water on the bottom of the oven to catch the fat drippings and keep the meat moist. This also leaves the oven clean.

MAKES 8 SERVINGS

1 (5- to 6-pound) duck, all visible fat removed, rinsed, and patted dry thoroughly outside and inside
Salt and freshly ground black pepper to taste
1 tablespoon dry sherry
1 teaspoon honey

½ tablespoon reduced-sodium soy sauce
1 small orange, quartered
½ apple, quartered
1 small onion, quartered
1 recipe Cherry Sauce (page 187) (optional)

Season cavity of duck with salt and pepper. Combine sherry and honey in a small bowl. Brush honey mixture all over duck breast, thighs, and legs; let dry 30 minutes. Then coat entire duck with soy sauce. Place on a plate and refrigerate to dry for 4 hours.

Preheat oven to 400F (205C). Stuff duck cavity with orange, apple, and onion. With a skewer or a fork, prick holes in the skin, especially in the fatty parts, being careful not to pierce the flesh.

Set duck on a roasting rack in a roasting pan filled with ½ inch of hot water. Roast duck, breast side up, 45 minutes. Rotate roasting pan 180° and roast another 45 minutes.

Remove duck from oven and let stand 30 minutes before cutting. Remove skin and any visible fat before eating. Serve duck with Cherry Sauce, if desired.

Per serving (duck meat only): 200 Calories, 23 g Protein, 11 g Total Fat (50% of Calories), 4 g Saturated Fat, 0 g Carbohydrates, 0 g Dietary Fiber, 88 mg Cholesterol, 64 mg Sodium

Salt-Cured Duck

This is an excellent favorite summer recipe, and its preparation is very simple. Although it takes three days to salt-cure, it is not labor intensive. The duck should be served cold. It makes an excellent cold appetizer or buffet food.

MAKES 14 APPETIZER SERVINGS

2½ tablespoons salt
2 tablespoons Sichuan peppercorns
1 teaspoon sugar
1 tablespoon dry sherry
1 cinnamon stick
1 star anise, crushed

1-inch piece fresh ginger, crushed
2 large scallions, including tops, lightly smashed and each cut into 4 pieces
1 (5-lb.) duck, all visible fat removed, rinsed, and patted dry thoroughly outside and inside

In a small dry skillet, roast salt and peppercorns over low heat, stirring and shaking pan frequently 4 to 5 minutes or until salt is slightly browned and peppercorns are faintly smoking. Transfer to a small bowl and add sugar, sherry, cinnamon stick, star anise, ginger, and scallions; stir until mixed well. Set aside.

Trim off excess neck skin from duck, and cut off tail. Press down hard on breast bone with both palms to snap breast bone and flatten duck. Rub salt and pepper mixture all over duck, including inside the cavity.

Place duck in a large bowl, cover, and marinate in the refrigerator 3 days, turning it once a day in the juice that accumulates in the bowl.

Drain duck, straining the liquid, and place duck in a clean heatproof bowl. Strain and discard liquid, reserving spices and scallions. Put half of scallion mixture in the cavity and remainder on top of duck breast.

Bring water in a steamer to a boil. Place bowl with duck in steamer and steam duck over medium heat about 1½ hours, replenishing the water and discarding the rendered fat and juice surrounding the duck as needed, or until duck is tender.

Discard scallions and spices. Transfer duck to a plate, cover, and chill it until cold before serving. Remove skin and all visible fat before eating.

> Per serving: 115 Calories, 13 g Protein, 6 g Total Fat (50% of Calories), 2 g Saturated Fat, 0 g Carbohydrates, 0 g Dietary Fiber, 50 mg Cholesterol, 494 mg Sodium

Cherry Sauce

This sauce is excellent with roasted duck.

MAKES 1 1/2 CUPS

1/3 cup sugar
2/3 cup red wine vinegar
2 cups Port wine
1/2 cup dried black Bing cherries
1/2 cup frozen orange juice concentrate
1 cup water

1/4 teaspoon ground cinnamon
2 cups fat-free, low-sodium chicken broth
1 teaspoon cornstarch dissolved in
  1 tablespoon water
Salt and freshly ground black pepper
  (optional)

In a heavy 1-quart saucepan over medium heat, cook sugar and vinegar until liquid has reduced to 1/4 cup. Add Port wine and bring to a boil. Reduce heat slightly and simmer until volume is reduced by half. Add cherries, orange juice concentrate, water, cinnamon, and broth. Cook over low heat 10 to 15 minutes, or until sauce is reduced to 1½ cups. Stir cornstarch mixture and stir into sauce. Cook, stirring, until slightly thickened and glossy. Taste and adjust seasoning with salt and pepper, if desired. Transfer to a serving dish and serve warm.

> Per tablespoon: 46 Calories, 0.5 g Protein, 0 g Total Fat (0% of Calories), 0 g Saturated Fat, 7.9 g Carbohydrates, 0.2 g Dietary Fiber, 0 mg Cholesterol, 7 mg Sodium

Smoked Duck

Smoked duck meat has a rich incomparable flavor. It is delicious warm, at room temperature, or cold. You can serve it as an appetizer or as part of a multicourse meal.

MAKES 6 APPETIZER SERVINGS

½ cup packed light brown sugar
½ cup raw rice
½ cup dried black tea leaves

1 boneless, skinless duck breast from cooked Salt-Cured Duck (page 186)

Line a wok or large pot and its lid with foil. In a small bowl, mix brown sugar, rice, and tea leaves and spread them in center of foil-lined pot. Spray a steaming rack with cooking spray and place rack in pan over smoking sugar mixture.

Place duck breast on rack and place pot over high heat until mixture starts to smoke. Cover, reduce heat to medium, and smoke duck 8 to 10 minutes. Reduce heat to low and smoke another 5 minutes. Turn off heat and let smoke subside for 3 minutes.

Take the covered pan, without opening it, and a plate outside. Uncover pan outside and transfer duck to the plate. Dispose of foil and its contents in the trash. Cut duck into bite-size pieces and serve.

Per serving: 115 Calories, 13 g Protein, 6.4 g Total Fat (50% of Calories), 2.4 g Saturated Fat, 0 g Carbohydrates, 0 g Dietary Fiber, 50 mg Cholesterol, 494 mg Sodium

Note: The color of the smoked duck should be an even, rich brown, light to dark mahogany, according to how intense a flavor you prefer. You can monitor the intensity of the smoke by adjusting the heat temperature or by adjusting the length of smoking time. To avoid a bitter taste, do not use high heat.

VARIATION
To smoke a whole skinless duck, follow the same instructions, except when you turn the heat to medium, smoke the duck 20 minutes, breast side down. Reduce heat to low and smoke another 5 minutes. Turn off heat and let smoke subside for 3 minutes.

Peking Duck

The old-fashioned Peking duck preparation calls for elaborate procedures, such as inflating the duck skin, and long hours of hanging and drying the duck in order to get the cooked skin to a satisfying crispness. Today we know that the skin contains too much fat and is not healthy to eat. Besides, it is not safe to eat a duck that has been hanging around for hours without refrigeration. The signature ingredient that gives this duck its delicious characteristic flavor is the deep earthy hoisin sauce. Wrapping the duck meat, scallion brushes, and hoisin sauce in a tender resilient thin pancake transforms a roast duck into delicious Peking duck.

MAKES 20 APPETIZER SERVINGS

20 Chinese Thin Pancakes (page 266)
Duck meat from 1 Chinese Roast Duck
 (page 185), cut into thin slices

15 young scallions, including tops, cut
 into 3-inch shreds
Hoisin Dipping Sauce (page 292)

Place thin pancakes, each folded in half, overlapping in a concentric pattern on a serving platter. Place duck slices neatly on a beautiful serving platter. Place scallions and Hoisin Dipping Sauce in separate dishes. Bring all ingredients to the table.

To eat, take a thin pancake and open it. Put a few pieces of duck meat and some scallion shreds on the pancake. Spread with 1 teaspoonful of sauce and roll it up.

Per serving: 141 Calories, 11 g Protein, 4.9 g Total Fat (31% of Calories), 1.7 g Saturated Fat, 13 g Carbohydrates, 0 g Dietary Fiber, 35 mg Cholesterol, 226 mg Sodium

Meat

 Because meat was scarce in China and most Southeast Asian countries, it was usually cut into thin slices or shredded and always supplemented by vegetables to absorb the flavor and add volume. This improved the dietary balance and made a little meat go a long way.

In this chapter I have included some modern twists that will spark your appetite. Many of these scrumptious dishes are prepared with refreshing fresh fruits. Small portions of meat keep these recipes within current guidelines and all of the meat dishes in this chapter have been modified to promote dietary balance. Remember that beef, pork, and lamb are considered red meats and can be high in cholesterol and fat content.

Papaya Beef

When ripened, the flesh of the green cooking papaya turns into a sweet orange-red fruit that blends exquisitely with tender beef. Serve this dish with jasmine rice.

MAKES 6 SERVINGS

1 pound beef tenderloin, trimmed of all visible fat and membranes
3 tablespoons Port wine
Freshly ground black pepper to taste
1 tablespoon premium oyster sauce
1 teaspoon brown sugar
1 tablespoon cornstarch
1 tablespoon reduced-sodium soy sauce
1/4 teaspoon granulated sugar

2 teaspoons cornstarch dissolved in 1/2 cup fat-free, low-sodium chicken broth
1 ripe green papaya
1 tablespoon safflower oil
2 scallions, including tops, cut into 1-inch lengths, white and green parts separated
2 slices fresh ginger, shredded

Cut beef into 1/2-inch-thick, 1-inch squares. In a medium bowl, combine beef, 2 tablespoons of the Port wine, black pepper, oyster sauce, brown sugar, and cornstarch. Refrigerate 30 minutes or longer.

In a small bowl, combine the remaining 1 tablespoon Port wine, soy sauce, granulated sugar, and cornstarch mixture for a seasoning sauce; set aside.

Cut papaya lengthwise in half and discard seeds. Using a melon baller, scoop out 3 cups of papaya balls; set aside.

Heat a heavy 10-inch nonstick frying pan over high heat until hot. Add oil and swirl to coat pan. Add white parts of scallions and ginger and cook, stirring, a few seconds, or until aromatic. Add beef; stir and toss rapidly to sear on all sides, about 1 minute. Stir seasoning sauce and stir into beef mixture. Stir in green parts of scallions. Cover and steam-cook 30 seconds. Fold in papaya, then transfer to a hot serving platter and serve immediately.

Per serving: 176 Calories, 17 g Protein, 6.7 g Total Fat (34% of Calories), 2 g Saturated Fat, 10 g Carbohydrates, 1 g Dietary Fiber, 42 mg Cholesterol, 392 mg Sodium

Orange-Flavored Crispy Beef

This is an outstanding recipe for entertaining. This dish was our best seller when I had my restaurant. Here tender juicy beef with a crisp coating on the outside is quickly tossed in an ambrosial sauce full of orange flavor. Usually this dish is deep fried. Here I modify it by broiling. The beef is wonderfully crisp, and broiling dramatically cuts down on fat calories.

MAKES 4 SERVINGS

¾ pound beef flank steak, trimmed of all visible fat and membranes

3 tablespoons reduced-sodium soy sauce

1 tablespoon dry sherry

¼ cup plus 1 tablespoon light brown sugar

2 teaspoons cornstarch

1 large egg white, lightly beaten

3 tablespoons cider vinegar

1 tablespoon plus 1 teaspoon peanut oil

¾ cup water chestnut flour (see Note, page 139)

4 dried red hot chilies

3 thin slices fresh ginger

2 large scallions, white part only, cut into 1-inch lengths

1 tablespoon julienned orange zest

4 teaspoons cornstarch dissolved in ¾ cup fat-free, low-sodium chicken broth

¼ teaspoon pure orange oil, preferably Boyajian brand

1 large seedless orange (optional), peeled, white pith removed, and segmented

Cut flank steak lengthwise into 2 or 3 long strips, each about 2 to 2½ inches wide. Holding a sharp Chinese cleaver or chef knife, slice strips crosswise with knife tilted at an angle to get broader slices, about ⅜-inch thick, 1½ inches wide, and 2 to 2½ inches long. Place beef in a glass pie plate. Add 1 tablespoon of the soy sauce, sherry, 1 tablespoon of the brown sugar, and cornstarch and mix evenly. Add egg white and stir until beef is evenly coated. Cover and refrigerate 1 hour or longer.

In a small bowl, combine remaining 2 tablespoons soy sauce, vinegar, and remaining ¼ cup brown sugar and stir until sugar is dissolved; set aside.

Preheat broiler to 500F (260C). Spray a 13 × 12-inch piece of foil with cooking spray.

In a small bowl, combine 1 tablespoon of the peanut oil and water chestnut flour; stir until evenly mixed. Dredge each beef piece in the flour mixture to coat well and lay beef in a single layer on prepared foil; set aside.

Heat a heavy 10-inch nonstick skillet over medium heat until hot. Add remaining 1 teaspoon peanut oil and swirl to coat skillet. Add chilies, ginger, scallions, and orange zest and cook, stirring, a few seconds, or until aromatic. Stir soy sauce mixture and add to pan; bring to a boil. Stir cornstarch mixture and stir into contents of skillet. Cook, stirring constantly, until sauce is smooth and slightly thickened. Drizzle in orange oil. Turn off heat and cover to keep warm.

Broil beef 3 minutes, or until coating is light brown. Turn each piece over and broil the other side 3 minutes, or until coating is crisp and light brown. Add beef to sauce in pan and mix quickly but gently until each piece is glazed with sauce. Add orange segments, if desired. Transfer to a hot serving platter and serve immediately.

Per serving: 386 Calories, 22 g Protein, 10 g Total Fat (23% of Calories), 3 g Saturated Fat, 51 g Carbohydrates, 1 g Dietary Fiber, 48 mg Cholesterol, 587 mg Sodium

Beef with Pineapple in Black Bean Sauce

Pineapple adds a fruity essence and interesting contrast to this dish. Each ingredient is cooked separately to preserve its own character, then combined with a delicious black bean sauce. It is a beautiful party dish. Serve it with jasmine rice.

MAKES 4 SERVINGS

¾ pound beef flank steak, cut diagonally across the grain into 2-inch-wide, ⅛-inch-thick slices
2 teaspoons light brown sugar
2 teaspoons premium oyster sauce
2 teaspoons cornstarch
1 tablespoon dry sherry
½ small pineapple, preferably Del Monte Gold extra sweet pineapple, peeled
4 teaspoons safflower oil
1 medium onion, cubed
½ pound asparagus, trimmed and cut diagonally into 2-inch lengths

1 teaspoon minced fresh ginger
1 clove garlic, minced
1 tablespoon Chinese fermented black beans
2 tablespoons reduced-sodium soy sauce
1 teaspoon sugar
Freshly ground black pepper to taste
1 teaspoon tapioca starch dissolved in ½ cup fat-free, low-sodium chicken broth
½ cup roasted red bell pepper strips

Place beef in a self-sealing plastic bag. Add brown sugar, oyster sauce, cornstarch, and sherry. Seal bag and turn to coat with the seasonings. Refrigerate 30 minutes or longer.

Cut pineapple in half lengthwise. Trim off core, then cut each half crosswise into ⅜-inch-thick slices; set aside.

Heat a heavy 10-inch nonstick frying pan over high heat until hot. Add 1 teaspoon of the oil and swirl to coat pan. Add onion and stir-fry 1 minute. Transfer to a large plate and set aside. Add asparagus and ⅓ cup water to pan, cover, and cook over high heat 1 minute, or until asparagus turns bright green. Transfer to the plate with onion.

Rinse and wipe pan dry. Add remaining 3 teaspoons oil, swirl to coat pan, and heat 15 seconds. Add ginger, garlic, and black beans and cook, stirring rapidly, a few seconds. Add beef and stir-fry, shaking pan to prevent sticking, until beef is no longer pink, about 2 minutes. (Do not overcook beef.) Add soy sauce, sugar, black pepper, and pineapple to beef and cook, stirring, 30 seconds. Stir tapioca mixture and stir into beef mixture. Cook, stirring, until sauce thickens and beef is coated with sauce. Stir in onion, asparagus, and bell pepper strips and heat until hot, stirring gently. Transfer to a large serving platter and serve immediately.

Per serving: 273 Calories, 23 g Protein, 10 g Total Fat (34% of Calories), 3 g Saturated Fat, 22 g Carbohydrates, 2 g Dietary Fiber, 48 mg Cholesterol, 767 mg Sodium

Filet Mignon with Chinese Vegetables

With the best quality of meat and fresh vegetables, you can't go wrong. This dish is easy to put together. The secret is to have all the ingredients ready within easy reach of your cooktop. Use high heat, a hot pan, and quick motions, and you will have a successful dish.

MAKES 4 SERVINGS

1 pound filet mignon, trimmed of all
    visible fat and membranes
3 tablespoons dry sherry
6 Chinese dried mushrooms, soaked in
    1 cup hot water 30 minutes
2 tablespoons reduced-sodium soy
    sauce
1 tablespoon premium oyster sauce
½ teaspoon sugar
Freshly ground black pepper to taste

2 teaspoons cornstarch
3 teaspoons safflower oil
2 thin slices fresh ginger
1 clove garlic, crushed
½ cup winter bamboo shoot slices
½ cup thin carrot slices
2 large stalks bok choy, cut diagonally
    into 1½-inch-long slices
1 cup fresh snow peas, strings removed

Cut beef into 1¼-inch cubes. In a medium bowl, combine beef and 1 tablespoon of the sherry; set aside.

Drain and squeeze mushrooms slightly to remove excess liquid, reserving ½ cup soaking liquid. Cut each mushroom in half; set aside.

In a small bowl, combine the remaining 2 tablespoons sherry, soy sauce, oyster sauce, sugar, pepper, cornstarch, and the mushroom soaking liquid and stir until sugar dissolves for a seasoning sauce; set aside.

Heat a heavy 10-inch nonstick skillet over high heat until hot. Add 2 teaspoons of the oil, swirl to coat pan, and heat for 15 seconds. Add beef; stir and toss rapidly to sear on all sides, about 1 minute. Transfer beef and pan juice to a plate.

Wipe pan clean. Add remaining 1 teaspoon oil and heat until hot. Add ginger and garlic and cook, pressing lightly in the oil, until aromatic, about 15 seconds. Add all the vegetables and the mushrooms; stir-fry 1 minute. Return beef and its juice to vegetables, cover, and steam-cook 1 minute. Stir seasoning sauce mixture and stir into beef mixture. Cook, stirring, until sauce is smooth and slightly thickened. Transfer to a serving dish and serve immediately.

Per serving: 269 Calories, 28 g Protein, 10 g Total Fat (34% of Calories), 3 g Saturated Fat, 16 g Carbohydrates, 3 g Dietary Fiber, 64 mg Cholesterol, 818 mg Sodium

Beef with Broccoli in Oyster Sauce

A premium-quality oyster sauce is crucial; it transforms ordinary beef into a gourmet delight.

¾ pound beef flank steak, trimmed of all visible fat and membranes
2 tablespoons dry sherry
2 teaspoons light brown sugar
1 tablespoon cornstarch
1 tablespoon premium oyster sauce
1 tablespoon reduced-sodium soy sauce
1 tablespoon cornstarch dissolved in ½ cup fat-free, low-sodium chicken broth
1 pound broccoli flowerets
1 tablespoon safflower oil
3 thin slices fresh ginger
2 scallions, white part only, cut into 1-inch lengths
Salt and freshly ground black pepper (optional)

Cut flank steak lengthwise into 2 or 3 long strips, each strip about 2 to 2½ inches wide. Holding a sharp Chinese cleaver or chef's knife, slice strips crosswise with knife tilted at an angle to get broader slices, about ¼ inch thick, 1½ inches wide, and 2 to 2½ inches long. In a medium bowl, combine beef, sherry, 1 teaspoon of the brown sugar, and cornstarch and stir until evenly coated. Cover and refrigerate at least 30 minutes.

In a small bowl, combine oyster sauce, soy sauce, remaining 1 teaspoon sugar, and cornstarch mixture and stir until sugar dissolves for a seasoning sauce; set aside.

In a pot of boiling water, blanch broccoli over high heat, covered, 2 minutes; drain and set aside.

Heat a heavy 10-inch nonstick frying pan over medium-high heat until hot. Add oil and swirl to coat pan. Add ginger and scallions and cook, stirring, a few seconds. Distribute beef evenly in pan and sear 1 minute, turning several times, until beef is no longer pink. Stir seasoning sauce mixture and stir into beef. Cook, stirring constantly, until sauce is thickened. Add broccoli to beef and cook, stirring, until heated through. Transfer to a serving platter and serve. Add salt and black pepper, if desired.

Per serving: 227 Calories, 23 g Protein, 9 g Total Fat (35% of Calories), 2 g Saturated Fat, 14 g Carbohydrates, 5 g Dietary Fiber, 48 mg Cholesterol, 595 mg Sodium

Beef with Leeks

Leeks are grown in sandy soil, with the soil mounded over their stems to produce their white color. Dirt gets in between the leaves so they must be thoroughly washed before use. Cut the white stem diagonally into thin slices and rinse thoroughly before cooking.

MAKES 4 SERVINGS

¾ pound beef flank steak, trimmed of all
    visible fat and membranes
2 tablespoons reduced-sodium soy sauce
2 tablespoons dry sherry
1 tablespoon cornstarch

1½ pounds leeks
3 teaspoons safflower oil
½ teaspoon salt
2¼ teaspoons sugar
2 tablespoons hoisin sauce

Cut flank steak along the grain into 2-inch-wide strips, then cut across the grain on an angle into ¼-inch slices; stack the pieces and shred. In a medium bowl, combine beef, 1 tablespoon of the soy sauce, 1 tablespoon of the sherry, and cornstarch and stir until evenly coated. Cover and refrigerate at least 30 minutes.

Trim off all but 1 inch of the green tops from leeks. Cut remaining white parts diagonally into thin slices. Put leek slices in a colander and rinse thoroughly under running water to remove any sand that is lodged in between the layers; drain well.

Heat a heavy 10-inch nonstick frying pan over high heat until hot. Add 1 teaspoon of the oil and swirl to coat pan. Add leeks, salt and ¼ teaspoon of the sugar and stir-fry until leeks are just slightly wilted, about 1 minute. Transfer to a platter.

Add remaining 2 teaspoons oil to pan over medium-high heat and swirl to coat pan. Add beef and stir-fry 1 minute. Make a space in the center; add hoisin sauce, remaining 2 teaspoons sugar, remaining 1 tablespoon sherry, and remaining 1 tablespoon soy sauce. Cook, stirring with a spatula, until sugar is dissolved. Mix with beef and cook another 30 seconds. Return leeks to beef and stir-fry until heated through. Transfer to a serving platter and serve.

Per serving: 310 Calories, 22 g Protein, 9 g Total Fat (26% of Calories), 3 g Saturated Fat, 34 g Carbohydrates, 3 g Dietary Fiber, 48 mg Cholesterol, 945 mg Sodium

Beef Stew Sichuan Style

This is a popular dish of Sichuan origin. The tender beef is flavorful and full of aromatic spices and herbs. Serve it as part of a multicourse meal with rice or steamed buns.

Make this dish a day ahead, refrigerate, and remove the solidified fat from the surface. It will keep one week in the refrigerator and up to two months in the freezer.

MAKES 8 SERVINGS

2 pounds boneless beef chuck, trimmed of all visible fat and cut into 1½-inch cubes

2½ quarts boiling water

5 scallions, including tops, lightly smashed

1 (1-inch) piece fresh ginger, crushed

3 whole star anise

½ teaspoon fennel seeds

1 tablespoon safflower oil

1 tablespoon Sichuan peppercorns

5 cloves garlic, coarsely chopped

2 tablespoons Chinese hot bean sauce

2 tablespoons dry sherry

4 tablespoons reduced-sodium soy sauce

1 tablespoon sugar

Salt (optional)

In a 4-quart pot, bring 2 quarts water to a boil. Blanch beef in the boiling water 2 minutes. Drain and rinse beef; discard water. Return beef to pot and add the 2½ quarts boiling water, scallions, ginger, star anise, and fennel seeds; bring to a boil. Reduce heat to low, cover, and simmer 2 hours. Discard ginger and scallions.

Meanwhile, heat a 1-quart saucepan over medium heat until hot. Add oil and swirl to coat pan; reduce heat to low. Add peppercorns, stir, and let them infuse in the oil about 1 minute, or until fragrant; do not let them burn. (If they darken too fast, remove the pot from heat.) Discard peppercorns, but reserve the oil in pan. Add garlic and cook, stirring, a few seconds. Add hot bean sauce and cook, stirring, until aromatic, about 30 seconds. Add sherry, soy sauce, and sugar and boil 30 seconds.

Add soy sauce mixture to the beef, cover, and simmer 1 hour more, or until beef is very tender. Adjust taste with a little salt or soy sauce, if desired.

Per serving: 216 Calories, 32 g Protein, 7 g Total Fat (27% of Calories), 2 g Saturated Fat, 5 g Carbohydrates, 1 g Dietary Fiber, 91 mg Cholesterol, 549 mg Sodium

VARIATION

This dish is also excellent served with its broth over a bowl of noodles. Served this way, it is known as the famous Sichuan Beef Noodle Soup.

Chinese Barbecued Pork

Instead of using the usual artificial red food dye, hoisin sauce and ketchup are used here to give this pork a natural, rich mahogany color. This is an excellent recipe. When we were roasting this pork at my restaurant, it smelled so good that customers told me I should patent the smell. You can cut this pork into thin slices for appetizers or for use in pork lo mein, or into small cubes for Pork Fried Rice (page 220).

MAKES 8 SERVINGS

2 (about 2 lbs. total) pork tenderloins, trimmed of all visible fat and membranes
2 cloves garlic, crushed
2 tablespoons reduced-sodium soy sauce
1 tablespoon dry sherry
1 tablespoon hoisin sauce
1 tablespoon Chinese fermented bean sauce

2 tablespoons ketchup
2 tablespoons orange juice
1 tablespoon sugar
2 tablespoons honey
½ teaspoon five-spice powder
1 teaspoon oriental sesame oil
Hot Mustard Sauce (page 292) and Plum Sauce (page 291) (optional)

Cut each pork tenderloin lengthwise in half to make 4 strips; place them in a self-sealing plastic bag. Add garlic, soy sauce, sherry, hoisin sauce, bean sauce, ketchup, orange juice, sugar, 1 tablespoon of the honey, and five-spice powder; turn to coat evenly. Refrigerate about 4 hours, turning several times.

Remove all but topmost rack from oven. Fill a roasting pan with a few inches of boiling water and place on bottom of oven to catch drippings and prevent smoking. (If you have an electric oven, place pan on bottom rack in lowest position.) Preheat oven to 350F (175C).

Insert a meat hook or drapery hook into larger end of each pork strip and hang strips from top rack over roasting pan. Roast strips 35 minutes. Increase oven temperature to 400F (205C) and roast 10 minutes more, or until a meat thermometer inserted in the thickest part of pork reads 160F (70C).

Transfer pork to a cutting board. Mix remaining 1 tablespoon honey with the sesame oil and brush it over each pork strip on all sides. Remove hooks and let pork stand 15 minutes before cutting crosswise into ¼-inch-thick slices for appetizers. Serve with Hot Mustard and Plum Sauces, if desired.

Per serving: 170 Calories, 27 g Protein, 3.5 g Total Fat (18% of Calories), 1 g Saturated Fat, 8 g Carbohydrates, 0 g Dietary Fiber, 74 mg Cholesterol, 382 mg Sodium

Kumquat Pork

This is a new twist on the Chinese classic. Instead of pineapple, fresh kumquats are used. Their tartness contrasts beautifully with the sweet marmalade. This is a dish for connoisseurs.

MAKES 4 SERVINGS

¾-pound pork tenderloin, trimmed of
   visible fat, cut into ½-inch-thick by
   1-inch-square pieces
1 tablespoon reduced-sodium soy sauce
1 tablespoon dry sherry
Freshly ground black pepper to taste
1 tablespoon lightly beaten egg white
1 tablespoon cornstarch
8 ounces fresh kumquats, thinly sliced,
   plus extra, for garnish
¼ cup sugar
1¼ cups water

3 teaspoons olive oil
2 teaspoons minced fresh ginger
3 cloves garlic, crushed
1 small onion, cubed
1 medium green bell pepper, seeded
   and cubed
1 tablespoon orange marmalade
1 tablespoon cider vinegar
½ teaspoon salt
1 teaspoon cornstarch dissolved in
   1 tablespoon water
Steamed jasmine rice (optional)

Place pork in a medium bowl. Add soy sauce, sherry, black pepper, egg white, and cornstarch and stir to coat well. Cover and marinate 30 minutes, turning once.

Place kumquats in a 2-quart saucepan. Add sugar and water and bring to a boil over medium heat. Reduce heat and simmer 15 to 20 minutes, or until just tender.

Heat a heavy 10-inch nonstick frying pan over medium-high heat until hot. Add 2 teaspoons of the oil, swirl to coat pan, and heat 10 seconds. Add pork pieces and stir-fry 2 to 3 minutes, or until no longer pink. Transfer pork to a plate.

Add remaining 1 teaspoon oil to pan and heat 15 seconds. Add ginger and garlic and cook, stirring, 15 seconds. Add onion and bell pepper and stir-fry 1 minute, or until bell pepper is bright green. Transfer to a plate and reserve.

Add kumquats with syrup, marmalade, vinegar, and salt to pan and bring to a boil, stirring to melt the marmalade. Scatter in the pork. Cover, reduce heat to medium-low, and simmer 5 minutes. Stir cornstarch mixture and stir into pork mixture. Cook, stirring, until lightly thickened. Return bell pepper to pan and heat through. Transfer contents of pan to a serving platter, garnish with fresh kumquats, and serve with rice, if desired.

Per serving: 254 Calories, 20 g Protein, 6 g Total Fat (20% of Calories), 1 g Saturated Fat, 31 g Carbohydrates, 3 g Dietary Fiber, 55 mg Cholesterol, 488 mg Sodium

Mu Shu Pork

This is a shredded meat and vegetable dish in which hoisin sauce provides the signature flavor. Traditionally this dish is served with Chinese Thin Pancakes (page 266), but it is also good with rice.

2 teaspoons olive oil

6 ounces pork tenderloin, thinly shredded

3/4 pound green cabbage, thinly shredded

4 slices fresh ginger, finely shredded

4 scallions, including tops, cut into 1-inch lengths, white and green parts separated

1/2 cup dried tree ear mushrooms, soaked 30 minutes, rinsed, and shredded

20 dried tiger lily buds, soaked 15 minutes, hard stems removed, and cut into 1 1/2-inch lengths

1 tablespoon reduced-sodium soy sauce

1 tablespoon dry sherry

1/4 teaspoon sugar

1 tablespoon hoisin sauce

Freshly ground black pepper to taste

1 teaspoon oriental sesame oil

8 Chinese Thin Pancakes or 16 pieces spring roll skins

Hoisin Dipping Sauce (page 292) (optional)

Heat a heavy 10-inch nonstick frying pan over high heat until hot. Add 1 teaspoon of the oil, swirl to coat pan, and heat 15 seconds. Scatter in pork and stir-fry about 1 minute, until each piece is separated and all pink traces are gone. Transfer to a large plate and reserve.

Add cabbage to pan and stir-fry, adding 2 tablespoons water if cabbage is too dry, 1 to 2 minutes, or just until softened. Transfer cabbage to the plate with pork.

Wash pan and dry with a towel. Heat pan over medium-high heat until hot. Add remaining 1 teaspoon oil and heat a few seconds. Add ginger and white parts of scallions and cook, stirring, until fragrant, about 15 seconds. Add mushrooms and lily buds and stir-fry about 30 seconds, or until heated through. Return pork and cabbage to pan and toss to mix. Add green parts of scallions, soy sauce, sherry, sugar, hoisin sauce, black pepper, and sesame oil. Stir-fry until heated through, about 2 minutes. Transfer to a hot serving dish.

To eat, place some pork mixture in the center of a thin pancake or double layers of spring roll skins. Drizzle some Hoisin Dipping Sauce over filling. Fold up one end, about 1½ inches, over the filling, then bring up the two sides to wrap filling snugly. Using your hands, eat as you would any roll-ups.

Per serving: 118 Calories, 8 g Protein, 2.5 g Total Fat (19% of Calories), 2.5 g Saturated Fat, 20 g Carbohydrates, 4 g Dietary Fiber, 14 mg Cholesterol, 194 mg Sodium

Chinese Aromatic Pot Roast

For pot roast, you can use chuck roast, but the Chinese prefer shin beef, which has a soft, resilient texture when cooked and contains a natural gelatin that thickens the sauce when cold. You can serve this with rice or noodles, or slice it paper thin to use in sandwiches.

MAKES 8 SERVINGS

1 tablespoon safflower oil
1 (1-inch) piece fresh ginger, crushed
3 scallions, including tops, lightly smashed
1 dried red chili
1 (2-pound) boneless shin beef or chuck roast, trimmed of all visible fat

½ cup dry sherry
¼ cup reduced-sodium soy sauce
3 tablespoons crushed rock sugar or 2 tablespoons brown sugar
2 whole star anise
½ teaspoon fennel seeds
4 cups boiling water

Heat a heavy 3-quart pot over high heat until hot. Add the oil and swirl to coat pan. Add the ginger, scallions, and chili and cook, stirring briskly, 30 seconds. Add beef and sear it on all sides until light brown. Reduce heat and add sherry; bring to a boil. Add soy sauce, sugar, star anise, fennel seeds, and enough of the boiling water to cover beef and bring to a boil. Reduce heat to low, cover, and simmer 2 hours, turning beef every 30 minutes for an even color, or until beef is tender but not falling apart. The texture should be firm, neither soft nor hard. Adjust the seasonings during the last 30 minutes by adding more soy sauce or sugar according to taste, if desired.

Transfer beef to a deep platter. Let cool 30 minutes before slicing and serving, or cover and refrigerate until beef is very firm and cold. Cut beef across the grain into thin slices and serve with a little of the jellied sauce on top. The sauce is also good on boiled noodles.

Per serving: 209 Calories, 26 g Protein, 8 g Total Fat (34% of Calories), 3 g Saturated Fat, 5 g Carbohydrates, 0 g Dietary Fiber, 68 mg Cholesterol, 419 mg Sodium

Twice-Cooked Pork

In this beautifully flavored dish, the pork is simmered first, then cut into thin slices and stir-fried with vegetables in a delicious bean sauce mixture that makes you reach for lots of steamed rice. Serve this dish with steamed cauliflower or stir-fried cabbage.

MAKES 6 SERVINGS

1 (1-lb.) pork tenderloin, trimmed of all visible fat
1 (¼-inch) piece fresh ginger, lightly smashed
2 medium scallions, including tops, lightly smashed
1 tablespoon Chinese hot bean sauce
2 tablespoons hoisin sauce

1 tablespoon reduced-sodium soy sauce
1 tablespoon dry sherry
2 teaspoons sugar
2 tablespoons water
2 teaspoons olive oil
1 large red bell pepper, chopped
1 large green bell pepper, chopped
2 large cloves garlic, coarsely chopped

Combine pork, ginger, and scallions in a 3-quart saucepan, cover with cold water, and bring to a boil. Reduce heat to low, cover, and simmer 20 minutes. Remove pork from the water and let cool 15 minutes, then cover with plastic wrap and refrigerate a few hours or until it is firm. (Do not slice until ready to stir-fry.)

Cut pork into ⅛-inch-thick slices; set aside. Mix hot bean sauce, hoisin sauce, soy sauce, sherry, sugar, and water in a small bowl and stir until sugar dissolves; set aside.

Heat a heavy 10-inch nonstick skillet over high heat until hot. Add 1 teaspoon of the oil and swirl to coat pan. Add the peppers and stir-fry about 1 minute, or until peppers are slightly charred and a bit blistered. Transfer peppers to a plate.

Add remaining 1 teaspoon oil to pan and add garlic. Press and turn lightly in the oil a few seconds. Reduce heat to medium. Add pork slices and stir-fry about 2 minutes, until pork is heated through. Make a well in the center, scrape in the hot bean sauce mixture, and cook, stirring, until bubbly. Stir and mix with the pork until evenly coated. Stir in bell peppers and cook until heated through. Transfer to a serving dish and serve immediately.

Per serving: 136 Calories, 17 g Protein, 3.7 g Total Fat (24% of Calories), 0.9 g Saturated Fat, 7 g Carbohydrates, 1 g Dietary Fiber, 49 mg Cholesterol, 390 mg Sodium

Red-Cooked Whole Pork Shoulder

Once I made this dish for my husband's birthday and we celebrated with my cooking class students. It was a big hit! Everybody raved about it and named it "Fred's Birthday Pork" and asked for the recipe. So here it is. The aroma and flavors from the ginger, scallions, wine, star anise, and Chinese mushrooms make this dish outstanding, Although it takes long hours of cooking, the whole dish does not involve a lot of work. You can cook it one or two days ahead, leave it in the pot to refrigerate, and remove the congealed fat on the surface before reheating. Reheat over low heat until heated through, about 30 minutes. You will agree this is the most delicious pork you've ever had. The meat and sauce are also excellent over rice.

MAKES 10 SERVINGS

1 (6- to 7-lb.) whole pork shoulder
½ cup dry sherry
½ cup reduced-sodium soy sauce
2 tablespoons dark soy sauce (optional)
1 (2-inch) piece fresh ginger, crushed
2 scallions, including tops, slightly smashed
2 whole star anise
3 cups boiling water
½ cup Chinese dried mushrooms, soaked in warm water 30 minutes

½ cup dried tree ear mushrooms, soaked in warm water 30 minutes
30 dried tiger lily buds, soaked in water 15 minutes
¼ cup crushed rock sugar or brown sugar
Salt to taste
Flower Rolls (page 260)

Bring 4 quarts water to a boil in a heavy 8-quart pot. Submerge pork and boil 10 minutes. Drain and rinse pork in cool water to eliminate scum. Wash pot.

Place 2 wooden chopsticks on the bottom of the 8-quart pot to prevent the pork from sticking. Place pork on the chopsticks; place pot over high heat. Add sherry, soy sauce, dark soy sauce, if using, ginger, scallions, star anise, and the 3 cups boiling water and bring to a boil. Adjust heat to low to maintain a very gentle simmer, cover, and simmer 4 hours, basting and checking every hour. Turn pork once midway through cooking, taking care not to tear the skin or meat.

Add both mushrooms and lily buds and cook 30 minutes longer, basting pork frequently. Add rock sugar or brown sugar to liquid and baste meat several times. Cover and cook another 30 minutes. Taste and adjust with salt.

Increase heat to bring sauce to a gentle boil and baste pork constantly about 5 minutes to deepen the color. Turn off heat and wait 10 to 15 minutes. Transfer meat carefully to a large deep serving platter. (I take out the meat with gloved hands.) Arrange lily buds and mushrooms around pork, discarding ginger, scallions, and star anise. Chill sauce. Remove solidified fat and reheat sauce. Pour sauce over pork before eating.

The tender pork can be pulled apart easily with chopsticks or a fork. Accompany this dish with Flower Rolls.

Per serving (meat only): 319 Calories, 38 g Protein, 12 g Total Fat (34% of Calories), 4 g Saturated Fat, 19 g Carbohydrates, 3 g Dietary Fiber, 76 mg Cholesterol, 516 mg Sodium

Scallion Exploded Lamb

Hi igh heat and rapid speed are crucial in cooking this dish in order to seal in the juices of the meat. Insufficient heat or cooking for too long will result in a watery dish. Do not overcook the scallions; they should keep their sweet, sharp character and bright green color.

MAKES 4 SERVINGS

¾ pound boneless lamb, trimmed of all visible fat and cut into ⅛-inch-thick slices
2 tablespoons dry sherry
1 tablespoon cornstarch
2 tablespoons reduced-sodium soy sauce
1½ teaspoons light brown sugar

1 tablespoon balsamic vinegar or cider vinegar
4 dried red chilies, seeds removed
4 large cloves garlic, coarsely chopped
½ pound scallions, including tops, cut into 1 ½-inch lengths, white and green parts separated
1 tablespoon safflower oil

In a medium bowl, combine lamb, 1 tablespoon of the sherry, and cornstarch, and stir to coat evenly. Set aside to marinate 30 minutes.

In a small bowl, combine soy sauce, remaining 1 tablespoon sherry, sugar, and vinegar and stir until sugar dissolves; set aside.

Put the chilies, garlic, white parts of scallions, and green parts of scallions in separate piles on a large platter within easy reach of the stove.

Heat a heavy 10-inch nonstick skillet over high heat until very hot but not smoking. Add oil, swirl to coat pan, and heat 15 seconds. Add chilies and garlic; quickly stir and press 3 seconds. Scatter in the lamb and stir-fry 30 seconds. Add white parts of scallions and stir-fry for 20 seconds. Add green parts of the scallions and stir-fry until their color deepens, about 30 seconds. Quickly add soy sauce mixture and stir vigorously about 1 minute, until lamb and vegetables have absorbed the seasonings. Pour into a heated serving dish and serve immediately.

Per serving: 236 Calories, 18 g Protein, 14 g Total Fat (52% of Calories), 6 g Saturated Fat, 9 g Carbohydrates, 2 g Dietary Fiber, 58 mg Cholesterol, 388 mg Sodium

Note: This delicious classic dish has a high percentage of calories from fat, so serving it in small portions and infrequently is recommended.

Mongolian Spicy Lamb

Charred bell peppers lend a smoky flavor that blends wonderfully with the hot spicy lamb. Use high heat when stir-frying lamb. The whole cooking process should only take about 5 minutes. Serve it with steamed jasmine rice.

MAKES 4 SERVINGS

¾ pound boneless lamb, trimmed of all visible fat and cut into ⅛-inch-thick slices
1 teaspoon sugar
1 tablespoon reduced-sodium soy sauce
1 tablespoon lightly beaten egg white
2 teaspoons cornstarch
1 tablespoon Chinese hot bean sauce
1 tablespoon hoisin sauce
1 tablespoon dry sherry
½ teaspoon cornstarch dissolved in ½ cup fat-free, low-sodium chicken broth
2 teaspoons safflower oil
1 orange bell pepper, chopped
1 yellow bell pepper, chopped
Salt to taste (optional)
3 scallions, including tops, cut into 1-inch lengths, white and green parts separated
1 teaspoon minced garlic

In a medium bowl, combine lamb, sugar, soy sauce, egg white, and cornstarch. Mix well and set aside 30 minutes.

In a small bowl, combine hot bean sauce, hoisin sauce, sherry, and cornstarch mixture and mix well; set aside.

Heat a heavy 10-inch nonstick frying pan over high heat. Add 1 teaspoon of the oil and swirl to coat pan. Add bell peppers and stir-fry over high heat until skins are charred a little and peppers are aromatic, about 2 minutes. Add salt to taste, if desired, and transfer to a plate; set aside.

Add remaining 1 teaspoon oil to pan, swirl to coat pan, and heat 15 seconds over high heat. Add white parts of scallions and garlic and cook, stirring, 15 seconds. Add lamb and stir-fry until brown, about 1 minute. Stir hot bean sauce mixture and stir into lamb mixture. Cook, stirring, until sauce is clear and slightly thickened. Return peppers and add green parts of scallions to pan and heat through. Transfer to a serving platter.

Per serving: 247 Calories, 18 g Protein, 15 g Total Fat (55% of Calories), 6 g Saturated Fat, 9 g Carbohydrates, 1 g Dietary Fiber, 58 mg Cholesterol, 585 mg Sodium

Note: This delicious dish has a high percentage of calories from fat, so serving it infrequently and in smaller portions is recommended.

Rice and Noodles

 A staple of China, rice is is an integral part of a family meal: It is eaten three times a day. Rice is rich in complex carbohydrates and is an important source of energy and of B vitamins. Rice is versatile. You can serve it in salads, soups, and stuffing. You can make a main course or side dish with it. You can even use it for desserts.

The Chinese use four types of rice: long-grain white rice, short-grain white rice, glutinous rice, and brown rice. The long-grain rices are firmer and less starchy (sticky) after cooking and hold up well when making stir-fried rice. Restaurants in the United States serve long-grain rice. Short-grain rice is oval in shape, softer and starchier when cooked, and much preferred by the Chinese for everyday eating and for making breakfast rice porridge. It is also excellent for making creamy rice pudding. Glutinous rice is very sticky and turns translucent when cooked. Its cohesive quality makes it suitable for stuffings and sweet snacks such as rice cakes and for rice dumplings, which is why it is often labeled "sweet rice," although it is not sweet. Brown rice can be served as an alternative to white rice. Brown rice has its bran intact, contains more vitamins and minerals, takes longer to cook, and is chewier than white rice. Try each of these types of rice. You will be able to tell the difference and choose the kind you most enjoy eating. Many delicious recipes that feature rice are presented in this chapter.

Meals in China always include steamed white rice. Leftover cold rice is used to make various kinds of fried rice to serve as snacks. To make a good fried rice, always start with cold cooked long-grain rice that has a firm texture so that it can hold up well when stir-fried.

In China, noodles are made from either rice flour or wheat flour. They are high in carbohydrates and low in fat. Whether stir-fried, pan-fried, deep-fried, steamed, cold, or used as a component in soups, noodles are always prepared with meat and vegetables in a delicious, healthy, nutritious way. This chapter contains a good selection of rice noodle and wheat noodle recipes. Try some Lo Mein Noodles (page 240) or Shrimp and Scallops on Crispy Noodles (page 242); these are great one-dish meals.

Basic Steamed Rice

Cooking rice is easy but there are several guidelines that help to make fluffier, lighter, and fresher-tasting rice. First, the rice must be rinsed with several changes of cold water until the water is no longer milky. Second, the ratio of water and rice should be based on experience. Most Asian Chinese judge the correct water level by the hand, not the cup. They place their hand flat on the rice in the pot; when the water comes to three-quarters of the way up the flat hand, that is the correct water level. My mother taught me this method, and it has worked perfectly for me each time. Use these guidelines as starting points, and determine by your own experience the best water ratio for your kitchen. Normally for 1 cup of rice, I add 1¼ cups cold water. Third, during cooking do not lift up the lid. The rice needs slow uninterrupted even simmering, for each grain must absorb enough moisture to become plump and tender.

MAKES 7 CUPS, OR 4 TO 6 SERVINGS

2 cups long-grain white rice

2½ cups cold water, or judge the water by hand

Put rice in a heavy 3-quart pot that has a tight-fitting lid. Rinse rice under running cold water, stirring until the water is no longer milky; drain rice. Add water, cover with lid, and bring to a rolling boil over medium-high heat. Reduce heat to its lowest level and simmer 20 minutes. Remove pot from heat and let stand, undisturbed, an additional 15 minutes or longer. Do not lift the lid at any stage or the heat will dissipate.

Uncover and gently fluff rice with a fork, lifting from the bottom and tossing gently to separate the grains. Serve the rice immediately, or let it sit in the covered pot, where it will stay warm for another half hour.

Per serving: 168 Calories, 3.1 g Protein, 0.2 g Total Fat (1% of Calories), 0 g Saturated Fat, 37 g Carbohydrates, 0.2 g Dietary Fiber, 0 mg Cholesterol, 2 mg Sodium

VARIATIONS

For steamed brown rice: Add 2½ cups water to 2 cups brown rice. Extend the simmering time to 30 minutes.

For steamed wild rice: Add 3½ cups water to 1 cup wild rice. Extend the simmering time to 45 minutes. (Wild rice is not really a grain but a grass seed from a different botanical family, though it is very nutritious.)

Note: Always fluff the rice while it is still warm and before serving. Leftover rice may be sealed and refrigerated for several days. It may be reheated by steaming it in a bowl over high heat until hot, or reheat it, covered, in a microwave oven. It is perfect for making fried rice.

Pork Fried Rice

To make a good fried rice always start with cold cooked long-grain rice that has a firm texture so that it can hold up well when stir-fried.

MAKES 6 SERVINGS

4 cups cold cooked long-grain rice
1 egg
2 egg whites
½ tablespoon dry sherry
1 tablespoon peanut oil
3 scallions, including tops, coarsely sliced

½ cup Chinese Barbecued Pork (page 202), or diced cooked ham
2 tablespoons reduced-sodium soy sauce
Salt and freshly ground pepper to taste
¼ cup fat-free, low-sodium chicken broth
½ cup thawed frozen green peas

Separate the grains of rice with wet fingers so that the rice does not stick on your fingers.

In a small bowl, beat whole egg, egg whites, and sherry. Spray a 10-inch heavy nonstick frying pan with cooking spray. Place pan over medium heat for 30 seconds. Add beaten eggs and stir constantly with a pair of chopsticks until eggs break into small pieces and are fluffy. Transfer to a plate and set aside.

Return pan to high heat. Add oil, swirl to coat pan, and heat 15 seconds. Add scallions and pork or ham and stir-fry 1 minute, or until scallions are aromatic and pork is heated through. Add rice and stir and flip with a wooden spoon and chopsticks until rice is hot. Add soy sauce, salt, pepper, and chicken broth; stir-fry 1 minute. Stir in the cooked eggs and peas and cook, stirring, until heated through. Transfer to a hot serving dish and serve.

Per serving: 267 Calories, 10 g Protein, 4 g Total Fat (14% of Calories), 1 g Saturated Fat, 46 g Carbohydrates, 1 g Dietary Fiber, 52 mg Cholesterol, 368 mg Sodium

TIP

The rice in the above recipe is white. If you like dark fried rice, add 1 tablespoon dark soy sauce or ¼ teaspoon thick soy sauce, and mix well during the stir-frying.

Pineapple and Shrimp Fried Rice

This is a delicious fried rice. The fresh juicy pineapple contrasts perfectly with the crisp crunchy cashews while the shrimp and spicy shrimp paste give this dish its tang and taste. For an elegant presentation serve this fried rice in a split hollowed pineapple shell with its leaves intact.

MAKES 6 SERVINGS

1 tablespoon peanut oil
1 medium onion, chopped
3 cloves garlic, chopped
2 fresh small red chilies, seeded and shredded
1 heaping teaspoon Spicy Shrimp Paste (page 301)
½ pound large shrimp, peeled and deveined
4 cups cold cooked long-grain rice, grains separated

2 cups fresh pineapple chunks, preferably extra-sweet Del Monte Gold brand
1 to 2 tablespoons fish sauce or to taste
½ teaspoon sugar
⅓ cup roasted cashew nuts
¼ cup thinly sliced scallion rings
Cilantro leaves, for garnish

Heat a heavy 10-inch nonstick skillet over high heat. Add oil and swirl to coat the pan. Add onion, garlic, and chilies and cook, stirring, until aromatic. Add shrimp paste and the fresh shrimp; stir-fry until shrimp turn pink, about 2 minutes. Transfer shrimp mixture to a plate and reserve.

Add rice to pan and stir-fry a few seconds. Add fish sauce and sugar and stir-fry until seasonings are distributed evenly and rice is heated through. Stir in shrimp mixture. Add pineapple, cashews, and scallion and stir to blend well. Transfer to a warm serving dish. Garnish with cilantro leaves.

Per serving: 271 Calories, 12 g Protein, 7 g Total Fat (22% of Calories), 1 g Saturated Fat, 42 g Carbohydrates, 1 g Dietary Fiber, 57 mg Cholesterol, 327 mg Sodium

Vegetarian Fried Rice

Here is a delicious vegetarian fried rice containing a variety of healthy vegetables.

MAKES 6 SERVINGS

3 teaspoons olive oil
8 ounces firm tofu, cut into ½-inch
  cubes and patted dry with paper
  towels
1 tablespoon Worcestershire sauce
1 large carrot, peeled and cut into ½-
  inch cubes
1 heaping cup small broccoli flowerets
1 summer squash, halved lengthwise,
  then cut crosswise into ¼-inch-thick
  slices

¼ cup vegetable stock
3 shallots, chopped
2 cups sliced firm mushrooms
1 cup sliced bok choy stalks
4 cups cold cooked long-grain rice,
  grains separated
2 tablespoons reduced-sodium soy
  sauce
Freshly ground black pepper to taste
½ cup dry-roasted peanuts

Heat a heavy 10-inch nonstick frying pan over high heat until hot. Add 2 teaspoons of the olive oil and swirl to coat pan. Add tofu cubes and pan-fry, stirring occasionally, 2 to 3 minutes, until tofu is browned and crisp. Add Worcestershire sauce and stir quickly until it is totally absorbed by tofu. Transfer to a large plate and set aside.

Add carrot, broccoli, and squash to pan and stir-fry 1 minute. Add vegetable stock and bring to a boil. Cover and cook 1 minute. Transfer contents of pan to plate with tofu.

Rinse pan and wipe dry. Add remaining 1 teaspoon oil to pan over high heat. Add shallots and stir-fry 1 minute. Add mushrooms and bok choy and stir-fry 1 minute or until mushrooms are about to release their juices. Add rice, soy sauce, and black pepper and stir-fry until rice is heated through. Return vegetables and tofu to the rice. Stir and mix gently until the whole mixture is heated through. Fold in peanuts and serve immediately.

Per serving: 269 Calories, 9 g Protein, 10 g Total Fat (32% of Calories), 1 g Saturated Fat, 38 g Carbohydrates, 3 g Dietary Fiber, 0 mg Cholesterol, 288 mg Sodium

Curried Fried Rice

Curried rice is a nice change of pace from plain rice. It perks up your taste buds. Accompany it with Tofu and Spinach Soup (page 55) for a light meal.

(page 55)

MAKES 6 SERVINGS

6 ounces skinless, boneless, chicken
   breast, cut into ½-inch cubes
1 teaspoon reduced-sodium soy sauce
1 teaspoon cornstarch
3 teaspoons olive oil
1 medium onion, diced
2 scallions, including tops, sliced into
   thin rings

1 tablespoon curry powder
4 cups cold cooked long-grain rice
2 tablespoons fish sauce or to taste
½ teaspoon sugar
⅓ cup thawed frozen green peas

In a small bowl, combine chicken, soy sauce, and cornstarch and mix until coated. Let stand 15 minutes.

Heat a heavy 10-inch nonstick skillet over high heat until hot. Add 2 teaspoons of the oil and swirl to coat pan. Add chicken cubes and stir-fry 2 minutes or until chicken is white and cooked through. Transfer chicken to a plate.

Add remaining 1 teaspoon oil and heat 15 seconds. Add onion and scallions and stir-fry 1 minute. Add curry powder and cook, stirring, 30 seconds, or until fragrant. Add rice, fish sauce, and sugar; stir-fry until rice is heated through and the seasonings are evenly distributed. Stir chicken into rice. Add peas; stir and toss until mixed. Transfer to a serving platter and serve.

Per serving: 205 Calories, 11 g Protein, 3 g Total Fat (13% of Calories), 0 g Saturated Fat, 33 g Carbohydrates, 1 g Dietary Fiber, 16 mg Cholesterol, 532 mg Sodium

Festival Rice

This is a fried rice that the Chinese prepare for special occasions, such as weddings, New Year celebrations, and festival holidays. It is nutritious and filling, and goes very well with roast chicken or turkey. It also makes a delicious stuffing for chicken or duck.

MAKES 10 SERVINGS

3 cups glutinous rice, rinsed thoroughly and soaked in 6 cups cold water overnight

4 ounces chicken breast, cut into ¾-inch shreds

1 teaspoon dry sherry

1 teaspoon cornstarch

1 tablespoon peanut oil

3 shallots, chopped

⅓ cup dried shrimp, soaked in ⅓ cup hot water 30 minutes, drained, and soaking liquid reserved

10 Chinese dried mushrooms, soaked in hot water 30 minutes, drained, and diced

4 ounces honey ham, cut into ½-inch cubes

1 cup cooked chestnuts, quartered

2 tablespoons reduced-sodium soy sauce

1 teaspoon sugar

Salt and freshly ground pepper to taste

½ cup cooked green peas

Cilantro leaves, for garnish

Drain rice. In a small bowl, combine chicken, sherry, and cornstarch; let stand 15 minutes.

Line a steamer or steaming basket with a double layer of wet cheesecloth or wet muslin; set aside.

Heat a wok or heavy 6-quart deep pot over high heat until hot. Add oil and heat 30 seconds. Add shallots and cook, stirring, 1 minute, or until fragrant. Add the chicken and stir-fry 1 minute, or until cooked through. Add shrimp, mushrooms, ham, and chestnuts and stir-fry until mixture is heated through. Add rice, the shrimp soaking liquid, soy sauce, sugar, salt, and pepper and stir-fry 2 to 3 minutes, until rice is heated through and evenly seasoned.

Transfer rice mixture into the lined steamer and make a small open space in the middle to allow steam to come up to ensure even steaming. Bring water to a boil over high heat, cover, and steam 30 minutes. Taste the rice. If it is still hard, sprinkle some warm water over rice and continue steaming 5 minutes more. Remove heat and let rice stand, covered, an additional 10 minutes. Stir in peas and transfer to a serving bowl. Garnish with cilantro and serve immediately.

Per serving: 301 Calories, 12 g Protein, 2 g Total Fat (7% of Calories), 0 g Saturated Fat, 55 g Carbohydrates, 3 g Dietary Fiber, 31 mg Cholesterol, 381 mg Sodium

TIP

During steaming, it is important to have enough boiling water in the steaming vessel at all times. Place a small dish in the boiling water; it will vibrate and creates a chattering sound from the force of the rolling boiling water. If the dish is quiet, it indicates the boiling water needs to be replenished; otherwise you might burn the bottom of the pot.

Basic Rice Porridge

Rice porridge, made by simmering a small quantity of rice with a large amount of water to produce a creamy gruel, is the basic breakfast for most Chinese and Southeast Asian people. It is warming and soothing and is considered a stabilizing influence on the stomach and digestive tract. It is good when one is feeling a little under the weather.

In China, the porridge is always served in individual rice bowls and accompanied by an assortment of tasty and highly seasoned hot or cold condiments, such as pickled cucumbers or turnips, fermented bean curd, stir-fried vegetables, fish, wheat gluten, soy sauce–cooked peanuts, red-cooked meats or poultry. Also, Western scrambled eggs, bacon, sausages, ham steak, smoked salmon, roasted peanuts, and feta, gorgonzola, or Parmesan cheeses make good accompaniments. Rice porridge is also served as a snack, lunch, or late-night supper.

MAKES 4 SERVINGS

½ cup long-grain or short-grain white rice, rinsed thoroughly

5 cups water, fat-free chicken broth, or vegetable stock

In a heavy 4-quart soup pot, combine rice and water and bring to a boil over high heat. Turn heat to medium-low, partially cover pot, and let rice simmer 10 minutes. Stir rice a few times and reduce heat to very low. Cover and barely simmer until rice is soft and creamy, about 1 to 1½ hours. Remove from heat and let stand 15 to 20 minutes before serving.

Per serving: 84 Calories, 1.6 g Protein, 0.1 g Total Fat (1% of Calories), 0 g Saturated Fat, 18.6 g Carbohydrates, 0.1 g Dietary Fiber, 0 mg Cholesterol, 1 mg Sodium

TIPS

Rice porridge may be made a few hours or a day in advance and refrigerated. It tends to get thick and gummy as it sits. Thin it out with a little boiling water as desired, then reheat over low heat until piping hot. For a thinner porridge, add more water; for a thicker version, reduce the amount of water.

You can also make the porridge with leftover cooked rice, using twice as much liquid as rice.

Fillet of Fish Porridge

This steaming hot rice porridge cooks the thin fillet of fish instantly. The fish used in this dish must be very fresh. In China this is usually served as a breakfast or late-night snack.

MAKES 4 SERVINGS

⅓ cup short-grain white rice, rinsed
   thoroughly
4 cups water
½ pound fresh fillet of flounder or sole,
   cut into thin slices

Salt and freshly ground pepper to taste
Lemon wedges, for garnish
2 tablespoons Crispy Shallots (page
   314), for garnish
½ cup cilantro leaves, for garnish

In a 4-quart saucepan, combine rice and water and bring to a boil over high heat. Reduce heat to medium, partially cover pan, and boil gently 5 minutes. Stir rice a few times, then turn heat to low to maintain a gentle simmer. Cover and simmer about 40 minutes. The porridge is ready when there is no separation of liquid and rice.

Add fish and cook, stirring gently, 30 seconds or until fish turns white, being careful not to break the fish. Remove from heat and season with salt and pepper. Cover and let stand 2 or 3 minutes, then pour into a serving bowl. Serve lemon wedges, crispy shallots, and cilantro in separate small dishes for garnishing.

Per serving: 105 Calories, 11 g Protein, 0.5 g Total Fat (4% of Calories), 0 g Saturated Fat, 13 g Carbohydrates, 0 g Dietary Fiber, 28 mg Cholesterol, 45 mg Sodium

Porridge Taiwanese Style

This exuberant porridge is easy to make. The crunchy, salty preserved Chinese radish perks up this delicate seafood porridge. Serve as a light dinner accompanied by a vegetable dish such as Green Beans with Garlic Sauce (page 88) or Stir-Fried Bok Choy (page 95).

MAKES 6 SERVINGS

1 teaspoon canola oil
4 shallots, cut into thin slices
1 tablespoon dried shrimp
6 ounces lean ground pork
4 ounces preserved Chinese daikon radish, rinsed and coarsely chopped
1 cup short-grain white rice, rinsed
3 quarts water

4 ounces cleaned calamari, each surface scored with crisscross marks and cut into squares
4 ounces sea scallops, cut crosswise into ¼-inch-thick slices
Salt and freshly ground pepper to taste
½ cup finely chopped celery

Heat a heavy 6-quart saucepan over high heat until hot. Add oil and heat 15 seconds. Add shallots and dried shrimp and stir-fry 2 minutes, or until shallots turn light brown. Add ground pork and preserved radish and stir-fry until pork is no longer pink. Transfer contents of pan to a plate and refrigerate.

Add rice and water to pan and bring to a boil. Reduce heat to medium-low, partially cover pan, and cook 5 minutes. Stir rice a few times. Reduce heat to low, cover, and simmer 1 hour, until rice is very creamy. Add calamari, scallops, salt, and pepper; cook, stirring gently, until calamari turns white, about 1 minute. Add pork mixture to rice and stir 30 seconds. Remove pan from heat, cover, and let porridge stand 1 or 2 minutes. Sprinkle in celery and serve.

Per serving: 203 Calories, 15 g Protein, 2 g Total Fat (9% of Calories), 0 g Saturated Fat, 30 g Carbohydrates, 1 g Dietary Fiber, 65 mg Cholesterol, 266 mg Sodium

Daikon Radish Cake

This is a traditional Chinese New Year's dish. Radish cake is served during this holiday season. It tastes especially good when cut into ¹/₂-inch-thick slices and pan-fried crisp on both sides. For a wonderful snack, serve it with Garlic-Soy Dipping Sauce (page 287), if desired.

MAKES 20 SERVINGS

¼ cup dried shrimp, soaked in ¼ cup water 30 minutes
3 tablespoons safflower oil
2 large shallots, thinly sliced
3 pounds Chinese daikon, peeled and cut into chunks

1 pound (4 cups) long-grain rice flour
⅓ cup cornstarch
2 teaspoons salt
1½ teaspoons sugar
½ teaspoon white pepper

Preheat oven to 350F (175C). Coat an 8-inch-square glass baking dish with cooking spray; set aside. Drain shrimp, reserving soaking liquid.

Heat a medium frying pan over medium heat until hot. Add 1 tablespoon of the oil and heat 15 seconds. Add shallots and shrimp and stir until aromatic and shallots are light brown; set aside.

In a food processor fitted with the steel blade, puree daikon until very smooth, about 1 minute, scraping down sides of bowl as necessary. Add rice flour, cornstarch, remaining 2 tablespoons oil, salt, sugar, and pepper and process until very smooth, about 1 minute.

Transfer mixture to the prepared baking dish. Scrape in the shallot mixture and its oil and stir briefly. Cover with foil. Place in a 13 × 9-inch baking pan filled with 1 quart of boiling water. Bake 2 hours, or until a wooden pick or tester inserted into the center comes out clean. Remove from water and let stand, covered, until lukewarm, about 1 hour. Cut into ½-inch-thick slices and serve.

Per serving: 129 Calories, 3 g Protein, 2.2 g Total Fat (15% of Calories), 0.2 g Saturated Fat, 24 g Carbohydrates, 2 g Dietary Fiber, 8 mg Cholesterol, 280 mg Sodium

Basic Rice Dumpling Dough

The dough is easy to make and you can serve the dumplings as snacks or desserts. The dumplings may be prepared one day in advance; refrigerate covered and cook just before serving.

MAKES I POUND RICE DUMPLING DOUGH

8 ounces (2 cups) glutinous rice flour
1 teaspoon safflower oil

½ cup cold water
¼ cup boiling water

To make by hand: In a medium bowl, combine rice flour, oil, and cold water and stir with chopsticks until water is absorbed. Add boiling water and continue stirring until flour becomes a coarse meal. Mix and squeeze with your hands until a dough forms.

To make in a food processor: Combine flour, oil, and cold water in a food processor fitted with the steel blade; process 15 seconds. Add boiling water and process until a dough forms, about 30 seconds. If dough is too soft, add more flour by tablespoons. If dough is too stiff, add more water by tablespoons.

Per recipe: 879 Calories, 14 g Protein, 5 g Total Fat (5% of Calories), 0 g Saturated Fat, 189 g Carbohydrates, 7 g Dietary Fiber, 0 mg Cholesterol, 105 mg Sodium

Sweet Rice Dumplings

$\int$ymbolic of joy and reunion, these little dumplings are traditional New Year and wedding celebration treats.

1 recipe Basic Rice Dumpling Dough   6 tablespoons honey
  (opposite page)

Divide dough in half. Roll each half into a 15-inch-long log, then cut each log crosswise into 15 pieces (or you can cut it into smaller sizes if you wish). Roll each piece in your palms to form a round ball.

Bring 8 cups of water to a rolling boil in a heavy 4-quart pot. Drop in the balls, a few at a time, and gently stir a few times to prevent sticking to the bottom. Simmer over medium heat about 5 minutes, or until they spin and float to the top of the water. Scoop them into 6 individual bowls. Cover with 1 cup of cooking water and sweeten with 1 tablespoon honey for each bowl.

Per serving: 147 Calories, 2 g Protein, 0.7 g Total Fat (5% of Calories), 0 g Saturated Fat, 31 g Carbohydrates, 1 g Dietary Fiber, 0 mg Cholesterol, 17 mg Sodium

Sesame Paste-Filled Dumplings

When you bite into one of these, the sweet wonderful flavor of the black sesame paste is like finding a delicious prize.

MAKES 6 SERVINGS

½ cup black sesame seed powder
½ cup sugar
2 tablespoons honey

1 tablespoon oriental sesame oil
1 recipe Basic Rice Dumpling Dough
(page 230)

In a small bowl, combine sesame seed powder, sugar, honey, and sesame oil. Stir until they come together and form a paste. Chill paste in refrigerator 30 minutes, or until firm. Divide paste into 30 portions and roll them in your palms to form small balls.

Divide dough in half. Roll each half into a 15-inch-long log; then cut each log crosswise into 15 pieces. Press each piece of dough into a small disk. Place a ball of sesame seed paste in the center, wrap dough around sesame paste by bringing the sides together and pinching to seal, then roll in your palms to make a small ball. Repeat until all 30 dumplings are formed.

Bring 8 cups of water to a rolling boil in a heavy 4-quart pot. Drop in balls, a few at a time, and gently stir a few times to prevent sticking to the bottom. Simmer over medium heat about 5 minutes, or until they spin and float to the top of the water. Scoop them into 6 individual bowls. Serve dumplings hot with some of the cooking water.

Per serving: 304 Calories, 4 g Protein, 7 g Total Fat (24% of Calories), 1 g Saturated Fat, 55 g Carbohydrates, 2 g Dietary Fiber, 0 mg Cholesterol, 20 mg Sodium

VARIATIONS

You can dye half of the dough with 1 drop red food coloring to make pink rice balls.

Replace sesame seed paste balls with about 1 cup canned sweetened red bean paste to make steamed Red Bean Paste–Filled Dumplings.

Cold Noodle Salad

Seasoned by a scrumptious sauce, this noodle salad is rich and full of nutty flavor and aroma.

MAKES 6 SERVINGS

Sesame Dressing (see below)
1/2 pound dried Chinese white noodles
2 tablespoons toasted sesame seeds
Cilantro sprigs, for garnish

SESAME DRESSING

2 tablespoons oriental sesame paste
1 teaspoon minced fresh garlic

2 tablespoons reduced-sodium soy sauce
2 teaspoons sugar
1/2 cup hot fat-free, low-sodium chicken broth or vegetable stock
1/8 teaspoon ground Sichuan peppercorns
1 tablespoon oriental sesame oil
Salt and cayenne pepper to taste

Prepare dressing: Place all ingredients in a blender and process until smooth; set aside.

In a 6-quart pot, bring 4 quarts water to a boil. Cook noodles until just tender to the bite, about 4 minutes. Drain and rinse with cold water until noodles are cold. Drain thoroughly. Place noodles in a large serving bowl.

Add sesame dressing to noodles and toss to mix. Sprinkle sesame seeds on top and garnish with cilantro. Serve at room temperature or chilled.

Per serving: 185 Calories, 6 g Protein, 8 g Total Fat (39% of Calories), 1 g Saturated Fat, 22 g Carbohydrates, 1 g Dietary Fiber, 4 mg Cholesterol, 422 mg Sodium

Sichuan Noodle Salad with Chicken

*T*his nutty and spicy noodle salad makes an excellent summer meal.

MAKES 6 SERVINGS

Sichuan Sesame Dressing (see below)
½ pound dried Chinese white noodles
1 to 2 cups cooked chicken, shredded
1 small firm cucumber, peeled, seeded,
    and shredded
1 cup thinly shredded carrots
1 cup shredded tender celery
2 tablespoons toasted sesame seeds

SICHUAN SESAME DRESSING

3 tablespoons oriental sesame paste
3 tablespoons reduced-sodium soy
    sauce

1 tablespoon rice wine vinegar
2 teaspoons sugar
1 tablespoon oriental sesame oil
½ cup hot fat-free, low-sodium chicken
    broth
1 teaspoon canola oil
2 tablespoons finely sliced scallion,
    white part only
½ tablespoon finely minced fresh ginger
½ tablespoon minced garlic
2 small red chilies, seeded and finely
    chopped

Prepare dressing: In a medium bowl, combine sesame paste, soy sauce, vinegar, sugar, sesame oil, and chicken broth and stir until smooth; set aside. Heat a 7-inch frying pan over medium heat until hot. Add canola oil and swirl to coat pan. Add scallion, ginger, garlic, and chilies and cook, stirring, until aromatic, about 20 seconds. Add sesame paste mixture and stir until sauce is combined. Transfer to a small serving bowl; set aside.

In a 6-quart pot, bring 4 quarts water to a boil, cook noodles until just tender to the bite, about 4 minutes. Drain and rinse with cold water until noodles are cold. Drain thoroughly. Place noodles in a large serving bowl.

To serve, arrange chicken, vegetables, sesame seeds, sesame dressing, and noodles in separate dishes in the center of the table. Diners can select their own salad ingredients and toss them on their own plates.

Per serving: 282 Calories, 16 g Protein, 12 g Total Fat (39% of Calories), 2 g Saturated Fat, 29 g Carbohydrates, 3 g Dietary Fiber, 24 mg Cholesterol, 576 mg Sodium

TIPS

Undercook the noodles a trifle, or until just barely tender to the bite. They will soften a bit more after draining. Chinese fresh noodles take only about 3 minutes to cook. Chinese dried noodles take 4 to 5 minutes to cook. To cook the noodles to the desired tenderness, keep tasting them during the cooking. After doing this several times you will be able to judge the cooking time.

Stir-Fried Rice Noodles

Chinese rice noodles are very thin, like angel hair pasta, but are more absorbent. Stir-fried in this recipe, they make a tasty light meal. Serve them with Stuffed Cucumber Soup (page 48) for a delicious lunch.

8 ounces dried Chinese rice sticks (rice vermicelli)

3 teaspoons canola oil

6 ounces chicken breast, shredded

4 Chinese dried mushrooms, soaked in warm water 30 minutes, drained, and shredded

½ cup shredded carrot

2 cups tightly packed shredded napa cabbage

⅓ cup water

2 scallions, including tops, cut into 1-inch lengths, white and green parts separated

1 cup fat-free, low-sodium chicken broth

2 tablespoons reduced-sodium soy sauce

Salt and freshly ground white pepper to taste

Soak noodles in cold water 35 minutes, until they are soft and separate easily. Drain well and set aside.

Heat a nonstick wok or heavy 6-quart nonstick pot over medium-high heat until hot. Add 1 teaspoon of the oil, swirl to coat pan, and heat 15 seconds. Add chicken and stir-fry about 2 minutes, or until chicken is white and cooked through. Transfer to a large plate and set aside.

Return pan to heat. Add mushrooms and carrot and stir-fry a few seconds. Add cabbage and water and stir-fry over high heat 1 minute, or until cabbage is softened. Transfer vegetables to plate with chicken.

Rinse pan and wipe dry. Return pan to high heat until hot. Add remaining 2 teaspoons oil and swirl to coat pan. Add white parts of scallions and cook, stirring, a few seconds, or until aromatic. Add chicken broth, soy sauce, and rice noodles. Slide a wooden spatula beneath the noodles, gently shaking and bringing them to the top, and repeat a few times, being careful not to break the noodles. Add salt and white pepper, if desired. Return chicken and vegetables to noodles. Add green parts of scallions and stir gently a few times. Cover, reduce heat to low, and simmer 2 to 3 minutes, or until all the liquid is absorbed. Transfer to a heated serving dish and serve.

Per serving: 376 Calories, 22 g Protein, 6 g Total Fat (14% of Calories), 1 g Saturated Fat, 60 g Carbohydrates, 3 g Dietary Fiber, 42 mg Cholesterol, 389 mg Sodium

TIPS

When opening the package of dried rice noodles, do so in a large grocery bag so they do not fly all over the kitchen.

The soaked rice noodles can also be cooked in chicken broth with meats and vegetables to make noodle soup.

Noodles with Spicy Peanut Sauce

This dish was very popular at our restaurant. It is easy to prepare and can be served as an appetizer, side dish, or entree if accompanied by shredded vegetables and meats. It is very satisfying. Serve this dish warm, at room temperature, or chilled.

MAKES 4 SERVINGS

⅓ cup smooth reduced-fat peanut butter
2 teaspoons minced garlic
½ cup fat-free, low-sodium chicken broth or water
2 tablespoons reduced-sodium soy sauce
¼ cup red wine vinegar

1 teaspoon honey
Hot chili sauce to taste
1 teaspoon oriental sesame oil
½ pound dried Chinese white noodles
2 tender celery stalks, finely shredded
½ cucumber, peeled, seeded, and shredded

In a small saucepan, heat peanut butter and garlic, stirring, until peanut butter dissolves and garlic is aromatic, about 1 minute. Add chicken broth or water, soy sauce, vinegar, honey, chili sauce, and sesame oil; simmer 1 minute. Cover and set aside.

In a 6-quart pot, bring 4 quarts water to a boil. Cook noodles until just tender to the bite, about 4 minutes. Drain and rinse with cold water until noodles are cold. Drain thoroughly. Place noodles in a large serving bowl.

Add peanut butter mixture to noodles and toss to combine. Garnish with shredded celery and cucumbers and serve immediately.

Per serving: 312 Calories, 11 g Protein, 9 g Total Fat (27% of Calories), 2 g Saturated Fat, 47 g Carbohydrates, 4 g Dietary Fiber, 0 mg Cholesterol, 710 mg Sodium

TIPS

Always cook noodles just before serving because noodles get soft and pasty after standing for hours. Always use plenty of water to cook noodles, at least 2 inches above the noodles.

Stir-Fried Singapore Noodles

This is a full-flavored, mouth-warming dish, using Chinese rice noodles. It is flavored with Indian curry spice and has small treasures of intensely flavored golden shrimp and shreds of tasty Chinese Barbecued Pork. It makes a perfect lunch or snack. Serve it with a leafy vegetable such as stir-fried napa or bok choy.

MAKES 4 SERVINGS

1 tablespoon canola oil
1 tablespoon dried shrimp, soaked in ¼ cup warm water, drained, and soaking liquid reserved
1 medium onion, cut into thin wedges
½ cup thinly shredded carrot
1 cup thinly shredded celery
1 tablespoon curry powder

1 cup fat-free, low-sodium chicken broth
1 teaspoon salt
8 ounces dried Chinese rice noodles, soaked in cold water 35 minutes and drained
1 cup thinly shredded Chinese Barbecued Pork (page 202) or deli ham

Heat a heavy 10-inch nonstick frying pan over medium-high heat until hot. Add oil, swirl to coat pan, and heat 15 seconds. Add shrimp and onion and stir-fry 1 minute, or until aromatic. Add carrot and celery and stir-fry until the vegetables are heated through. Add curry powder and stir-fry until aromatic, about 30 seconds.

Add chicken broth, salt, and reserved shrimp soaking liquid and bring to a boil. Add rice noodles and stir gently in turning and folding motions until all seasonings and vegetables are evenly distributed. Reduce heat to low, cover, and simmer 2 to 3 minutes, or until liquid is absorbed by the noodles. Fold in barbecued pork or ham and stir a few more times. Transfer to a serving platter and serve.

Per serving: 402 Calories, 19 g Protein, 10 g Total Fat (26% of Calories), 2 g Saturated Fat, 59 g Carbohydrates, 2 g Dietary Fiber, 52 mg Cholesterol, 661 mg Sodium

Lo Mein Noodles

Lo mein, meaning "stir-fried noodles" in Guangdong dialect, are well seasoned and entwined with pieces of juicy meat and crisp vegetables. They make a scrumptious snack, main course, or side dish. To prepare this dish successfully you must drain the noodles well and spread them out to dry a little until firm and no more moisture droplets remain. Use a high-quality cooking utensil that conducts high heat rapidly and cook and toss with spirited motions. The whole stir-frying process should only take 4 to 5 minutes.

MAKES 4 SERVINGS

½ pound fresh Chinese egg noodles
1 tablespoon canola oil
2 thin slices ginger
1 clove garlic, crushed and coarsely chopped
2 scallions, including tops, cut into 2-inch lengths
1 cup shredded chicken breast, or thigh meat or seafood

1 tablespoon dry sherry
½ cup thinly shredded carrot
2 cups thinly sliced bok choy
2 teaspoons reduced-sodium soy sauce
1 tablespoon premium oyster sauce
½ teaspoon sugar
2 cups fresh bean sprouts

Bring a large pot of water to a rolling boil over high heat. Add noodles and stir with chopsticks to separate and untangle them. Cook about 3 minutes, or until just barely tender to the bite. Drain immediately and rinse with cold water to stop cooking. Drain thoroughly. Spread noodles out on a baking sheet to dry 30 minutes.

Heat a heavy 10-inch nonstick skillet over high heat until hot. Add oil and heat 30 seconds. Add ginger, garlic, and scallions and stir-fry a few seconds; do not let garlic burn. Add chicken and stir-fry 1 minute. Add sherry and stir-fry 15 seconds. Add carrot and bok choy and stir-fry 1 minute. Make a well in the center, add soy sauce, oyster sauce, and sugar and stir-fry a few times.

Add noodles and immediately slide a wooden spatula from the side of the pan beneath the noodles, chicken, and vegetables, and mix by raising them up and shaking the spatula from side to side to drop them back into the pan. Repeat these sweeping motions until noodles are heated through. Add bean sprouts and toss and stir 45 seconds. Transfer to a heated serving dish and serve immediately.

Per serving: 309 Calories, 26 g Protein, 6 g Total Fat (17% of Calories), 1 g Saturated Fat, 37 g Carbohydrates, 3 g Dietary Fiber, 55 mg Cholesterol, 801 mg Sodium

Shrimp and Scallops on Crispy Noodles

Here the noodles are first boiled, then pan-fried like a noodle pancake until crisp and brown on both sides. They are then topped with a shrimp, scallop, and vegetable mixture and served. This is an all-time favorite for both Easterners and Westerners.

MAKES 4 SERVINGS

½ pound thin fresh Chinese egg noodles

8 jumbo shrimp, peeled, deveined, and halved lengthwise

2 teaspoons cornstarch

2 tablespoons plus 4 teaspoons dry sherry

8 large sea scallops, cut crosswise into ¼-inch-thick slices

1 tablespoon plus 1 teaspoon peanut oil

2 scallions, including tops, cut into 1-inch lengths

2 thin slices fresh ginger

6 Chinese dried mushrooms, soaked in hot water 30 minutes, drained, and shredded

½ cup sliced carrot

1 small summer squash, cut crosswise into ¼-inch-thick slices

2 cups fat-free, low-sodium chicken broth

2 tablespoons reduced-sodium soy sauce

½ teaspoon sugar

Salt and freshly ground black pepper to taste

¼ pound (about 3 cups) baby bok choy or spinach, blanched

2 tablespoons cornstarch dissolved in 2 tablespoons water

1 teaspoon oriental sesame oil

In a 6-quart pot, bring 4 quarts water to a boil. Cook noodles until just tender to the bite, about 3 minutes. Rinse with cool water, then drain well. Spread noodles out to dry on a baking sheet 30 to 60 minutes. This may be done in advance and the noodles refrigerated.

In a medium bowl, combine shrimp, 1 teaspoon of the cornstarch, and 2 teaspoons of the sherry. In another small bowl, combine scallops, remaining 1 teaspoon cornstarch, and 2 teaspoons of the sherry. Set both aside 15 minutes.

Heat a 10-inch heavy nonstick frying pan over high heat until hot. Add 1 tablespoon of the oil, swirl to coat pan, and heat 30 seconds. Add noodles, coiling them into a large pancake, and pan-fry 1 minute, pressing noodles with a spatula frequently. Reduce heat to medium-high and continue to fry, pressing and jiggling pan frequently, about 4 minutes, or until bottom is brown and crisp. Flip noodle nest over and fry another 4 minutes, or until this side is as crisp as the other side. Transfer to a hot large shallow serving platter.

Heat remaining 1 teaspoon oil in the skillet over high heat until hot. Add scallions and ginger and stir-fry 15 seconds. Add mushrooms, carrot, and squash and stir-fry 1 minute. Add chicken broth, remaining 2 tablespoons sherry, soy sauce, sugar, salt, and pepper and bring to a boil. Spread shrimp and scallops evenly on top of vegetables, cover, and cook 1 minute, or until shrimp are pink. Add bok choy or spinach and stir gently to distribute. Stir cornstarch mixture and stir into seafood mixture. Cook, stirring gently, until sauce is slightly thickened. Drizzle in sesame oil, then transfer contents of pan onto top of the crisp noodle pancake. Cut pan-fried noodle pancake into wedges for easy serving.

Per serving: 354 Calories, 25 g Protein, 7 g Total Fat (18% of Calories), 1 g Saturated Fat, 47 g Carbohydrates, 5 g Dietary Fiber, 79 mg Cholesterol, 891 mg Sodium

Noodles with Clam Sauce

*T*hese clams are stir-fried in their shells with seasonings and steam-cooked briefly until their shells open. Then freshly cooked noodles are added and tossed in the clam sauce. This dish is absolutely delicious.

MAKES 4 SERVINGS

3 teaspoons olive oil
1 green bell pepper, cut into small
    squares
½ red bell pepper, cut into small
    squares
2 scallions, white part only, cut into
    1-inch lengths
2 thin slices ginger
1 teaspoon minced garlic
1 small red chili, thinly sliced (optional)
2 tablespoons Chinese fermented black
    beans

4 tablespoons dry sherry
1 cup water
1 tablespoon reduced-sodium soy sauce
    or to taste
2 teaspoons premium oyster sauce
1 teaspoon sugar
Freshly ground pepper to taste
24 littleneck clams, scrubbed clean
¾ pound fresh noodles

Heat a heavy 10-inch nonstick frying pan over high heat until hot. Add 1 teaspoon of the oil and swirl to coat pan. Add bell peppers and stir-fry 1 minute, or until their color brightens and peppers are heated through. Transfer to a plate and set aside.

Add remaining 2 teaspoons oil to pan over medium-high heat, swirl to coat pan and heat 15 seconds. Add scallions, ginger, garlic, chili, if using, and black beans and stir-fry 45 seconds, or until fragrant. Add sherry, water, soy sauce, oyster sauce, sugar, pepper, and clams. Cover and steam-cook over high heat 3 to 4 minutes, or until shells have opened. Discard any clams that do not open. Add bell peppers to clams. Remove from heat and cover partially to keep warm.

Meanwhile, in a 6-quart pot, bring 4 quarts water to a boil. Cook noodles until just tender to the bite, about 3 minutes. Drain noodles and add them to the clams. Toss to distribute evenly. Serve immediately.

Per serving: 362 Calories, 15 g Protein, 5 g Total Fat (13% of Calories), 1 g Saturated Fat, 60 g Carbohydrates, 3 g Dietary Fiber, 34 mg Cholesterol, 828 mg Sodium

VARIATIONS

Substitute mussels or a 1½-pound live lobster, cut up, for the clams.

Grilled Tofu with Sesame Noodles

This rich flavorful grilled tofu is reminiscent of barbecued beef and pork, but does not contain any cholesterol and is low in fat. Served with an array of fruits and vegetables, this dish makes a healthy meal.

MAKES 6 SERVINGS

4 tablespoons reduced-sodium soy sauce

1 tablespoon dry sherry

1 tablespoon premium oyster sauce

1 tablespoon hoisin sauce

1 teaspoon light brown sugar

1 teaspoon minced garlic

½ teaspoon five-spice powder

1½ pounds extra-firm tofu, cut into 12 (½-inch-thick) slices

¾ pound dried Chinese white noodles

1 tablespoon oriental sesame oil

1 teaspoon granulated sugar

½ cup fat-free, low-sodium chicken broth

1 tablespoon toasted sesame seeds

2 pears, peeled, cored, and sliced

3 carrots, blanched and shredded

2 to 3 scallions, including tops, thinly sliced

In a small bowl, combine 1 tablespoon of the soy sauce, sherry, oyster sauce, hoisin sauce, brown sugar, garlic, and five-spice powder and stir until blended; set aside.

Heat a heavy 10-inch nonstick frying pan over high heat until hot. Spray pan with cooking spray. Fry tofu slices 2 to 3 minutes per side, or until light brown. Remove pan from heat and let cool slightly. Cover tofu with the soy sauce mixture, making sure each piece is evenly coated. Refrigerate at least 30 minutes or up to 2 hours, turning several times.

In a 6-quart pot, bring 4 quarts water to a boil. Cook noodles until just tender to the bite, about 4 minutes. Drain and rinse with cold water until noodles are cold. Drain thoroughly. Place noodles in a large pasta bowl and add remaining 3 tablespoons soy sauce, sesame oil, sugar, and chicken broth. Toss and mix well. Sprinkle sesame seeds on top.

Heat a grill until hot and spray rack with cooking spray. Grill tofu slices, basting several times, until grill marks show on both sides.

Place tofu on the noodles and arrange pears, carrots, and scallions in separate dishes around the pasta bowl. Diners can help themselves, making up their own plates.

Per serving: 320 Calories, 15 g Protein, 6 g Total Fat (17% of Calories), 1 g Saturated Fat, 51 g Carbohydrates, 4 g Dietary Fiber, 0 mg Cholesterol, 811 mg Sodium

Chicken Noodle Soup

We served this soup on our lunch buffet table at our restaurant. Some customers came in just for this soup, and consumed two or three bowls of it for lunch.

⅓ pound dried Chinese rice sticks (rice vermicelli), soaked in cold water 30 minutes

4 Chinese dried mushrooms, soaked in ¾ cup hot water 30 minutes

1 tablespoon canola oil

2 scallions, including tops, thinly sliced, white and green parts separated

2 stalks celery, chopped

2 carrots, peeled and shredded

½ teaspoon white pepper, or to taste

5 cups fat-free, low-sodium chicken broth

1 tablespoon reduced-sodium soy sauce

1 cup diced cooked chicken

Salt and freshly ground black pepper (optional)

Drain noodles and set aside. Drain mushrooms and squeeze to remove excess water, reserving the soaking liquid. Cut the mushrooms caps into thin shreds and set aside.

Heat a 4-quart heavy soup pot over medium-high heat until hot. Add oil, swirl to coat pan, and heat 15 seconds. Add white parts of scallions, stir briefly, and let cook until aromatic, about 15 seconds. Add mushrooms, celery, carrots, and white pepper and stir-fry until aromatic, 2 minutes. Add chicken broth, soy sauce, and mushroom soaking liquid and bring to a boil. Add rice noodles, stir gently a few times, and bring to a boil again. Reduce heat, add chicken, and simmer 2 minutes. Add green parts of scallions. Taste and adjust seasonings with salt and pepper, if desired. Serve immediately.

Per serving: 211 Calories, 12 g Protein, 4 g Total Fat (18% of Calories), 1 g Saturated Fat, 32 g Carbohydrates, 2 g Dietary Fiber, 21 mg Cholesterol, 202 mg Sodium

Notes: When cooked, rice noodles break easily, so stir gently just to blend.

Rice noodles made in China and rice noodles made in Thailand or Vietnam are slightly different. The latter require heating only a minute or two; once softened in the hot broth, remove from heat to avoid overcooking them.

Breads and Buns

 Dumplings, breads, buns, and pancakes occupy an important place in Chinese cooking. Because homes in China did not have ovens, the Chinese relied on a steamer or a flat iron griddle to make their breads. Even today, in China, one is enticed by the aroma of flaky Scallion Pancakes from a far-away street vendor.

If you can bake breads you can make these oriental breads and buns. They are different from Western-style baked goods, but they are deliciously different and nutritionally sound.

Basic Steamed Bun Dough

Steamed buns are to northern China what rice is to southern China—the carbohydrate staple of the region. Since the dough is steamed, not baked, there is no crust on the bun, just a delicious white, soft, resilient bread.

MAKES ABOUT $1^1/_2$ POUNDS OF DOUGH

1 teaspoon active dry yeast
1 cup lukewarm water
3 tablespoons sugar
1 tablespoon safflower oil

¾ cup bread flour
2½ cups all-purpose flour
1 teaspoon baking powder

Food-processor method: Combine yeast, warm water, sugar, and oil in the work bowl of a food processor fitted with the steel blade. Let stand 10 minutes, or until foamy. Add flours and process until dough forms a mass and pulls away from the sides of the work bowl, about 1 minute. Let rest 15 minutes. Then process again 30 seconds.

Turn dough out onto a lightly floured board. Knead by hand 3 minutes, until dough is smooth, elastic, and fingertip firm. If dough is sticky, add a dusting of flour.

Hand method: In a small bowl, combine yeast, water, sugar, and oil and stir to dissolve the yeast. Let stand 10 minutes, or until foamy.

In a large bowl, whisk flours together. Mound flour mixture on a work surface; make a deep well in the center. Add 2 tablespoons of dissolved yeast mixture to well. With two fingers, stir in flour from walls of well gradually. When water is absorbed and a paste formed, repeat with more yeast mixture until you have a soft but not sticky dough. Knead dough on a lightly floured surface 10 to 15 minutes, until dough is smooth, elastic, and fingertip firm.

Place dough in a lightly oiled large bowl three times the size of the dough, turning once to coat both sides of dough with oil. Seal bowl with plastic wrap and let rise until dough doubles in volume, about 1 hour, and a fingertip indentation does not spring back.

Punch down dough until flat. Reseal bowl and let dough double in volume a second time. The second rising is not necessary, but it will produce a distinctly lighter bread.

Punch down dough and turn onto a lightly floured surface. Flatten it with the palm of your hand. Sprinkle baking powder over surface. Fold dough over and knead vigorously 5 minutes, incorporating baking powder and restoring dough to its original smooth, elastic, and finger-tip-firm texture. Dust work surface with flour when necessary. Now the dough is ready to be shaped into buns and rolls.

Silver Thread Rolls

This is the most interesting bread I have ever seen among the Eastern and Western breads. The whole oblong bread looks like an ordinary small loaf on the outside, but when it is sliced open, the inside is completely filled with thin threads of dough, like cutting a spaghetti squash. In northern China this steamed bread is known as a "silver thread roll." Sometimes the roll is deep fried until the outside is golden and crisp, and it becomes a "golden roll." Children especially love this bread because they like the fun of picking out the threads and eating them. It may sound complicated, but once you make this once, you will find it easy to repeat.

MAKES 4 ROLLS

1 recipe Basic Steamed Bun Dough (page 250)

Flour, for dusting
Cooking spray

Shape dough into a 16-inch-long log. With a sharp knife cut the log into 8 equal pieces, dusting each piece with flour to prevent sticking. With the help of a ruler, roll first 4 pieces into 6 × 4-inch rectangles, dusting board if dough sticks. Spray rectangle tops with cooking spray, then fold each rectangle in half to make 4 (3 × 4-inch) rectangles. Spray again with cooking spray, then fold each in half again to yield 4 (1½ × 4-inch) rectangles. Cover with a dry towel and set aside.

Roll remaining 4 pieces of dough into 6 x 4-inch rectangles, cover with a dry towel, and set aside.

With a sharp knife, shred each of the folded rectangles crosswise into ¼-inch-wide strips, cutting through to the board and leaving shreds side by side without separating them, making 4 groups of shredded strips. Cover with a dry towel and let rest 5 to 10 minutes.

Working with 1 group of shreds and 1 smooth rectangle at a time, pick up ⅓ of the shreds, grasping them by their folded ends, then very gently stretch them until they are about 5½ inches long. Place them in the middle of a smooth rectangle, lengthwise, then anchor them to the rectangle by pressing edges of shreds to adhere to ends of smooth rectangle. Grasp, stretch, and anchor second third, then final third, piling them on top each time. Now pick up the sides of smooth rectangle parallel to shreds and fold them over the shreds, then overlap sides a little to seal. Now carefully turn whole package over to keep seam side down; pinch the 2 ends shut and tuck them under dough. Now you have a smooth oblong loaf of dough filled with dough shreds. Repeat process with remaining 3 sets of dough.

Place rolls on a steaming rack sprayed with cooking spray, leaving 2 to 3 inches between them for expansion. Cover with a clean dry towel and let rise until light and springy to the touch, 30 to 60 minutes, depending on the temperature of the room.

Bring the water in the steamer to a vigorous boil over high heat. Steam buns over high heat 15 minutes. Remove from heat and wait 5 minutes before opening steamer. Uncover and transfer buns to a platter. Do not let water droplets on lid fall on buns.

Per roll: 404 Calories, 10 g Protein, 4 g Total Fat (10% of Calories), 0 g Saturated Fat, 80 g Carbohydrates, 2 g Dietary Fiber, 0 mg Cholesterol, 53 mg Sodium

Chinese Barbecued Pork Buns

This is a very popular snack or appetizer item in Chinese restaurants known as *Char Shao Bao*. The filling is a luscious sweet brown gravy with bits of barbecued pork. The filling can be made a day in advance and refrigerated. This smooth, cotton-soft, springy roast pork bun is so delicious that you can sink your teeth into it with great satisfaction.

MAKES 20 BUNS

1 tablespoon all-purpose flour
1 tablespoon cornstarch
¾ cup water
2 tablespoons reduced-sodium soy sauce
1 tablespoon premium oyster sauce
1 tablespoon hoisin sauce
1 tablespoon sugar

½ teaspoon salt
1 tablespoon oriental sesame oil
10 ounces Chinese Barbecued Pork (page 202), diced into ¼-inch cubes (2 cups)
Flour, for dipping
1 recipe Basic Steamed Bun Dough (page 250)

In a small saucepan, dissolve flour and cornstarch in ¾ cup water. Add soy sauce, oyster sauce, hoisin sauce, sugar, salt, and sesame oil. Cook over medium heat, stirring constantly, until sauce thickens, about 3 minutes. Add diced pork and stir to mix well. Remove from heat to cool slightly. Transfer to a bowl, cover, and refrigerate 2 hours or longer, until mixture is cold and firm.

Divide dough in half and, using the palms of your hands, roll each piece of dough into a 10-inch-long log. Cut each log crosswise into 1-inch-thick pieces. Dip cut sides in flour and press pieces with your palm to flatten them slightly. Roll out each one into a 4½-inch disk, making the center slightly thicker than the edges.

Put 1 disk in your cupped hand and mound 1 tablespoon of filling in the center. Pleat the edges of the disk firmly all around filling and bring all sides of the disk up around filling to enclose it, with the pleats coming together at the top. Pinch and twirl the pleats into a tiny knot on top to seal. Repeat with remaining dough and filling. Place finished buns, 1 inch apart, on a lightly floured baking sheet. Cover with a dry towel and let buns rise 20 to 30 minutes, depending on the temperature of the room.

Place buns on a steaming rack sprayed with cooking spray, leaving 1 inch between them. Bring water in steamer to a vigorous boil over high heat. Steam buns over high heat 15 minutes. Remove from heat and wait 5 minutes before opening steamer. Uncover and transfer buns to a platter. Do not let water droplets on lid fall on buns.

Serve immediately, refrigerate 3 to 4 days, or freeze up to 1 month. Reheat by steaming until piping hot, or microwave, covered.

Per bun: 134 Calories, 6 g Protein, 3.6 g Total Fat (24% of Calories), 0.9 g Saturated Fat, 19 g Carbohydrates, 0 g Dietary Fiber, 13 mg Cholesterol, 255 mg Sodium

VARIATION

Substitute drained, cooked lean ground pork or turkey or 2 cups Chinese canned sweetened red bean paste for barbecued pork.

Steamed Miniature Buns

These dainty petite buns are filled with a meat-and-jellied-stock mixture. During steaming the jelly melts into a delicious gravy, resulting in a luscious juicy bun. Be cautious of the steaming hot juice when biting into the buns; sometimes they squirt or drip on your clothes. They make a satisfying snack, or serve them in soup as "soup buns" (see Variation, opposite page) for a light meal.

MAKES 24 BUNS

½ cup Jellied Meat Stock (see opposite), finely diced
12 ounces lean ground turkey or pork
1 large scallion, including top, finely sliced
2½ tablespoons reduced-sodium soy sauce
1 tablespoon dry sherry
Salt and freshly ground pepper to taste
1 teaspoon oriental sesame oil

1 tablespoon cornstarch dissolved in ¼ cup water
1 recipe Basic Steamed Bun Dough (page 250)
Ginger Sauce I (page 288) (optional)

JELLIED MEAT STOCK

1 (¼-oz.) package unflavored gelatin
2 cups fat-free chicken or meat stock

Prepare Jellied Meat Stock: In a small saucepan, sprinkle gelatin over ½ cup of the stock and let stand 1 minute. Add the remaining 1½ cups stock and boil over medium heat, stirring constantly, until gelatin is completely dissolved. Pour into a bowl; chill until firm, about two hours. Makes 2 cups.

In a medium bowl, combine turkey or pork with scallion, soy sauce, sherry, salt, pepper, sesame oil, and cornstarch mixture and mix thoroughly. Fold in the jelly stock. Cover and chill in the refrigerator 2 hours to firm up the mixture.

Divide dough into 2 pieces. On a lightly floured board, roll each piece into a smooth 12-inch-long log, then slice it crosswise into 1-inch-thick pieces. Dip the cut sides in flour and press pieces with your palm to flatten them slightly. Roll each into a 3½-inch disk, making the center thicker than the edge.

Put 1 disk in your cupped hand and mound 1 teaspoon of filling in the center. Pleat the edges of the disk firmly all around filling and bring all sides of the disk up around filling to enclose it, with the pleats coming together at the top. Pinch and twirl the pleats into a tiny knot on top to seal. Repeat with remaining dough and filling.

Place buns, pleated side up, on a steaming rack coated with cooking spray, leaving ¾ inch between them. Bring water in steamer to a vigorous boil over high heat. Steam buns over high heat 15 minutes. Remove from heat and wait 5 minutes before opening steamer. Uncover and transfer buns to a platter. Do not let water droplets on lid fall on buns. Serve immediately with Ginger Sauce, if desired.

Per bun: 91 Calories, 4 g Protein, 1.3 g Total Fat (12% of Calories), 0.2 g Saturated Fat, 15 g Carbohydrates, 0 g Dietary Fiber, 8 mg Cholesterol, 175 mg Sodium

VARIATION
SOUP BUNS

Heat a heavy 3-quart soup pot until hot. Add 1 teaspoon oil and swirl to coat pan. Add 1 sliced scallion and 1 cup sliced mushrooms and stir-fry until aromatic. Add 6 cups fat-free, low-sodium chicken broth and bring to a boil. Add ½ cup shredded egg sheet and 4 ounces spinach leaves and cook 1 minute. Divide buns among 4 large soup bowls; ladle soup and vegetables over buns. Serve immediately.

Boiled Meat Dumplings (Shui Jiao)

These dumplings are made with a cold-water dough so that during cooking the dough can withstand the boiling water and can still be cooked to al dente. The Cantonese call this boiled dumpling *Shui Gao*, which is synonymous with "water dog" in their dialect; thus the name "water dog" appears on menus in Cantonese restaurants.

MAKES 40 DUMPLINGS

1 recipe meat filling from Tricolored Meat
   Dumplings (page 16)
1½ cups bread flour
1 cup all-purpose flour

1 cup cold water
Garlic-Soy Dipping Sauce (page 287) or
   Ginger Sauce I (page 288)

Prepare filling as for Tricolored Meat Dumplings. Chill at least 2 hours to firm up mixture.

Combine flours in work bowl of a food processor fitted with steel blade and pulse to mix. While the motor is running, add cold water through the feedtube and process 30 to 40 seconds, or until dough forms a soft ball. Let stand 10 minutes, then process another 30 seconds.

Turn out dough onto a floured surface. Knead 3 minutes, dusting dough and board lightly with flour to prevent sticking, until dough is very smooth, elastic, and earlobe-soft. Seal dough in a plastic bag and chill 2 hours in the refrigerator.

Transfer dough to a lightly floured board and knead gently a few seconds. Divide dough into 3 equal pieces with a sharp knife. Work with 1 piece at a time, keeping remaining pieces covered to prevent drying.

Dust board lightly with flour. Press first piece of dough into a flat disk, then roll it into an even ¹⁄₁₆-inch-thick sheet, dusting lightly with flour as necessary to prevent sticking. Using a 3-inch round cutter, cut out as many rounds as possible, cutting them as close as possible to minimize scraps. Squeeze scraps into a ball, place in a plastic bag, and set aside. Repeat with remaining 2 pieces of dough. Dust rounds lightly with flour to prevent sticking and keep them covered (do not overlap them for too long, or they will stick together). Gently knead scraps together into a single ball, roll out dough, and cut out circles until all the dough has been used.

Put 1 tablespoon of filling in the center of each circle, fold it over the filling and pinch to seal edges securely so that meat juice will not seep out during cooking. Place dumplings on a baking sheet without them touching one another.

In a 6-quart pot, bring 5 inches of water to a rolling boil. Stir water in a circular motion while adding the dumplings. Add just enough to make a single layer in the water. Cover and bring water to a boil. Add ½ cup cold water, cover, and bring to a boil again. Repeat cooling and boiling twice more, until dumplings rise to the surface. Transfer dumplings to a platter and serve with your choice of sauce. Some cooking liquid may be served with the dumplings, if desired.

Per dumpling: 36 Calories, 3 g Protein, 0.8 g Total Fat (20% of Calories), 0.2 g Saturated Fat, 4 g Carbohydrates, 0 g Dietary Fiber, 7 mg Cholesterol, 69 mg Sodium

Note: Freeze the dumplings on a baking sheet, then place them in a plastic freezer bag and freeze up to 1 month. Cook them frozen when you need them.

# Flower Rolls

These are delicious, tender, semisweet rolls artistically shaped to look like a flower.

MAKES 10 ROLLS

1 recipe Basic Steamed Bun Dough   Cooking spray
    (page 250)

Divide dough into 2 parts. Roll each part into a rectangle measuring about 12 × 8 inches. Spray top of both rectangles with cooking spray, then beginning at a long edge, roll up each sheet of dough tightly, jelly-roll style, into a cylinder about 1½ inches in diameter. Cut each roll crosswise with a sharp knife into 10 (1-inch-thick) pieces.

Stack 1 piece on top of another with cut sides facing front and back, then firmly press a chopstick crosswise down the middle of the rolls. The rolled ends of the top piece will lift up. (In steaming, these top and bottom folds will puff and open up like flowers.) Repeat with remaining pieces until all 10 flower rolls are formed. Set rolls on a steamer rack that has been sprayed with cooking spray, leaving 1 inch space between the them. Cover rolls with a dry towel and let rise until double in size, about 30 minutes, depending on the temperature of the room.

Bring water in steamer to a vigorous boil over high heat. Steam buns, in batches if necessary, over high heat 15 minutes. Remove from heat and wait 5 minutes before opening steamer. Uncover and transfer buns to a platter. Do not let water droplets on lid fall on buns.

Once steamed, buns will keep in an airtight plastic bag 1 week in refrigerator and several weeks in freezer. To reheat, steam 10 minutes, or microwave on HIGH a few seconds, depending on the power of your oven.

Per roll: 135 Calories, 3 g Protein, 1.5 g Total Fat (10% of Calories), 0 g Saturated Fat, 27 g Carbohydrates, 0 g Dietary Fiber, 0 mg Cholesterol, 18 mg Sodium

Basic Baked Bun Dough

This dough is placed in the refrigerator to rise slowly overnight for a finer crumb and a lofty bun.

MAKES 2 POUNDS BUN DOUGH

2 teaspoons (1 package) active dry yeast
1 cup lukewarm water
½ cup sugar
3 tablespoons safflower oil

1 egg, beaten
4 cups bread flour or unbleached all-purpose flour

Combine yeast, lukewarm water, and sugar in the work bowl of a food processor fitted with the steel blade. Let stand 10 minutes, or until foamy. Add oil and egg and pulse a few times to mix. Add flour, 2 cups at a time, and process until dough forms a mass and pulls away from the sides of the work bowl, about 1 minute. Let rest 15 minutes. Then process again 30 seconds.

Turn out dough onto a lightly floured board. Knead by hand 3 minutes, until dough is smooth, elastic, and springy. If dough is sticky, add a dusting of flour.

Place dough in a lightly oiled large bowl nearly double its size, turning once to coat both sides of dough. Cover tightly with plastic wrap and refrigerate overnight.

Bring dough to room temperature and let it rise until it doubles in bulk, 2 to 4 hours, depending on the room temperature. Use dough for making various baked buns.

Per recipe: 2442 Calories, 53 g Protein, 50 g Total Fat (19% of Calories), 7 g Saturated Fat, 451 g Carbohydrates, 2 g Dietary Fiber, 274 mg Cholesterol, 74 mg Sodium

Baked Beef Curry Buns

These tender baked sweet buns are filled with luscious yellow curried ground beef in a delicious brown gravy. Just one bite and you will ask for more. They make a scrumptious snack.

MAKES 24 BUNS

2 teaspoons safflower oil
1 large onion, finely diced
12 ounces lean ground beef
1½ tablespoons curry powder
2 tablespoons reduced-sodium soy sauce
2 teaspoons premium oyster sauce
½ teaspoon salt
¾ teaspoon sugar
2 tablespoons tapioca starch dissolved in 1½ cups fat-free, low-sodium chicken broth

1 recipe Basic Baked Bun Dough (page 261)
1 egg yolk beaten with 2 teaspoons water and ½ teaspoon sugar for the egg wash
Sesame seeds or poppy seeds for sprinkling

Heat a heavy 10-inch non-stick skillet over high heat until hot. Add oil and swirl to coat pan. Add onion and stir-fry until aromatic and translucent, about 5 minutes. Transfer onion to a 9-inch pie plate; set aside. Add beef to pan and cook, stirring to separate the beef, about 5 minutes until no longer pink. Tilt pan to drain off the fat and liquid. Add curry powder to beef and cook, stirring, until fragrant. Return onion to beef; add soy sauce, oyster sauce, salt, and sugar and cook, stirring, until beef has absorbed all the seasonings. Stir tapioca starch mixture and stir into beef mixture. Cook, stirring, until gravy is very thick. Cool slightly, then cover with plastic wrap directly on it, and refrigerate 2 hours or up to a day in advance.

Divide dough into 2 pieces. While you work with 1 piece, cover the other with a dry towel. On a lightly floured board, roll the first piece into a large even sheet about ¼ inch thick. With a 3½-inch round cutter, stamp out as many circles as possible, cutting them as close as possible to minimize scraps. Place circles on a large baking sheet and cover with a dry towel. Repeat process with second piece of dough until all circles are made. Gather scraps and squeeze them into a smooth ball. Let rest under a dry towel for 15 minutes, then roll out and make more circles until all dough is used up.

Work with 1 circle at a time, leaving the rest covered. With one hand on top of rolling pin, roll toward center of dough circle, but not all the way to the center, freeing your other hand to turn wrapper after each roll, leaving a thicker quarter-size area unrolled at the center (so that edges are thinner than center).

Holding disk in your cupped hand, put 1 tablespoon of filling on top of center, then bring the edges together, enclosing the filling in the center and pinch and twist the dough to close opening. Turn twisted side down and place 1½ inches apart on 2 nonstick baking sheets. Shape and fill remaining buns, one at a time. Cover with a dry cloth and let them rise until they are soft and puffy, about 30 minutes.

Preheat oven to 350F (175C) 15 minutes before baking. Put a shallow pan of boiling water on bottom of the oven, so buns will bake in a steamy environment and not become too dry.

Lightly brush tops and upper sides of buns with egg wash and sprinkle with sesame or poppy seeds. Place buns, 1 sheet at a time, in oven and bake 5 to 6 minutes. Quickly rotate baking sheet from front to back to ensure even coloring. Bake another 5 to 6 minutes, or until tops are light brown. Serve immediately or let buns cool slightly, then wrap and refrigerate. Reheat in a preheated 250F (120C) oven until thoroughly hot, 5 to 6 minutes, or use a microwave oven.

Per bun: 147 Calories, 5 g Protein, 5 g Total Fat (33% of Calories), 1.3 g Saturated Fat, 20 g Carbohydrates, 0 g Dietary Fiber, 23 mg Cholesterol, 153 mg Sodium

Note: When steaming or baking buns in batches, refrigerate the remaining buns to prevent over rising, which causes the buns to collapse.

Scallion Pancakes

In China these aromatic flaky pan-fried scallion pancakes are a national favorite. They are as popular as pizza is in America, but they are much easier and quicker to make. They are great complements to soups and salads, and they make scrumptious after-school snacks.

MAKES 6 (5-INCH) PANCAKES

3½ cups all-purpose flour
1 cup boiling water
¼ cup cold water
2 tablespoons peanut oil

1 tablespoon salt
1½ teaspoons sugar
3 cups thinly sliced scallions (about 12 scallions)

Make dough: Add the flour to the work bowl of a food processor fitted with the steel blade. While the motor is running, add boiling water through the feedtube and process 45 seconds. Let stand 5 minutes. Turn on machine and add the cold water and process until the dough forms a ball.

Turn out dough onto a floured work surface and knead 2 minutes, or until dough is smooth and earlobe-soft, dusting the board lightly with just enough flour to prevent sticking. Cover with plastic wrap and let rest at least 30 minutes.

Form dough into an even 3-inch-diameter roll. Using a sharp knife, cut crosswise into 6 equal pieces. Turn each piece, cut side up, on the lightly floured board.

Work with 1 piece at a time. Hold piece, cut side up, in one floured hand and gently flatten dough into a circle. Place circle on a lightly floured board and roll it out into a thin 8-inch round sheet, dusting the board and rolling pin lightly with flour to prevent sticking.

Place ½ teaspoon oil in center of dough. Use your finger to spread oil evenly over the entire surface, then sprinkle evenly with a rounded ¼ teaspoon salt and a scant ¼ teaspoon sugar. Spread ½ cup of scallions evenly over top. Roll up dough, jelly-roll style: snug but not tight. Keep seam side down and pinch ends shut. Grasp 1 end of roll and wind other end around it in a flat spiral. Tuck tail end underneath and press lightly with your hand to flatten the spiral. Gently roll out spiral into a 5-inch circle, ¼ to ½ inch thick; set aside. Repeat with remaining pieces.

Heat a heavy 8-inch frying pan over medium heat until hot, 1 to 2 minutes. Add ½ teaspoon oil, swirl to coat pan. Add 1 pancake, cover, and cook 2 to 3 minutes, or until golden brown and crisp. Flip pancake over and fry the other side, covered, until golden brown and crisp, shaking pan frequently during cooking. Transfer to a plate and keep warm. Cook remaining pancakes. Serve immediately. Leftovers can be reheated in a 350F (175C) oven until thoroughly hot, 4 to 5 minutes.

Per ¼ piece scallion pancake: 73 Calories, 2 g Protein, 1 g Total Fat (16% of Calories), 0 g Saturated Fat, 14 g Carbohydrates, 0 g Dietary Fiber, 0 mg Cholesterol, 267 mg Sodium

Chinese Thin Pancakes

These pan-baked thin flour wrappers are a must for some marvelous dishes such as Peking Duck (page 189), Mu Shu dishes (pages 99 and 206), and Beef with Leeks (page 199).

MAKES 30 THIN PANCAKES

2½ cups bread flour or unbleached all-purpose flour

1 cup boiling water
Cooking spray

Measure flour into a large bowl. Add boiling water gradually as you stir with chopsticks or a wooden spoon until mixture resembles lumpy meal. Squeeze the mass into a large ball and turn out onto a lightly floured surface. Knead dough with the heel of your hands, dusting lightly with flour to prevent sticking, about 7 minutes, or until it is no longer sticky. Dust board only as necessary to prevent sticking, or dough may become too stiff. Cover with a clean damp cloth and let rest 30 minutes.

Knead dough another 5 minutes, or until it is smooth, elastic, and earlobe-soft. Roll dough into a large, even ⅛-inch-thick circle. With a 3½-inch-round cutter, stamp out as many circles as possible, cutting them as close as possible to minimize scraps. Transfer cut circles to a tray, line them neatly touching one another in a single layer. Gather scraps together into a ball and wrap in plastic wrap to rest 15 minutes, then roll out and make more circles until all dough is used up.

Spray surfaces of circles thoroughly and evenly with cooking spray. Starting with 2 oiled circles, invert one on top of the other like a sandwich, with oiled surfaces together. Repeat until all circles are paired. Then roll out each paired circle on a lightly floured surface into a double pancake about 7 inches in diameter and ¹⁄₁₆ inch thick, dusting board and top of pancake lightly with flour as necessary to prevent sticking (do not use too much flour or pancakes will be tough). Repeat until all the pairs have been rolled out.

Heat an ungreased heavy skillet over low heat until hot. Place a pancake in skillet and dry-bake it about 45 seconds, until pancake begins to bubble up in several places. Turn pancake over and bake the other side 30 seconds, until bottom is speckled with small light-brown spots. Transfer pancake to a plate and cover. Repeat with remaining pancakes. As pan tempers, pancakes will cook a bit more quickly; reduce heat if pancakes are browning too fast.

After pancakes are cooked, peel each into 2 individual pancakes. Stack them with speckled side up and cover with a clean towel or seal cooled pancakes in a plastic bag until ready to use.

> Per pancake: 34 Calories, 1 g Protein, 0.1 g Total Fat (2% of Calories), 0 g Saturated Fat, 7 g Carbohydrates, 0 g Dietary Fiber, 0 mg Cholesterol, 0 mg Sodium

Notes: Adjust heat level carefully; if the pan is too hot the pancake will be covered with large burned spots, and if it is not hot enough the pancake will dry out during cooking. The pancakes should be tender. At the beginning you may have to test a few pieces to determine the right temperature.

These pancakes may be made hours or days in advance, stacked, wrapped, and sealed airtight. Store in the refrigerator or freezer. Reheat by steaming 8 to 10 minutes, or until soft and resilient.

Chinese Sesame Flaky Bread

These crispy, flaky sesame breads are the ingenious creation of Chinese chefs. The flavorful roux is cooked first and then folded into a fresh dough. It enhances the bread and provides the flakiness. These are traditionally eaten as a breakfast food, split open and stuffed with a deep-fried dough cruller, and accompanied by a bowl of sweetened hot soybean milk. These flatbreads are also great with soups, or split along their natural folds and stuffed with lunch meat, lettuce, and tomato to make scrumptious sandwiches. And they are most enjoyable when stuffed with barbecued beef.

MAKES 18 PIECES

ROUX

⅓ cup peanut oil
¾ cup all-purpose flour

DOUGH

5 cups all-purpose flour
1 cup boiling water
⅔ cup very cold water
1½ teaspoons salt
½ cup toasted sesame seeds

Make roux: Heat a small heavy saucepan over medium heat until hot. Add oil and heat until oil is hot enough to foam a pinch of flour, 2 to 3 minutes. Add ¾ cup flour and cook, stirring constantly, about 5 minutes, until mixture has a nutty toasty smell and turns light brown. Watch carefully and do not cook to dark brown. Remove pan from heat and let cool, stirring occasionally.

Make dough: Add 5 cups flour to the work bowl of a food processor fitted with the steel blade. While the motor is running, add boiling water through the feedtube and process 2 minutes, then add cold water. Process until dough forms a soft ball. Let stand 10 minutes, then process another 30 seconds. Turn out dough onto a floured surface. Cover with plastic wrap and let rest at least 30 minutes.

Knead dough 5 minutes. Roll out dough into a large ¹⁄₁₆-inch-thick square. Stir roux, then spread it evenly on top of the dough square. Sprinkle salt evenly over roux. Roll up jelly-roll style. Using a sharp knife, slice roll crosswise into 18 pieces. Cover with plastic wrap and let rest 5 minutes.

Put 1 dough piece on a lightly floured board with uncut side up. Start rolling from the center of dough toward the front and then fold over in half. Roll again from the center toward the front, then fold over again. Now turn dough on its side and roll from the center to the front, fold over, and repeat the same rolling procedure (rolling and folding four times).

Dip the smooth bottom into sesame seeds. With the side of your hand, press the length of the dough and roll it out lengthwise into a rectangular flatbread, 5 inches long and 3 inches wide. Repeat with remaining pieces dough one by one until all are shaped.

Preheat the oven with a baking sheet on the middle rack to 425F (220C) for 20 minutes. Place breads on the hot baking sheet and bake 8 minutes. Turn breads over and bake 5 more minutes, or until light brown. Remove from oven and serve immediately. If your oven is small, bake them in 2 or 3 batches.

Per piece: 175 Calories, 4 g Protein, 4.9 g Total Fat (25% of Calories), 0.7 g Saturated Fat, 29 g Carbohydrates, 0g Dietary Fiber, 0 mg Cholesterol, 178 mg Sodium

Chinese Sesame Bagels

Did you know that bagels originated in China? The bread was developed in the Ming Dynasty in the year 1500 by a famous general. To win the war, he wanted each of his troops to carry sufficient food to keep up their strength. He ordered the baker to bake breads with a hole in their middle. These were given to the soldiers strung on necklaces to wear around their neck. Then, whenever they were hungry they could just pull one off to eat.

When I was a college student in Taiwan, for a snack after school I would always buy a warm sesame bagel from a nearby bakeshop. In Taiwan, bagels were eaten plain for snacks; butter and cream cheese were not available. Having grown up on a rice diet, eating a bagel was like a special treat for me.

MAKES 10 BAGELS

2 packages active dry yeast
3 tablespoons sugar
1½ cups warm water (120 to 130F; 50 to 55C)
3½ cups bread flour

1 tablespoon salt
1½ tablespoons sugar
1 egg white beaten with 1 teaspoon water for the egg wash
⅓ cup sesame seeds for sprinkling

Combine yeast, sugar, and warm water in the work bowl of a food processor fitted with the steel blade and stir until yeast is dissolved; let stand 10 minutes, until a brown foam rises to the surface. Add flour and salt and process until dough forms a mass and pulls away from the sides of the work bowl, about 1 minute. Let rest 10 minutes, then process again 30 seconds.

Turn out dough onto a lightly floured board. Knead by hand 3 minutes, until dough is smooth, elastic, and fingertip firm. If dough is sticky, add a dusting of flour.

Place dough in a lightly oiled large bowl three times the size of the dough, turning once to coat both sides of dough with oil. Seal bowl with plastic wrap and let rise until double in volume, about 1 hour.

Meanwhile, bring 3 inches water to a boil in a large pot. Add sugar, cover, and reduce heat to barely simmering.

Turn dough onto a floured work surface and punch down with extended fingers. Divide dough into 10 pieces and shape each into a ball. Allow dough to rest about 5 minutes before flattening with the palm of your hand.

With your finger, poke a hole in the center of each ball through the dough, enlarge it a bit, and twirl the dough around your finger on the floured surface until the hole is an inch or so in diameter. It should look like a bagel. Put bagels together without touching one another on a lightly floured surface, cover with a dry towel or plastic wrap, and leave at room temperature only until dough is slightly raised (half-proofed), about 10 minutes. Do not overproof or the bagel texture will not be as dense and chewy as a good bagel should be.

Preheat oven to 450F (230C). With the water boiling gently, lift 1 bagel at a time with a spatula and slip into the hot water. Do not do more than 2 or 3 bagels at a time; they need room to expand. Keep water at a simmer. The bagel should sink and then rise again after a few seconds. Simmer 1 minute, then flip them over and continue cooking them 2 more minutes. Lift bagels carefully out of water with a skimmer, drain briefly on a towel, then place them very gently on a nonstick baking sheet to keep them from deflating. Repeat with all of the bagels.

Bake bagels on middle rack of oven 10 minutes. Brush them with egg wash and sprinkle generously with sesame seeds.

Bake bagels until tops are a light brown color, about 5 to 8 minutes. Turn bagels over and bake another 3 to 5 minutes. Remove them from oven when they are brown and shiny, about 18 to 20 minutes total baking time.

Per bagel: 174 Calories, 4.7 g Protein, 0.4 g Total Fat (2% of Calories), 0 g Saturated Fat, 36 g Carbohydrates, 0 g Dietary Fiber, 0 mg Cholesterol, 647 mg Sodium

Desserts

The Chinese have a wide variety of sweets and pastries they eat as snacks between meals but usually not as desserts at the end of a meal. Instead, oranges or other fruits, cut into pieces, are frequently served at the conclusion of a meal.

I have included a variety of these sweet snack recipes, which are based on fruits, nuts, beans, and rice. These recipes are low in fat, rich in protein, and contain lots of health-building fiber. Best of all, they will satisfy your cravings for sweets, and you can serve them as desserts or eat them as snacks anytime.

Almond Float

This is a refreshing almond-flavored gelatin. It has the texture of soft tofu and in China it is called "almond tofu." It is served in a sugar syrup with mixed fruits, and is quite delightful.

MAKES 6 SERVINGS

2 (¼-oz.) packages unflavored gelatin
3 cups water
½ cup reduced-fat evaporated milk
¼ cup sugar

1 tablespoon pure almond extract
2 (15-oz.) cans good-quality fruit cocktail
 in juice, chilled

In a 2-quart saucepan, sprinkle gelatin over water and let stand 5 minutes. Bring to a boil over medium heat, stirring constantly, until gelatin has dissolved. Reduce heat to very low and add evaporated milk and sugar. Cook, stirring, until sugar dissolves. Add almond extract, then transfer mixture to an 8-inch-square baking dish coated with cooking spray. Cover and refrigerate about 4 hours, or until firm or up to 1 day ahead.

When ready to serve, cut milk jelly into diamond shapes or squares and place them in a crystal serving bowl. Add chilled fruit cocktail with its juice and stir gently to blend.

Per serving: 124 Calories, 3.5 g Protein, 0 g Total Fat (0% of Calories), 0 g Saturated Fat, 27.3 g Carbohydrates, 1.1 g Dietary Fiber, 2 mg Cholesterol, 40 mg Sodium

VARIATION

Serve the milk jelly in individual crystal glasses with slices of fresh strawberries, kiwi fruit, nectarines, and fruit syrup, and garnish each glass with fresh mint leaves.

Pineapple-Filled Cookies

These shortbread cookies are a specialty of Tainan, a city in the southern part of Taiwan where delicious pineapples and pineapple cookies are produced. They are light and crisp on the outside and moist and fragrant on the inside. Serve them with hot jasmine tea.

MAKES 20 COOKIES

1½ cups all-purpose flour
¼ teaspoon salt
1 teaspoon baking powder
2 egg whites
¼ teaspoon cream of tartar

1 egg yolk
⅔ cup packed light brown sugar
⅓ cup corn oil
1 teaspoon pure vanilla extract
½ cup pineapple preserves, chilled

Preheat oven to 375F (190C). Coat a baking sheet with cooking spray. Sift together flour, salt, and baking powder into a medium bowl and set aside.

In another medium bowl, beat egg whites with an electric beater at medium speed until soft peaks form. Sprinkle with cream of tartar and continue beating until stiff glossy peaks form; set aside.

In a large bowl, combine egg yolk, sugar, oil, and vanilla and beat until smooth. Fold egg white mixture into egg yolk mixture, a large spoonful at a time, until incorporated. Fold in flour mixture, ¼ cup at a time, until just moist. Chill dough 2 hours or more.

Roll out chilled dough between 2 pieces of waxed paper to ¼-inch thickness. Using a 3-inch cutter, cut out as many circles as possible. Gather scraps into a ball, roll it out, and cut again until all of the dough is used.

Fill each circle with ½ teaspoon pineapple preserves, fold sides and ends over filling to seal, and shape it into 2 × 1-inch rectangle. Dip your fingers in flour frequently to prevent sticking. Place cookies 1 inch apart, seam side down, on prepared baking sheet

Bake cookies 10 minutes. Turn cookies over and bake another 3 minutes. Transfer cookies to a wire rack to cool, then serve.

Quick Real Almond Cookies

Most almond cookies are made with lard. Here I use only pure vegetable oil and ground almonds with the flour to make crispier, lighter, and healthier almond cookies. They are rich in calories so enjoy them as a treat, in moderation!

MAKES 20 COOKIES

1 cup all-purpose flour
1 cup (5½ oz.) whole almonds
¾ cup sugar
1 whole egg plus 1 egg white, lightly beaten
⅓ cup corn oil

½ teaspoon baking powder
½ teaspoon baking soda
¼ teaspoon salt
1 teaspoon pure almond extract
20 almond halves

Preheat oven to 375F (190C) for 15 minutes. Coat a baking sheet with cooking spray.

In a food processor fitted with the steel blade, combine flour, almonds, and sugar; process to a fine powder. Add beaten egg and egg white, oil, baking powder, baking soda, salt, and almond extract; process just until incorporated.

Gently shape dough into 20 walnut-size balls and place 2 inches apart on baking sheet. Place 1 almond half in center of each cookie and gently press down to make an impression in the cookie. Bake 10 to 12 minutes, or until light brown. Transfer cookies to a wire rack to cool and crisp.

VARIATION
WALNUT COOKIES

Replace 1 cup whole almonds with 1 cup walnuts and replace almond extract with vanilla extract. Use walnut halves for garnish.

Mango Mousse

The flavors of mango and orange complement each other. Blended together they make refreshing summer dessert.

8 ounces thawed frozen mango chunks
1 cup orange juice
1 tablespoon unflavored gelatin powder
⅓ cup water
½ cup half and half
2 tablespoons coconut cream

5 tablespoons superfine sugar
3 egg whites
Dash of salt
¼ teaspoon cream of tartar
Strawberry slices and mint leaves, for garnish

Place mango chunks in a food processor fitted with the steel blade. Pulse a few times until coarsely chopped. Add orange juice and process until mixture is very smooth, about 1 minute.

In a small dish, let gelatin soften in the water 5 minutes. Place dish in a saucepan with ½ inch of boiling water over low heat. Stir until gelatin dissolves, then stir gelatin into mango mixture and process 1 minute, or until finely blended. Transfer mango mixture to a bowl, cover, and refrigerate 30 to 40 minutes, or until almost set.

In a medium bowl, using an electric mixer, beat half and half, coconut cream, and 2 tablespoons of the sugar on high speed 1 minute. Fold into mango mixture. Cover and refrigerate 30 minutes, or until almost set.

In another medium bowl and with clean beaters, beat egg whites until foamy. Sprinkle salt and cream of tartar on top and continue beating until stiff peaks form. Carefully beat in remaining 3 tablespoons sugar, 1 tablespoon at a time. Gently fold egg whites into mango mixture until just mixed. Pour into 8 individual serving cups. Cover and chill at least 4 hours, or until mousse is set. Garnish with strawberries and mint leaves.

Per serving: 105 Calories, 2.9 g Protein, 2.2 g Total Fat (19% of Calories), 1.5 g Saturated Fat, 18.4 g Carbohydrates, 0.6 g Dietary Fiber, 8 mg Cholesterol, 35 mg Sodium

Note: Raw eggs may carry salmonella, a bacterium that will cause severe illness. The very young, the very old, anyone who is immune-compromised or has a serious illness should never eat raw eggs.

Mango-Banana Smoothie

A refreshing low-cal fruit drink for breakfast, after dinner, or for serving to guests anytime.

MAKES ABOUT 2 CUPS

1 cup chilled orange juice
1 small banana
½ cup chilled mango puree

1 teaspoon honey
2 tablespoons fresh lime juice
2 to 3 ice cubes

Combine all ingredients in a blender and process on high speed until smooth, about 1 minute.

Per ½ cup: 79 Calories, 2 g Protein, 0 g Total Fat (4% of Calories), 0 g Saturated Fat, 20 g Carbohydrates, 1 g Dietary Fiber, 0 mg Cholesterol, 3 mg Sodium

TIP

Fresh mangoes are seasonal, but frozen mango chunks are available year-round.

Eight-Treasure Pudding Flambé

This is a classic Chinese dessert, traditionally served on special occasions at formal dinners. The pudding is made with soft sticky glutinous rice filled with a sweetened red bean paste and garnished with a variety of preserved fruits and nuts. The number eight is considered a lucky number among the Chinese, so we use eight different items as the treasures in the pudding. You can select treasures of your own choosing, usually fresh or preserved fruits and nuts, such as plums, dates, candied orange slices, canned loquats, peaches, figs, almonds, or pecans.

MAKES 10 SERVINGS

1½ cups glutinous rice, rinsed thoroughly

2 cups cold water

2 tablespoons sugar

1 tablespoon safflower oil

¼ cup walnuts, coarsely chopped

12 canned sweetened lotus seeds

10 candied red cherries, each cut in half

10 candied green cherries, each cut in half

30 raisins

10 candied pineapple chunks, each cut in half

10 dried apricots, soaked in water until soft and each cut in half

1 cup Chinese canned sweetened red bean paste

Sugar Syrup (see below)

¼ cup dark rum (optional)

SUGAR SYRUP

1 cup water

¾ cup sugar

1 teaspoon almond extract

1 tablespoon cornstarch dissolved in 3 tablespoons water

Place rice in a heavy 10-inch skillet with a tight-fitting lid, add cold water, and bring to a boil. Reduce heat to the lowest setting, cover, and cook 20 minutes. Remove pan from heat and let stand 15 minutes without lifting the lid. Stir in sugar and oil until evenly blended. Cover and set aside.

Spray the inside of a 4- to 6-cup heatproof bowl with cooking spray. Carefully arrange nuts, seeds, and fruits in a beautiful design on bottom and sides of bowl. Put nuts in center, then circle nuts with the different fruits listed above in order, and in a single layer to cover as much area as possible. Carefully spoon ⅔ of the sweetened rice on top of the fruits and nuts, pressing down gently without disturbing the neat design. Make a shallow pie plate–shaped indentation in the rice from center to within 1 inch of edge, and fill this with sweetened red bean paste. Spread remaining rice on top of paste and press down gently to seal. This can be done a day in advance.

To cook: Set bowl of pudding in a steamer and steam over medium heat 1 hour, or until heated through, replenishing water when necessary during steaming. Remove bowl from steamer. Invert a beautiful serving platter on top of bowl. Holding platter and bowl firmly together, turn upside down to transfer pudding to the serving platter.

Make syrup: In a 1-quart saucepan, bring water to a boil. Add sugar and stir until dissolved. Add almond extract. Stir cornstarch mixture and stir into syrup. Cook, stirring, until smooth and slightly thickened. Spoon syrup over pudding.

For a festive touch, warm rum in a small skillet; pour it over the pudding and set it aflame. When flame subsides, cut pudding into small wedges and serve immediately. This pudding is excellent hot but can be eaten at room temperature or cold.

Per serving: 337 Calories, 4 g Protein, 3 g Total Fat (20.24% of Calories), 0 g Saturated Fat, 66 g Carbohydrates, 2 g Dietary Fiber, 0 mg Cholesterol, 5 mg Sodium

VARIATION
Make the pudding in a microwave-proof bowl and cook it in the microwave oven, covered, on HIGH power 15 minutes, or until it is heated through.

Fat-Free Bean Fudge

This is a delicious fudge made from adzuki beans. It has the taste, texture, and look of regular fudge but without the fat. It provides real nutrition instead of empty calories. Enjoy the fudge with hot green tea.

MAKES 32 (1-INCH) SQUARES

8 ounces (1 cup) dried adzuki beans,
    soaked overnight
2 (1/4-oz.) packages unflavored gelatin
1 1/4 cups sugar

1/4 teaspoon salt
1 teaspoon pure vanilla or almond
    extract

Rinse soaked beans and cover them with 2 inches of water in a heavy 3-quart saucepan. Bring to a boil over medium-high heat, then reduce heat to the lowest setting and simmer slowly, until beans are very soft and have begun to burst, 2 to 3 hours. Cool slightly.

In a food mill set over a heavy 4-quart deep pot puree beans; discard skins and coarse particles that do not pass through the food mill. If you do not have a food mill, puree beans and cooking liquid in a blender, then press pulverized beans through a fine strainer to remove skins. Add additional warm water if mixture is too thick. Discard skins and coarse particles.

Cook pureed bean paste in a heavy saucepan over medium heat, stirring frequently to prevent scorching, until very thick, about 30 minutes.

In the 3-quart saucepan, stir together gelatin, sugar, and salt. Add 1 cup water and bring to a boil over medium heat, stirring constantly, until gelatin has completely dissolved. Add bean paste and return to a boil. Cook, stirring constantly, over medium-low heat until it is very thick and fudgy and forms large round bubbles that burst with a gentle poof, about 1 1/2 hours. The mixture should be reduced to about 3 cups.

Remove bean mixture from heat. Stir in vanilla or almond extract. Transfer mixture to an 8 × 4-inch glass loaf pan lightly coated with cooking spray. Cool and refrigerate, covered, overnight or until firm. Cut into 1-inch-square pieces.

Per square: 55 Calories, 2 g Protein, 0.1 g Total Fat (2% of Calories), 0 g Saturated Fat, 12 g Carbohydrates, 2 g Dietary Fiber, 0 mg Cholesterol, 18 mg Sodium

Sweet Bean-Filled Rice Balls

Glutinous rice flour makes desserts that are unique. Here, the soft chewy rice dough is filled with a delectable sweet red bean paste. These rice ball confections go wonderfully with hot green tea.

MAKES 20 BALLS

3 tablespoons tapioca starch
½ cup boiling water
1 tablespoon safflower oil
2 tablespoons sugar
2½ cups glutinous rice flour

1½ cups canned Chinese sweetened red bean paste
⅔ cup coconut flakes
10 maraschino cherries, each cut in half

In a small bowl, combine tapioca starch and boiling water and stir immediately to form a thick paste. Transfer paste to a food processor fitted with the steel blade. Add oil, sugar, and rice flour; process until mixture is smooth and can be gathered into a ball, about 45 seconds.

Turn out mixture onto a lightly floured board and knead until smooth and soft. Divide dough into 20 pieces. Roll each into a ball and cover with plastic.

Divide sweet bean paste into 20 portions. Work with 1 piece of dough at a time, keeping remaining pieces covered so they stay soft and pliable. Flatten each ball with the palm of your hand into a thin circle. Place 1 portion of sweet bean paste in center of dough. Pinch and pleat edges, gather them together, and pinch to seal. Repeat until dough and filling are finished.

Put dumplings, seam side down, without touching one another, on a steaming rack sprayed with cooking spray. Steam over boiling water on high heat about 10 minutes, or until dough is cooked through. Remove from steamer and cool slightly. Coat each ball with coconut and garnish with a half cherry on top.

Per ball: 124 Calories, 2 g Protein, 2 g Total Fat (15% of Calories), 1.4 g Saturated Fat, 20 g Carbohydrates, 1 g Dietary Fiber, 0 mg Cholesterol, 23 mg Sodium

New Year's Cake

In China it is traditional to serve this sweet rice cake during the New Year celebration. It symbolizes happiness and prosperity for the coming year. The cake can be cut into 1/2-inch slices and served warm or at room temperature. It will keep, well wrapped, for three weeks in the refrigerator. Reheat by pan-frying it or heat it in a microwave.

MAKES 20 SERVINGS

1 pound (4 cups) glutinous rice flour
1/2 cup boiling water
2 cups packed light brown sugar

2 tablespoons safflower oil
1 cup cold water
1 tablespoon banana extract

Preheat oven to 350F (175C). Coat an 8-inch-square baking dish with cooking spray; set aside.

Combine rice flour and boiling water in a food processor fitted with the steel blade and process 15 seconds. Scrape down rice flour from sides and loosen up rice flour on bottom of bowl. Add brown sugar, oil, cold water, and banana extract; process 1 minute, or until the mixture is very smooth. Transfer to the prepared baking dish and cover with foil.

Fill a 13 × 9-inch baking pan with 1 quart boiling water. Set dish containing the rice mixture in the hot water. Bake for 2 hours or until a knife inserted in the center comes out clean or with some translucent rice cake stuck to the blade. If it still looks milky and raw, bake another 5 minutes. Let cake cool in dish 4 hours. Cut into slices. Serve cake warm or at room temperature. It gets hard when refrigerated, but can be softened in the microwave oven.

Per serving: 150 Calories, 1 g Protein, 1 g Total Fat (8% of Calories), 0.1 g Saturated Fat, 33 g Carbohydrates, 1 g Dietary Fiber, 0 mg Cholesterol, 15 mg Sodium

TIP

After cutting the rice cake into pieces, coat the pieces with powdered sugar; then they won't stick together.

Strawberry-Flavored Rice Cake

This is my New Year's cake. The strawberries give it a wonderful flavor and a tender texture, and adzuki beans provide added nutrition.

1 pint strawberries, washed, stems removed, and sliced

1 pound (4 cups) Mochiko (Japanese) sweet rice flour

2 cups sugar

3 tablespoons safflower oil

½ cup water

1 cup cooked adzuki beans

3 tablespoons almond slices

1 tablespoon toasted sesame seeds

Preheat oven to 350F (175C). Spray an 8-inch-square baking dish with cooking spray.

In a food processor fitted with the steel blade, pulse strawberries until chopped, 1 minute, then puree until smooth. Add rice flour, sugar, oil, and water; process until smooth, about 1 minute. Stir in adzuki beans by hand, being careful not to break them. Transfer mixture to the prepared baking dish and sprinkle almond slices and sesame seeds on top.

Fill a 13 × 9-inch baking pan with 1 quart boiling water. Set dish containing rice mixture in the hot water and tent with foil. Bake 2 hours, or until a knife inserted in center comes out with translucent rice cake stuck to the blade. If it still looks milky and raw, bake another 10 minutes. Let cake cool in the dish 4 hours. Cut into squares. Serve warm or at room temperature. It gets hard when refrigerated, but can be reheated in the microwave oven.

Per serving: 270 Calories, 4 g Protein, 4 g Total Fat (15% of Calories), 0 g Saturated Fat, 56 g Carbohydrates, 4 g Dietary Fiber, 0 mg Cholesterol, 15 mg Sodium

Rainbow of Fortune Cookies

Fortune cookies are easy to make and can add great fun to special occasions. Type your own humorous messages for birthdays, anniversaries, employee raffles, or job assignments. Let the fun begin!

MAKES 14 COOKIES

¼ cup all-purpose flour
½ tablespoon cornstarch
3 tablespoons sugar
⅛ teaspoon baking powder
Pinch of salt
1 egg white, beaten just until frothy

2 tablespoons corn oil
½ teaspoon banana extract
½ teaspoon mint extract
Green food coloring
½ teaspoon strawberry extract
Red food coloring

Preheat oven to 325F (165C). Have ready 1 nonstick baking sheet, 1 plastic dough scraper, 1 water glass, 1 muffin pan, and 12 to 14 fortunes typed on 3 × ½-inch strips of paper.

Into a small bowl, sift together flour, cornstarch, sugar, baking powder, and salt. Add egg white and oil and stir gently until smooth.

Divide batter into 3 equal portions in 3 small separate bowls. Add banana extract to the first bowl, mint extract and 1 tiny drop green food coloring to the second bowl, and add strawberry extract and 1 tiny drop red food coloring to the third bowl. Stir each batter until blended and set aside.

Make just 2 or 3 cookies at a time. For each cookie, spoon 2 teaspoons of batter onto the baking sheet. Using the back of a teaspoon, spread batter evenly into a 3½-inch round.

Bake cookies about 10 minutes, or until edges just begin showing hints of light brown. Use a spatula or dough scraper to remove 1 cookie at a time. Place a "fortune" on the cookie, then fold it over and bring edges together, enclosing the fortune in the cookie, then bend bottom of cookie on rim of a water glass to make a fortune-cookie shape. Immediately fold the other cookies. You must work quickly while cookies are still warm.

Place each folded cookie, pointed ends down, in cup of muffin pan to maintain the shape until cookies are completely cooled and firm.

Per cookie: 40 Calories, 0.4 g Protein, 2 g Total Fat (45% of Calories), 0.3 g Saturated Fat, 5.3 g Carbohydrates, 0 g Dietary Fiber, 0 mg Cholesterol, 5 mg Sodium

TIP

Fold cookies before they cool down and become too stiff. If that happens, you can restore flexibility by returning them to the oven for 10 to 15 seconds.

Condiments, Seasonings, and Sauces

A taste of chutney, a bite of relish, a bit of hot sauce—small amounts of these exotic condiments and seasoning sauces can accentuate your meals, stimulate your appetite, and make dining more enjoyable. They round out a well-designed menu.

Garlic-Soy Dipping Sauce

This pungent garlic dipping sauce gives a flavorful kick to understated foods such as steamed meatballs and dumplings. The garlic used here must be firm and fresh. Make fresh dipping sauce each time you serve it.

MAKES ABOUT 6 TABLESPOONS

3 tablespoons good-quality reduced-sodium soy sauce
2 tablespoons white-wine vinegar
1 teaspoon sugar
Freshly ground pepper to taste

1 tablespoon water or fat-free, low-sodium chicken broth
1 to 2 teaspoons finely chopped fresh garlic
½ teaspoon oriental sesame oil

In a small dish, combine soy sauce, vinegar, sugar, pepper, and water or broth and stir until sugar dissolves. Stir in garlic and sesame oil. Cover and let stand 15 minutes before using to let the flavor develop.

Per teaspoon: 5 Calories, 0 g Protein, 0.1 g Total Fat (22% of Calories), 0 g Saturated Fat, 1 g Carbohydrates, 0 g Dietary Fiber, 0 mg Cholesterol, 99 mg Sodium

Ginger Sauce I

This sauce is good as a dip sauce for meatballs, for Daikon Radish Cake (page 229), or for many steamed vegetables.

MAKES ½ CUP

3 tablespoons reduced-sodium soy
  sauce
2 tablespoons cider vinegar
1 teaspoon sugar
¼ teaspoon hot chili sauce

2 teaspoons finely grated, peeled, fresh
  young ginger
1 tablespoon water or fat-free, low-
  sodium chicken broth

In a small bowl, combine all the ingredients and stir until sugar dissolves.

Per teaspoon: 3 Calories, 0 g Protein, 0 g Total Fat (0% of Calories), 0 g Saturated Fat, 1 g Carbohydrates, 0 g Dietary Fiber, 0 mg Cholesterol, 84 mg Sodium

Ginger Sauce II

This sauce is good on meat dumplings, shrimp dumplings, Dumpling Blossoms (page 19), Pearl Balls (page 36), and blanched or steamed seafood such as blanched calamari, steamed fish, or fish balls.

MAKES ½ CUP

2 tablespoons grated, peeled, fresh
  young ginger
2 tablespoons reduced-sodium soy
  sauce

2 tablespoons rice wine vinegar
1 tablespoon sugar
1 teaspoon oriental sesame oil

Combine all the ingredients in a small bowl and stir until sugar dissolves.

Per teaspoon: 6 Calories, 0 g Protein, 0 g Total Fat (0% of Calories), 0 g Saturated Fat, 1 g Carbohydrates, 0 g Dietary Fiber, 0 mg Cholesterol, 55 mg Sodium

Teriyaki Sauce

This is a popular all-purpose seasoning sauce used as an ingredient in Chinese and Japanese cooking. Use it to marinate meats or seafood, or use it as a glaze. Keep some in the refrigerator in a jar with a plastic cap; metal lids tend to corrode.

MAKES 1¼ CUPS

⅓ cup pale dry sherry
½ cup reduced-sodium soy sauce
1½ tablespoons brown sugar

1½ teaspoons tapioca starch dissolved in ½ cup fat-free, low-sodium chicken broth

Warm sherry in a 1-quart nonreactive saucepan over medium heat. Remove from heat and ignite sherry with a match. Swirl pan back and forth until flames subside. Add soy sauce, sugar, and broth mixture. Cook, stirring constantly, until sauce is bubbly and slightly thickened. Remove from heat and let cool. Transfer to a jar, seal tightly, and refrigerate until ready to use.

Per tablespoon: 13 Calories, 1 g Protein, 0 g Total Fat (0% of Calories), 0 g Saturated Fat, 2 g Carbohydrates, 0 g Dietary Fiber, 0 mg Cholesterol, 266 mg Sodium

Lemon Sauce

Make this fruity sweet and tart sauce for Lemon Chicken (page 161) or fish, or serve it as a dipping sauce for spring rolls, wontons, and fish rolls. A drop of yellow food coloring gives this sauce a color boost.

MAKES 1 CUP

½ cup fresh lemon juice
½ cup pineapple juice
5 tablespoons sugar
¼ teaspoon salt
¼ teaspoon hot chili sauce

1 tablespoon tapioca starch or arrowroot starch dissolved in 1½ tablespoons water
1 drop yellow food coloring (optional)

Combine lemon juice, pineapple juice, sugar, salt, and chili sauce in a small saucepan over medium heat. Bring to a boil and stir until sugar dissolves. Reduce heat and simmer 1 minute. Stir tapioca starch or arrowroot starch mixture until smooth and stir into lemon juice mixture. Cook, stirring, until sauce is thickened and glossy. Add yellow food coloring, if using, and stir to distribute.

Per tablespoon: 22 Calories, 0 g Protein, 0 g Total Fat (0% of Calories), 0 g Saturated Fat, 6 g Carbohydrates, 0 g Dietary Fiber, 0 mg Cholesterol, 34 mg Sodium

 # Plum Sauce

This plum sauce is quite different from those available in the Asian markets, and I think you will enjoy it. Use good plums for this recipe. Do not remove the skins; they impart a wonderful flavor and deep red color to the sauce. You may double or triple this recipe since it freezes very well.

MAKES 1$^{1}/_{2}$ CUPS

1 cup pitted and finely chopped fresh plums
¼ cup dried apricots, soaked in warm water 1 hour and finely chopped
¼ teaspoon cayenne pepper

½ teaspoon salt
2 tablespoons water
½ cup sugar
⅓ cup distilled white vinegar

In a nonreactive heavy saucepan, combine plums and apricots. Add cayenne pepper, salt, and water and bring to a boil. Reduce heat to low and simmer, uncovered, 15 minutes, stirring occasionally. Stir in sugar and vinegar and simmer stirring occasionally, 25 to 30 minutes, or until sauce reaches a chutneylike consistency. Remove from heat and let cool. Transfer sauce to a sealed glass jar and refrigerate. The sauce keeps up to 6 months in the refrigerator, or freeze up to 2 years.

Per tablespoon: 24 Calories, 0 g Protein, 0.1 g Total Fat (4% of Calories), 0 g Saturated Fat, 6 g Carbohydrates, 0 g Dietary Fiber, 0 mg Cholesterol, 45 mg Sodium

Hot Mustard Sauce

Serve this mustard sauce as condiment for appetizers or finger foods.

MAKES ¹/₂ CUP

3 tablespoons Coleman's dry mustard
¼ cup medium-dry sherry
2 teaspoons rice vinegar

Pinch of salt and sugar or to taste
1 teaspoon oriental sesame oil

Combine all ingredients in a small glass bowl. Stir until a smooth paste forms. Seal airtight and let sauce mellow at least 30 minutes before serving.

Per teaspoon: 7 Calories, 0.2 g Protein, 0.4 g Total Fat (56% of Calories), 0 g Saturated Fat, 0.2 g Carbohydrates, 0 g Dietary Fiber, 0 mg Cholesterol, 0 mg Sodium

Hoisin Dipping Sauce

This is a marvelous dipping sauce for poultry, meats, seafood, and tofu dishes. It will keep for months in a sealed jar in the refrigerator.

MAKES ³/₄ CUP

½ cup hoisin sauce
2 tablespoons sugar

½ teaspoon oriental sesame oil
2 tablespoons water

Combine hoisin sauce, sugar, sesame oil, and water in a small serving dish; stir until sugar dissolves. Cover with plastic wrap and microwave 30 seconds.

Per teaspoon: 14 Calories, 0.2 g Protein, 0.2 g Total Fat (11% of Calories), 0 g Saturated Fat, 3 g Carbohydrates, 0 g Dietary Fiber, 0 mg Cholesterol, 111 mg Sodium

Dijon Mustard Vinaigrette

Serve this mustard vinaigrette on duck or chicken salads. It's also delicious on shrimp salads.

1 tablespoon Dijon mustard
3 tablespoons reduced-sodium soy
  sauce
2 teaspoons Coleman's dry mustard

1½ teaspoons honey
1 tablespoon balsamic vinegar
2 teaspoons oriental sesame oil
Salt and freshly ground pepper to taste

Whisk all ingredients in a small glass bowl until blended. Seal airtight and let mellow 30 minutes before using.

Per teaspoon: 9 Calories, 0.4 g Protein, 0.6 g Total Fat (54% of Calories), 0.1 g Saturated Fat, 0.8 g Carbohydrates, 0 g Dietary Fiber, 0 mg Cholesterol, 99 mg Sodium

Sweet and Sour Sauce

This is an excellent sweet and sour sauce for meats, poultry, and seafood. It can be used in cooking or as a dipping sauce. Stored in a covered jar, it will keep for two weeks in the refrigerator.

MAKES 1½ CUPS

½ cup sugar
½ cup distilled white vinegar
2 tablespoons reduced-sodium soy
  sauce

2 tablespoons dry sherry
3 tablespoons ketchup
1 tablespoon tapioca starch dissolved in
  ½ cup water or pineapple juice

Combine sugar, vinegar, soy sauce, sherry, and ketchup in a nonreactive saucepan. Bring to a boil over medium heat. Stir tapioca mixture and stir into vinegar mixture. Cook, stirring constantly, until sauce is smooth, clear, and glossy.

Per tablespoon: 22 Calories, 0 g Protein, 0 g Total Fat (0% of Calories), 0 g Saturated Fat, 5 g Carbohydrates, 0 g Dietary Fiber, 0 mg Cholesterol, 82 mg Sodium

Mango Relish

This refreshing mango relish makes a good complement for barbecued meats or seafood. Always peel mangoes before you eat them. The skin contains a substance that can cause an allergic skin reaction.

MAKES ABOUT 2 CUPS

1 large firm ripe mango
2 tablespoons finely diced red onion
1 teaspoon finely chopped crystallized
  ginger
½ teaspoon chopped serrano chili

2 tablespoons chopped fresh cilantro
1 tablespoon fresh lime juice
1 teaspoon sugar
Pinch of salt and freshly ground pepper
  to taste

Hold mango firmly, straight up. Using a sharp knife cut off flat-side half of mango (the mango pit is flat) as close to pit as possible. Cut crisscross sections at ⅓-inch intervals in the flesh down to, but not through, the peel. Push peel up from underneath skin so that mango pieces separate and open up; cut off mango pieces. Turn mango around and do the same on the other half, then cut off any remaining flesh left around the pit. Dice fruit into ⅓-inch cubes. Discard peels and pit.

In a medium bowl, combine mango cubes, onion, ginger, chili, cilantro, lime juice, and sugar; toss to combine. Season with salt and pepper.

Per ¼ cup: 22 Calories, 0 g Protein, 0.1 g Total Fat (3% of Calories), 0 g Saturated Fat, 6 g Carbohydrates, 0.6 g Dietary Fiber, 0 mg Cholesterol, 0.8 mg Sodium

Mango Chutney

This sweet and tart chutney is excellent served with roast duck or barbecued chicken.

MAKES ABOUT 3 CUPS

1 teaspoon olive oil
1½ teaspoons minced fresh ginger
1 teaspoon minced garlic
½ teaspoon toasted cardamom seeds, ground
¼ teaspoon toasted cumin seeds, ground
½ teaspoon curry powder
3 large firm mangos, cut into 2-inch long ⅜-inch-thick strips, with peels and pits discarded

¼ teaspoon cayenne pepper or to taste
¼ teaspoon salt or to taste
1 tablespoon reduced-sodium soy sauce
¾ cup packed light brown sugar
½ cup distilled white vinegar
½ cup golden raisins
1 tablespoon diced crystallized ginger

Heat a heavy 3-quart nonreactive saucepan over medium heat until hot. Add oil, swirl to coat pan, and heat 15 seconds. Add ginger and garlic and stir a few seconds. Add cardamom, cumin, and curry powder and cook, stirring, until aromatic, about 15 seconds. Add mango pieces and stir to evenly distribute spices. Cook 2 minutes. Add cayenne pepper, salt, soy sauce, brown sugar, vinegar, raisins, and crystallized ginger. Stir gently to dissolve sugar and evenly distribute and bring to a boil. Reduce heat to low and simmer, uncovered, 40 to 45 minutes, stirring occasionally, until mangos are soft and look translucent and liquid has reduced and became syrupy.

Remove from heat and let cool. Transfer chutney to a glass jar and seal. Keep up to 2 weeks in the refrigerator, or freeze up to 2 months.

Per tablespoon: 24 Calories, 0.2 g Protein, 0.2 g Total Fat (6% of Calories), 0 g Saturated Fat, 6 g Carbohydrates, 0 g Dietary Fiber, 0 mg Cholesterol, 26 mg Sodium

Mango Sauce

A fruity refreshing sauce full of vitamin C. The lime juice gives it an extra kick. It's great on roast chicken or duck.

1 large mango, peeled and cubed
1 teaspoon olive oil
1 small shallot, minced
½ teaspoon finely minced peeled fresh ginger

2 tablespoon firmly packed brown sugar
⅛ teaspoon salt
Juice of 1 lime
2 tablespoons chopped fresh cilantro

In a food processor fitted with the steel blade, puree mango cubes until smooth.

Heat a 1-quart saucepan over medium heat until hot. Add olive oil, shallot, and ginger and cook, stirring, a few seconds, or until fragrant. Add mango puree, brown sugar, and salt and stir until sugar is dissolved and sauce is hot. Stir in lime juice and cilantro and serve.

Per tablespoon: 12 Calories, 0 g Protein, 0.2 g Total Fat (14% of Calories), 0 g Saturated Fat, 3 g Carbohydrates, 0 g Dietary Fiber, 0 mg Cholesterol, 10 mg Sodium

Spicy Orange Sauce

A delicious, pungent dipping sauce for Shrimp Toast (page 24), or Crispy Fish Rolls (page 32).

¼ cup orange marmalade
1½ teaspoons horseradish

1 tablespoon ketchup
⅛ teaspoon salt

Place orange marmalade in a microwave-safe bowl. Melt in a microwave oven on HIGH 30 seconds. Add remaining ingredients, stir, and mix well.

Per tablespoon: 12 Calories, 0 g Protein, 0 g Total Fat (0 % of Calories), 0 g Saturated Fat, 3 g Carbohydrates, 0 g Dietary Fiber, 0 mg Cholesterol, 34 mg Sodium

Spicy Cucumber Relish

This refreshing sweet and sour cucumber relish is an excellent palate stimulator. Serve it with barbecued meats or poultry.

2 cups cucumbers, peeled, seeded, and thinly sliced

2 shallots, thinly sliced

1 small hot chili, seeded and chopped

⅓ cup vinegar

3 tablespoons sugar

¼ teaspoon salt or to taste

Place the cucumber, shallots, and chili in a small glass bowl.

In a small saucepan, heat vinegar, sugar, and salt over medium heat, stirring constantly, until sugar is dissolved. Boil 1 minute. Remove from heat and let cool completely. Pour over cucumber mixture, mix gently, and marinate 1 hour. Chill completely before serving.

Per tablespoon: 6 Calories, 0 g Protein, 0 g Total Fat (0% of Calories), 0 g Saturated Fat, 2 g Carbohydrates, 0.1 g Dietary Fiber, 0 mg Cholesterol, 17 mg Sodium

 Sweet Peanut Sauce

This delicious, sweet, creamy sauce is excellent on grilled chicken, pork, lamb, or calamari. But don't eat too much; it's high in calories and fats. It can be stored in a sealed jar and kept frozen for months.

MAKES 1¼ CUPS

¼ cup reduced-fat creamy peanut butter
2 tablespoons red curry paste
1 tablespoon coconut cream or canola oil
1 cup reduced-fat coconut milk

2 tablespoons sugar
2 teaspoons fish sauce
2 tablespoons lime juice
Salt to taste

Mix peanut butter and red curry paste in a small bowl to make a peanut-curry paste.

Heat coconut cream or canola oil in a 1-quart saucepan over medium heat until hot. Stir in peanut-curry paste and cook until aromatic, 1 minute. Add coconut milk, sugar, fish sauce, lime juice, and salt and bring to a vigorous boil. Reduce heat and cook, stirring, until sauce is reduced and thickened, 2 to 3 minutes. Remove from heat and serve.

Per tablespoon: 45 Calories, 1 g Protein, 2.9 g Total Fat (59% of Calories), 2 g Saturated Fat, 4 g Carbohydrates, 0 g Dietary Fiber, 0 mg Cholesterol, 143 mg Sodium

Spicy Shrimp Paste

This fiery tasty condiment is indispensable in an Asian kitchen. It is used as a food enhancer in cooking or as a condiment, such as a dipping paste for raw vegetables. Sealed in a glass jar, it will keep for months in the refrigerator. Try it on fried rice, noodles, or curried dishes for a spicy treat.

MAKES $^1/_2$ CUP

2 tablespoons dried shrimp, finely chopped
6 cloves garlic, chopped
4 dried small hot chilies, chopped
1 teaspoon sugar

3 tablespoons fish sauce
3 tablespoons fresh lime juice
2 fresh red or green small hot chilies, seeded and chopped

In a mortar or blender, pound or grind shrimp, garlic, dried chilies, and sugar until mixture is fragmented and well blended. Gradually stir in fish sauce and lime juice, spoonful by spoonful, until you have a consistent mixture. Transfer to a small serving bowl. Just before serving, stir in fresh chilies. Store in an airtight jar in the refrigerator.

Per teaspoon: 8 Calories, 1 g Protein, 0 g Total Fat (0% of Calories), 0 g Saturated Fat, 1 g Carbohydrates, 0 g Dietary Fiber, 3 mg Cholesterol, 195 mg Sodium

Glossary

Adzuki (Azuki) Beans

Small dried dark red beans that are high in protein and B vitamins, adzuki beans are widely used by the Chinese and Japanese for cooking with rice and for making into sweet bean paste for sweets and desserts. They are available in oriental and health food stores.

Baby Corn

These are miniature young corn cobs. They are available in cans, packed in lightly salted water. They have a lovely sweet fragrance and taste. Use in salads, in stir-frying with other ingredients, or in soups. Unused corn may be covered with cool water and refrigerated 1 week. Change water every 3 days.

Balsamic Vinegar

An aromatic dark colored vinegar made from grape juice, it is aged in wooden barrels and is available in supermarkets. In Chinese cooking, Chinese aromatic Zhenjian black rice vinegar can be used as a substitute.

Bamboo Shoots

Bamboo shoots are the shoots of bamboo plants dug from the earth. They are sold in cans. Once opened, the bamboo shoots should be covered with water and refrigerated. Change the water frequently, and they will last for weeks.

Basil, Holy

Also known as Chinese basil or Thai basil, it is available in Asian markets. It has purplish stems and small, pointed, oval, serrated-edge leaves with an intense flavor reminiscent of anise. Use in salads or in stir-frying with other ingredients, or as a garnish. Sweet basil can be substituted.

Bean Curd (Tofu)

White, milky, custardlike blocks made from the milk of strained soy beans, it is very nutritious and inexpensive. It is bland but absorbent, adaptable to all types of cooking. It may be made at home or bought from supermarkets. Opened bean curd should be covered with fresh water. If changed daily, it will last refrigerated 2 to 3 days.

Bean Curd (Pressed) Cake

Compressed bean curd has a very low water content. The water is extracted from the bean curd by pressing with a weight long enough to make the bean curd become firm and compact. Sometimes they are flavored with soy sauce or five-spiced soy sauce. All are good in stir-frying with vegetables or in salads.

Bean Curd Sticks

Made from layers of soybean milk that have been dried, they are tan in color, smooth, hard, and brittle. After soaking in water for 2 hours or overnight, they become softened and chewy. Use in stewed or braised dishes with other ingredients.

Bean Paste, Red and/or Sweet

A dark reddish-brown paste made of pureed red adzuki beans and sugar, it is sold in cans and keeps indefinitely if refrigerated in a sealed container. It is used for sweet fillings, as in Eight-Treasure Pudding Flambé (page 278) or Sweet Bean-Filled Rice Balls (page 281).

Bean Sauce

Made from fermented soybeans, flour, and salt, it is a major seasoning agent of the northern and Sichuan cuisines. It gives food a distinctive flavor. It is sold in cans. Transferred to a covered jar and refrigerated, it keeps indefinitely. I like Szechuan brand bean sauce.

Bean Sauce, Hot

A Sichuan specialty, crushed red chilies are added to the regular bean sauce. It is an important ingredient in Sichuan cooking, giving food a subtle spiciness. It is sold in cans. Transferred to a covered jar and refrigerated, it keeps indefinitely. I like the Szechuan brand.

Bean Threads

Noodles made from mung bean starch, they are also known as glass noodles, cellophane noodles, or plastic noodles. They must be soaked in water before using, and are often cut into smaller lengths before cooking.

Black Beans, Fermented

These pungent fermented black soybeans come in two forms, plain or covered with salt. They serve as a wonderful seasoning agent that pairs beautifully with garlic. They keep indefinitely in a tightly covered jar on the shelf.

Bok Choy

A calcium-rich, white-stalked, broad, green-leafed Chinese cabbage, it is sweet and juicy. Use in salads or stir-fried dishes. It keeps well up to 2 weeks if tightly wrapped and refrigerated.

Chestnuts, Dried Blanched

Shelled, blanched, and dehydrated chestnuts must be soaked and simmered before they are used. They are sold by weight in plastic bags in Asian markets. Substitute fresh chestnuts, if desired.

Chilies, Dried Chinese Red

Small, scarlet red chilies, about 2 inches long, they are very aromatic and very spicy. They are sold by weight in plastic bags. They are always added to the hot pan at the beginning to season the oil before other ingredients are added in a stir-fried dish. They can be used to make chili oil. They keep indefinitely in a tightly covered jar on the shelf.

Chili Sauce (Paste), Chinese

Made from ground fresh red chilies, salt, and vinegar cooked in an oil base, it is very spicy, with bright red color and has the refreshing taste of fresh peppers. Once opened, store it in the refrigerator.

Chili, Serrano

A slender, dark green chili about $1^1/_2$ inches long and $^3/_4$ inch wide; a jalapeño chili can be substituted.

Chives, Common, and Garlic Chives

Common chive plants have delicate 8-inch-long slender leaves and round lavender flowers. Garlic chives, known as Chinese chives, have broader (about 1/4-inch) flat leaves and white flowers. The flowers are edible and should be used before or just as they open, or they become dry and fibrous. Common chives used in garnishes have a mild onion flavor. Garlic chives have a pungent onion-garlic flavor and are used in stir-frying alone or with other ingredients.

Cilantro (Chinese Parsley)

This flat-leafed, long-stemmed herb has an intense earthy aroma. Use primarily in flavoring foods or as a garnish. Every part of the cilantro—seeds, leaves, stems, and roots—can be used in cooking.

Coconut Milk

Extracted from grated coconut meat blended with boiling water, it is not to be confused with the clear liquid inside a coconut. When the coconut milk is left to stand, a thick cream will rise to the top—coconut cream—which can be skimmed off. Dilute canned coconut milk with an equal amount of water to make light (thin) coconut milk.

Daikon Radish, Fresh

A giant Chinese white radish, measuring from 6 to over 12 inches, it has paper-thin skin and a light texture like that of the Western white radish. It is widely used in soups, pickling, or stir-frying, either alone or with other ingredients. In Japan, it is eaten raw in salads, shredded as a garnish, or grated as an accompaniment to fish dishes. It keeps about 2 to 3 weeks wrapped and refrigerated.

Daikon Radish, Preserved

Shredded daikon radish preserved in salt and brown sugar, and sun dried. It is available in vacuum-packed plastic bags in Asian markets. Very salty, it is used sparingly in stir-frying with other ingredients, or as a condiment for rice porridge. It keeps indefinitely if well sealed and refrigerated.

Dates, Red Chinese

A glossy fruit with blood-red skin, smooth texture, and sweet taste, Chinese dates come in various sizes and colors. The ones used in this book are small red dates resembling chicken hearts, known in Chinese as "chicken heart dates." Store them in an airtight container at room temperature. They keep indefinitely.

Dry Sherry

Use as a good substitute for Chinese Shaoxing rice wine in flavoring foods and marinating meats. In Chinese cooking, use genuine Chinese rice wine or a good-quality dry sherry with rich aroma and taste. Avoid buying bottles labeled "cooking wine." They have poor taste and added salt.

Fish Sauce

A thin, brown, clear liquid with a pungent aroma, it is extracted from salted anchovies or shrimp. It is used for cooking and as a condiment. It is called *nuoc nam* in Vietnam, *nam pla* in Thailand, and *patis* in the Philippines. It is available in Asian markets. I like the Three Crabs and Golden Boy brands imported from Thailand.

Five-Spice Powder

A pungent spice made from ground anise, fennel, cloves, cinnamon, and Sichuan peppercorns. It is used sparingly to give food a distinctive aroma and flavor. Keep it in a tightly sealed jar on the shelf.

Ginger, Fresh

Fresh ginger is a mainstay of Chinese cooking. They should be rock-hard, with a smooth, thin, tannish skin. The Chinese never peel the fresh ginger unless it's for grated ginger. To peel the ginger, use a metal spoon to scrape it; the skin will come off easily. Fresh ginger will keep up to 2 weeks if kept dry and refrigerated. You can store it, wrapped, in the freezer for months. When needed, take it out and let it stand 5 minutes for easy slicing, then put the remainder back in the freezer.

Hoisin Sauce

Made from soybeans, flour, sugar, salt, garlic, and chilies, this dark reddish-brown, thick creamy sauce gives food a glowing reddish color and a sweet piquant flavor. It is widely used in Chinese cooking for barbecuing and seasoning, or in dipping sauces for Peking Duck (page 189) and Mu Shu Pork (page 206). After opening, hoisin sauce will keep indefinitely in a sealed jar in the refrigerator. I like Koon Chun brand, which comes in a 15-ounce jar or in a 5-pound can.

Lemongrass

A long grasslike herb with a strong lemon flavor and aroma, it grows in most tropical countries. Only the white bulbous base and the tender part of the stalk are used because the leaves are tough. The lemongrass stalks are available fresh from Asian markets and should be kept in the refrigerator. If you can't find lemongrass, substitute the thin outer peel of fresh lemons.

Lotus Seeds

They are the small round pale-yellow seeds, about the size of chick-peas, from the lotus flower. They are available dried in plastic bags or blanched in cans and are mainly used for desserts. Sometimes they are used in making nutritious herbal soups.

Long Beans, Chinese

Foot-long, stringless green beans, they are also known as yard-long beans. Tender fresh long beans should be smooth-skinned, uniformly green, and about $^1/4$-inch across when you buy them. Irregularly bumpy, wrinkled, or thicker beans are tough. To use, simply cut into 3-inch lengths. Tender green beans can be substituted

Mango

A tropical fruit with a tough, thin skin. It is dark green when unripe; yellow or a reddish-orange and green when ripe. The ripe flesh is juicy, aromatic, and luscious. Mangoes are available canned or fresh, in season. They are also available frozen in some better supermarkets. They are great for making mango sauces or purees.

Mesclun

A combination of baby and bitter greens, it may contain baby spinach, escarole (curly endive/chicory), mâche (corn salad), arugula, dandelion leaves, radicchio, chervil and/or oak-leaf lettuce. Use for salads or garnishes.

Mint (Peppermint and Spearmint)

Peppermint has a strong minty taste and has toothed $2^1/2$-inch-long leaves. Spearmint is milder in flavor and has crinkly, pointed 2-inch-long leaves. They are used mostly in salads or garnishing.

Mirin

A Japanese sweet rice wine made from glutinous rice, it is used widely in Japanese cooking to add sweetness and an attractive glaze to foods. Pale dry sherry sweetened with sugar can be used as a substitute.

Miso

A high-protein fermented soybean paste made from fermented soybeans and grains, it is used as a flavoring or marinade. It comes in different hues and textures, each with its own aroma and flavor. Miso should be added to dishes at the last possible moment, or eaten uncooked, because boiling destroys the digestion-aiding enzymes. After opening, miso should be covered airtight and refrigerated.

Mushrooms, Chinese Dried

These dried mushrooms range in width from 1 to 3 inches. Their color varies from black to speckled brown or gray. The medium-sized, thick-capped mushrooms have the best flavor. They are bagged by sizes and have an earthy aroma and meaty texture with which fresh shiitake mushrooms do not compare. Dried mushrooms must be softened before using. Soak in hot water to cover about 30 minutes. The soaking liquid, with its concentrated mushroom flavor can be strained and saved for use in soups or stir-fries. Dried mushrooms are sold by weight and keep indefinitely in a sealed plastic bag in a cool, dry place.

Mushrooms, Enoki

Slender and extremely delicate mushrooms, they have a cream-colored stalk about 5 inches long and $1/16$ inch thick, topped by a tiny buttonlike cap. You can find them fresh vacuum-packed in 3-ounce plastic packages both in oriental and Western markets. They have a mild flavor and are great additions to soups. Cut off the spongy base of the stems before using.

Mushrooms, Mu-Er (Cloud Ears, Tree Ears, or Wood Ears)

These crinkly tree fungi are thin and brittle. They are sold packaged in plastic bags. After soaking in warm water 30 minutes, they expand into resilient clusters of dark brown petals resembling dark clouds. Mu-er mushrooms have no real flavor, but they mix well with other ingredients and can absorb any seasonings that you use. If well sealed, they keep almost indefinitely.

Mushrooms, Straw

These small silky mushrooms with black pointed caps are grown in beds of rice straw; hence the name. They come in cans in two forms: peeled or unpeeled. I prefer the peeled straw mushrooms because they look prettier and a have pleasant crunchy texture that blends well in stir-fried dishes or soups. They are available in Asian markets or some better supermarkets.

Mustard, Chinese

Chinese hot mustard is hotter than prepared Western varieties. It is made with English mustard powder diluted with water and vinegar. Put 3 tablespoons of the mustard powder in a small dish, stir in 4 tablespoons water and 1 tablespoon distilled white vinegar until it forms a thin, smooth paste. Let it mellow at least 1 hour before serving. Keep it tightly covered and store in the refrigerator. The powder is available in cans or plastic bags in Oriental markets.

Napa Cabbage

A popular creamy-white oblong crinkled-leaf Chinese cabbage, it has a mild but distinct taste. It is used in salads, stir-frying, soups, or simmering with meats, and is excellent pickled. It will keep 2 weeks if stored in a dry airtight plastic bag and refrigerated.

Nori

A dried, pressed, rosy purple variety of seaweed, it comes in sealed plastic bags, usually 10 sheets per package. It is used as a wrapper for sushi or shredded as a garnish for soups. It keeps indefinitely.

Oyster Sauce

A thick brown sauce made of oyster extracts and other ingredients. Used as a seasoning, it provides color and flavor to foods. It comes in bottles and large cans and keeps indefinitely in the refrigerator. I use Lee Kum Kee's premium brand oyster sauce.

Papayas

There are many varieties of papaya, ranging from 6 to 10 inches long. The unripe (green) papaya is used as a vegetable in curries or eaten raw in green papaya salad. The ripe fruit is firm, juicy, and yellow, sometimes orange. It is commonly eaten raw, sometimes with sugar and a squeeze of lime juice, or with salt and ground chilies. The sap of the plant contains a large quantity of papain, which is used as a natural tenderizer for meats.

Prawns

Large shrimp, 3 to 4 inches in length, are called prawns in Asian markets.

Radicchio

An Italian cultivated variety of chicory, it grows into small crinkled loose heads with red leaves and white ribs. The striking beautiful leaves have a crisp texture and slightly bitter flavor. They are often used in salads with other salad greens.

Rice, Glutinous

Snow white–colored rice also called "sweet rice," it becomes very soft and sticky when cooked. It is used for desserts and savory stuffings. It is available in Asian markets.

Rice Flour

Regular rice flour is made from long-grain rice. This flour does not become sticky after it is cooked. It is suitable for making radish rice cakes or rice drinks. It is available in Asian markets.

Rice Flour, Glutinous

Made of short-grain glutinous rice, this flour is used in making sweet snacks. After steaming or boiling the dough becomes resilient and chewy. It is available in Asian supermarkets in 1-pound packages.

Rice Paper

Brittle, translucent round sheets, they are made of rice flour, water, and salt. After immersion in warm water for a few seconds, they become resilient and pliable. They are used as wrappers for spring rolls.

Rice Sticks (Rice Vermicelli)

These are thin dry white noodles made from rice flour. They are sold typically in 1-pound cellophane bags, three or four loosely packed wads to the bag. They need to be soaked in cool water before cooking. Avoid vigorous mixing during cooking, for they easily break into short lengths.

Rice Vinegar

A distilled vinegar made from white rice, it is used in cooking and pickling. It is excellent in salad dressings. Japanese rice vinegar is milder and less concentrated than Chinese rice vinegar.

Rock Sugar

Made from raw sugar, these chunks of crystallized sugar are used widely in simmered or stewed meats and poultry. They have a unique subtle sweetness that granulated sugar lacks, and they give food a special sheen and glaze. Rock sugar should be broken into small bits before it is added to a sauce. Wrap it in a heavy lint-free cloth and smash it with a hammer. Stored away from heat, light, and moisture, it keeps indefinitely.

Salt

Although all my recipes in this book call for regular salt, I generally prefer to cook with kosher salt, which is very granular and has a pure, mild-tasting flavor that balances well with Chinese seasonings. Kosher salt is sold in 3-pound boxes at most supermarkets.

Sea salt is very salty, twice as salty as kosher salt; it does not blend well with most Chinese seasonings. If you must use sea salt, use it sparingly.

Sesame Oil, Oriental

This thick, brown aromatic oil is made from roasted sesame seeds. It is used more for seasoning than for cooking. It comes in bottles and large cans. The aroma remains indefinitely if the oil is tightly covered at all times and stored in a cool dark place.

Sesame Paste, Oriental

Chinese sesame paste is aromatic, rich, and tasty. It is used in making dressings for noodles, vegetables, or meats. If you can't find the oriental sesame paste, substitute tahini paste or peanut butter creamed with a little sesame oil.

Shallots

Shallots available in Asia have reddish-brown skins and purple flesh and are smaller and stronger in flavor than those found here in America. They are called "red onions" in Asia. When browned in oil, they have a sweet enticing aroma and are widely used in Asian cooking. Regular shallots can be substituted.

Shrimp, Dried

Highly prized by the Chinese as a seasoning, these small, golden-orange shrimp are salted and dried under the sun so that their flavor is intensified by the process. They should be soaked in hot water or sherry to cover at least 30 minutes to release their flavor before being cooked with other ingredients. The soaking liquid can be used for cooking also. They are sold by weight in plastic packages and keep well if they are stored dry in a sealed plastic bag in the refrigerator or freezer.

Sichuan Peppercorns

A regional product of the Sichuan province, they are unrelated to the familiar white and black peppercorns. They are the reddish-brown fragrant berries of the prickly ash tree. They leave a pleasantly numbing taste rather than a burning sensation on the tongue. The flavor and aroma come from their petallike husks. Store Sichuan peppercorns in an airtight container away from heat, light, and moisture.

Sichuan Preserved Mustard Greens

A specialty of Sichuan, they are preserved in salt and chili powder, greenish in color, and very crisp in texture. They are used as cooking ingredients or as tasty condiments for soups, noodles, or salads. They come in cans or in plastic bags and keep indefinitely in a covered jar in the refrigerator.

Soy Sauces (Light, Dark, and Thick)

Soy sauces are made from fermented soybeans, wheat, and salt. They are the major seasonings in Chinese and Japanese cooking. They are used for marinating and cooking and for dipping sauce. They range in quality, flavor, and degree of saltiness. The brand I use is Kimlan reduced-sodium soy sauce imported from Taiwan.

The light (or thin) soy sauce has a clear brown color and a pleasant soy aroma. It is used for seasoning delicate dishes.

The dark (or thick) soy sauce is thicker in consistency than light soy. If you shake a bottle of soy sauce and the brown color clings to the glass, it is dark soy sauce. Its aroma is subtly sweet and it is used whenever a deep brown color is wanted, such as in fried rice or in braising or stewing poultry and meat dishes.

There is a third kind, called "thick soy sauce" on the bottle. It comes in a 16-ounce jar. It is made from molasses, salt, and soybean extract and is manufactured by the Koon Chun sauce factory in Hong Kong. It has the consistency of molasses, and is used much the same way as the thinner dark soy, except in smaller amounts. It is available in Oriental markets.

Star Anise

A hard, starlike brown pod, it has eight points, each point of which holds a glossy brown seed. Both the pod and the seed are used. It has a strong licoricelike aroma. It is used in simmering meats and poultry. Store in a tightly covered jar.

Tahini

A ground paste made from hulled sesame seeds, it is used in most Middle Eastern sauces and dips. It is available in most Middle Eastern stores and health food stores. After opening, store it, tightly covered, in the refrigerator.

Tapioca Flour (Starch)

The paste of the cassava root made into a flour, it looks like cornstarch. It is used in desserts and as a thickening agent. It is available in Asian markets.

Tienjin Preserved Vegetable

Chopped celery cabbage preserved with salt, garlic, and spices, it comes in a small dark-brown ceramic crock and has a tasty garlic flavor. It is especially good in simmering meats or poultry or in soups. If well sealed, it keeps indefinitely in the refrigerator.

Tiger Lily Buds (Golden Needles)

These are the unopened flower buds of the tiger lily, picked before dawn. The fresh ones can be sautéed or added to soups as garnishes. Dried tiger lily buds must be reconstituted in water before using. They are wonderful in stir-fried dishes or when simmered with other ingredients, as in Red-Cooked Whole Pork Shoulder (page 210). They are sold in plastic bags, available in Oriental markets.

Tofu: *See* Bean Curd

Water Chestnut Flour

Dry starch or flour made of ground water chestnuts, it is used for coating foods when you want the coating to be exceptionally crisp. It is sold in 1-pound packages in Asian markets.

Wheat Gluten

A high-protein food used widely in vegetarian cooking, it is made by washing out the starch from gluten flour until only the adhesive substance remains. There is a large variety of delicious prepared wheat gluten in bottles and cans available in Asian markets. Both boiled and deep-fried wheat glutens are also available in Asian and health food stores.

Zest

The oil-rich outer peel of a citrus fruit, without the white pith. Remove it with a grater or zester. It is used in flavoring or garnishing.

Crispy Shallots

In a small skillet, heat $1/2$ cup peanut oil to 375F (190C). Or test with a small piece of shallot: if it foams instantly without burning, the oil is ready. Remove pan from heat, add 6 thinly sliced shallots, and stir gently until golden and crisp, about 3 minutes. Transfer shallots to paper towels to drain. Makes about $1/3$ cup. The oil can be strained and used as shallot-flavored oil for salad dressings or cooking.

Egg Sheets

Egg sheets should be as thin as French crêpes. They are often used as wrappers or shredded and used as garnishes for salads or soups. To make an egg sheet: Heat $1/2$ teaspoon oil in a 7-inch frying pan over medium heat until hot and swirl to coat the bottom of the pan. Add 1 beaten egg, swirl immediately to coat the pan as thinly as possible. Sprinkle with salt and pepper to taste, and cook until the egg is set, about 45 seconds. Flip the egg sheet over and cook the other side 15 seconds. Remove from heat. Use as needed.

Roasted Red Bell Peppers

Choose heavy meaty sweet bell peppers for roasting. The light ones are thinner and do not have as much flesh. Place peppers under the broiler or on the grill and broil or grill 3 inches from heat until charred, 7 to 9 minutes. Turn and char the other side another 5 to 7 minutes. Place them in an unused paper bag, close the bag, and place it on a tray in the kitchen sink (the peppers will leak juices). Let their own heat continue to cook them until they are cooled.

With your fingers, peel off the skins (if they are charred enough, the skin should come off very easily) and pull the stems and seeds out and discard. Do not rinse the peppers; rinsing washes off their sweet juice, vitamins, and nutrients. Use them in salads, stews, stir-fries, sauces, or dips. They can be frozen up to 6 months in a freezer container.

Roasted Sichuan Peppercorns

Heat Sichuan peppercorns in a heavy ungreased skillet over low heat, shaking pan occasionally, about 5 minutes, until they are faintly smoking and aromatic. Cool, then crush them with mortar and pestle, or grind them in a spice mill. Store in an airtight jar.

Sichuan Pepper-Salt

It is used widely in China for seasoning roasted poultry or crispy foods. Heat 3 tablespoons kosher salt in a 6-inch heavy frying pan over low heat until the salt is hot and turns off-white, about 5 minutes. Add 2 teaspoons Sichuan peppercorn husks (without the seeds). Shake the pan and stir the contents constantly until the peppers start to smoke faintly. Turn off the heat and let cool. Crush the salt mixture with a mortar and pestle or grind with a spice mill. Bottle and use as needed.

Toasted Sesame Seeds

Heat a 6-inch heavy ungreased frying pan over medium heat until hot enough to sizzle a bead of water and evaporate instantly on contact, about 1 minute. Add 3 tablespoons white sesame seeds. Shake and swirl the pan constantly until they are pale gold and have a good aroma. Use for sprinkling or grind to a paste for seasoning. Store in an airtight jar and keep refrigerated.

Metric Conversion Charts

Comparison to Metric Measure				
When You Know	**Symbol**	**Multiply By**	**To Find**	**Symbol**
teaspoons	tsp	5.0	milliliters	ml
tablespoons	tbsp	15.0	milliliters	ml
fluid ounces	fl. oz.	30.0	milliliters	ml
cups	c	0.24	liters	l
pints	pt.	0.47	liters	l
quarts	qt.	0.95	liters	l
ounces	oz.	28.0	grams	g
pounds	lb.	0.45	kilograms	kg
Fahrenheit	F	5/9 (after subtracting 32)	Celsius	C

Fahrenheit to Celsius	
F	**C**
200–205	95
229–225	105
245–250	120
275	135
300–305	150
325–330	165
345–350	175
370–375	190
400–405	205
425–430	220
445–450	230
470–475	245
500	260

Liquid Measure to Liters		
¼ cup	=	0.06 liters
½ cup	=	0.12 liters
¾ cup	=	0.18 liters
1 cup	=	0.24 liters
1¼ cups	=	0.30 liters
1½ cups	=	0.36 liters
2 cups	=	0.48 liters
2½ cups	=	0.60 liters
3 cups	=	0.72 liters
3½ cups	=	0.84 liters
4 cups	=	0.96 liters
4½ cups	=	1.08 liters
5 cups	=	1.20 liters
5½ cups	=	1.32 liters

Liquid Measure to Milliliters		
¼ teaspoon	=	1.25 milliliters
½ teaspoon	=	2.50 milliliters
¾ teaspoon	=	3.75 milliliters
1 teaspoon	=	5.00 milliliters
1¼ teaspoons	=	6.25 milliliters
1½ teaspoons	=	7.50 milliliters
1¾ teaspoons	=	8.75 milliliters
2 teaspoons	=	10.0 milliliters
1 tablespoon	=	15.0 milliliters
2 tablespoons	=	30.0 milliliters

Index

About the Author

Rose Lee was raised in Taipei, Taiwan, where gourmet chefs from all regions of Mainland China offer the best dishes of their regions. She is a graduate of Ming-Chuan University, and studied cooking with Fu Pei-Mei, Taiwan's celebrated television cooking pioneer. Rose graduated from Pei-Mei's cooking school in 1966.

In 1969, Rose came to the United States. She has taught and demonstrated Chinese cooking in many areas of the United States. She opened Rose Lee's Cooking School at Westborough, Massachusetts, in 1983, and later she opened a restaurant. She has made a Chinese Cooking series for a local cable television station.

Presently, Rose is a teacher, a caterer, a restaurant consultant, and a writer. Now she is concentrating on promoting a healthy Asian diet based on traditional Chinese eating patterns.

She is married and has three children.